C
Spo
of the Gulf

Jack Smart
and
Frances Altorfer

The publisher has used its best endeavours to ensure that the URLs for external websites referred to in this book are correct and active at the time of going to press. However, the publisher and the author have no responsibility for the websites and can make no guarantee that a site will remain live or that the content will remain relevant, decent or appropriate.

For UK order enquiries: please contact Bookpoint Ltd, 130 Milton Park, Abingdon, Oxon OX14 4SB. Telephone: +44 (0) 1235 827720. Fax: +44 (0) 1235 400454. Lines are open 09.00–17.00, Monday to Saturday, with a 24-hour message answering service. Details about our titles and how to order are available at www.teachyourself.com

For USA order enquiries: please contact
McGraw-Hill Customer Services,
PO Box 545, Blacklick, OH 43004-0545, USA.
Telephone: 1-800-722-4726. Fax: 1-614-755-5645.

For Canada order enquiries: please contact
McGraw-Hill Ryerson Ltd,
300 Water St, Whitby, Ontario L1N 9B6, Canada.
Telephone: 905 430 5000. Fax: 905 430 5020.

Long renowned as the authoritative source for self-guided learning – with more than 50 million copies sold worldwide – the **Teach Yourself** series includes over 500 titles in the fields of languages, crafts, hobbies, business, computing and education.

British Library Cataloguing in Publication Data: a catalogue record for this title is available from the British Library.

Library of Congress Catalog Card Number: on file.

First published in UK 1999 as *Teach Yourself Gulf Arabic* by Hodder Education, part of Hachette UK, 338 Euston Road, London NW1 3BH.

First published in US 1999 by The McGraw-Hill Companies, Inc.

This edition published 2010.

Typeset by MPS Limited, A Macmillan Company.

Printed in Great Britain for Hodder Education, an Hachette UK Company, 338 Euston Road, London NW1 3BH.

Hachette UK's policy is to use papers that are natural, renewable and recyclable products and made from wood grown in sustainable forests. The logging and manufacturing processes are expected to conform to the environmental regulations of the country of origin.

Impression number 10 9 8 7 6 5 4 3 2 1

Year 2014 2013 2012 2011 2010

Contents

For Mairi and Kirsty

Acknowledgements

Many people and organizations helped us in various ways in the preparation of this book, and we should like to express our sincere gratitude to them.

We would especially like to thank the al-Battashi family for their generous hospitality and for help with the text; Joan Crabbe, Jim and Margaret Fraser, Marijcke Jongbloed and the Sharjah National History Museum and Desert Park, Mike Pinder, Brian Pridham, Adrian Gully and Mairi Smart who helped us with realia; Bobby Coles, Ruth Butler and Jennifer Davies at the Centre for Arab Gulf Studies and Sheila Westcott in the Department of Arabic at the University of Exeter who were endlessly helpful and resourceful, and the embassies of the United Arab Emirates, Bahrain, and Yemen who kindly gave us information and materials.

We are also very grateful to the Coca-Cola Company, McDonalds Corporation, Penguin Trading Est. and National Mineral Water Co. Ltd. of Oman, and Vimto for giving us permission to use copyright material.

Thanks are also due to our editors Sarah Mitchell, Sue Hart and Helen Green, and Ginny Catmur for this latest edition, for their encouragement and patience, to Fred and Dorothea Altorfer, and to Lynne Noble for her generous help behind the scenes.

Meet the authors

The authors are both linguists of long experience, and are familiar with the Arab countries, their society, religion and culture.

Jack Smart has taught Arabic at university level for more than 30 years, specializing in the learning of the language, his students ranging from beginners to candidates for a doctoral degree. He is familiar with the written language from its earliest pre-Islamic period to the present day, and has researched widely into spoken Arabic dialects, in several of which he is fluent. He has lived and worked in Egypt, Sudan and the Gulf countries, and has made short or extended visits and study trips to virtually all of the other Arab states.

Frances Altorfer has also lived in the Middle East. She knows several European languages as well as Swahili and Arabic, and has many years of experience of teaching languages, using the most up-to-date teaching methods.

Working in partnership, Jack has provided the linguistic material, and Frances the teaching expertise. The result is, we are sure, a balanced self-teaching book with a broad scope, mainly linguistic, but also with useful sections on the Arab and Islamic culture, in a clear and easily digestible format.

Only got a minute?

Arabic is spoken by more than 200 million people, across North Africa, the Arabian Peninsula and the Middle East. In several other countries it is an official language. It is read and written by more than 1,000 million Muslims across the world. It is the language of the Koran, the holy scripture of the Islamic religion. All Muslims use Arabic in their devotions.

Arabic is a Semitic language, one of an ancient group of languages spoken across North Africa, the Arabian peninsula and South-West Asia. Its main surviving sister language is modern Hebrew. Modern Arabic exists on two levels. The first is the written Arabic of books, newspapers and the media, known as Modern Standard Arabic; the second is colloquial or spoken Arabic, which varies across the Arab world and is not normally written. Although spoken Arabic differs between countries, all dialects descend directly from Ancient Arabic. This book deals with one of the larger dialect groups, spoken in the Gulf States, Saudi Arabia and Iraq.

Arabic is written from right to left, cursively, like European handwriting, i.e. most letters are joined up. There is no equivalent of European printed text, with separated letters. There are no capital letters. The alphabet has 28 consonants. The short vowels, such as *a* as in *hat*, are not normally written. The Arabic script *looks* difficult, but is actually quite easy to master. Spelling is no problem as there are few irregularities.

There are some 'strange' sounds in Arabic which do not occur in English, but these can be mastered with practice. Vocabulary can be difficult as Arabic comes from a different language group from English, but – especially in spoken Arabic – there are many 'borrowed' words, such as **bank**, and **siinama** (*cinema*), to help you along.

10 Only got ten minutes?

Why learn Arabic?

Why do you want to learn Arabic? There could be several reasons.

- It may be that you are going to work in a country where Arabic is the everyday language, and you would like to be able to communicate with the people. To read such basic things as street signs, newspaper headings and so on you need some knowledge of the written language, the basics of which are also dealt with in this book.
- You may simply want to learn Arabic because you intend to visit one of the Arabic-speaking countries as a tourist. Besides the wonderful pharaonic monuments in Egypt, the marvels of Roman and Arab civilizations extend across North Africa and the Middle East.

If you know one form of spoken Arabic, you will find it quite easy to adapt to the dialect of whichever Arabic-speaking country you happen to be in, as you will have a good grounding in the basics of the language. All the dialects are ultimately based on the ancient written language, and grammatical features such as the way the verbs work do not differ greatly wherever you are. For instance, in the Arabic taught in this book, the word for *they go* is **yiruuHuun**; in other dialects – even a few within the Gulf region itself – it is **yiruuHuu**, without the final **-n**. This is typical of these minor variations – and in any case, you will be understood whichever you use.

What kind of Arabic will you learn?

The Arabic taught in this book is representative of the spoken Arabic of the Gulf region, the Kingdom of Saudi Arabia and most of Iraq, and even within this area, there are regional differences. The dialects of the Yemen, perhaps, differ the most. If you learn the Arabic in this book, you will be understood in the whole area. If you are to be in a specific area for a long period, you should listen to and adopt the local usages. For instance, the word given for *there is/are* is **fiih**. If you are in Bahrain you will hear **hast**, in Iraq you will hear **aku**, and in parts of Oman **shayy** – but **fiih** will do fine wherever you are.

In addition to the native speakers, Arabic is read and written by Muslims all over the world as a language of religion.

- There are millions of Muslims in Pakistan, Afghanistan and in the Far East, in Malaysia and Indonesia. If you are a Muslim, you have to read the Koran and pray in Arabic. Translations are only used for reference or to help with understanding the Arabic.
- All the commentaries on the Holy Text, and other literature on interpretation and rules for daily life are written in and have to be read in Arabic.

It is a matter of pride for Muslims to regard Arabic as a prestige language.

In the same way that Welsh and Spanish and English use mostly the same script but are not closely related to one another, other languages of mainly Islamic countries, such as Persian (Farsi) and Urdu, and previously Turkish, use adapted versions of the Arabic script, but are not linguistically related to Arabic. While Persian and Urdu are still written in slightly adapted forms of the Arabic alphabet, Turkish adopted a modified European alphabet in 1928. If you know Arabic, you can often get the gist of a newspaper article written in one of those languages. This is because they have many words borrowed from Arabic, due to the shared Islamic culture.

Writing Arabic

Many people are put off by the apparently difficult script. In fact, this is one of the most rewarding aspects of learning Arabic. Once you have mastered the 28 letters, it is easy to write Arabic – which has few of the spelling oddities of English (think of *write/right* or *cough/through*, for example).

Arabic – except in the Holy Koran and ancient poetry – is always written without the short vowels, such as the *a* in *hat* or *i* in *tin*. This is not as bizarre as you might think: in English we are already used to this with text messaging (*txt msg*). The vowels can usually be predicted because there is a very limited number of permitted word shapes in Arabic. In fact, all true Arabic words fall into fewer than 50 patterns (i.e. combinations of consonants and vowels).

The Arabic heritage

The Arabs began to study their language early in their history, so the basics of grammar were laid down in the eighth century, which is also when the first dictionary was written.

Written Arabic has existed for about 12 centuries without a great deal of change. The West owes Arabic a major debt, as Arabic carried the torch of classical learning when Europe entered the Dark Ages. Many early Greek mathematical, medical and philosophical texts were translated by Arab writers and scientists. Without these scholars, they would have been lost to us. Much that we know of today in the fields of chemistry, medicine, astronomy and other branches of scientific endeavour stems from these early Arab scholars.

Although they did not invent them, the Arabs also gave us what we call Arabic numerals, including the concept of *zero*, which derives from the Arabic **Sifr**. This is more obvious in the word *cipher*, which originally meant the same thing.

Arabic has lent many words to European languages, particularly Spanish and Portuguese, as a result of the Arab occupation of the Iberian Peninsula which lasted for over 700 years. There are also a surprising number in English. *Magazine*, *calibre*, *algebra*, *arsenal* and *admiral*, for instance, all come from Arabic.

The Arabic word for *the* is **al-** , in Arabic script ال, which you can see in many borrowings, such as *algebra*, *Alhambra* and *algorithm*. It is always joined on to the next word, so you never see it alone.

Arabic literature

Popular Arabic literature familiar in the West is mainly confined to the *Arabian Nights*, a collection of tales from many sources and not highly regarded in the Arab world until quite recently, due to their popular folk origins. The poetry of Omar Khayyam, the next best known piece of Middle Eastern literature in the West, is in fact Persian, not Arabic.

Arabic literature began with poetry in the pre-Islamic era. There were no novels or drama until the 20th century.

The Muslim religion technically prohibits the artistic representation of anything living. Although this was ignored in many Muslim areas, it led to a highly developed art of calligraphy. This is evident in inscriptions on religious buildings, and indeed in all walks of Arab life.

If you learn Arabic, you will be able to learn more about all these things.

Spoken Arabic

The position of spoken or colloquial Arabic is slightly confusing for Westerners to understand. In Britain, for example, by no means everyone speaks Standard English in everyday life, but most people can do so if required, albeit with varying accents (Scottish, Irish,

Welsh, etc.). In the Arab world, no one uses Standard Arabic in speech and indeed, even highly educated people find it difficult to sustain in, for instance, academic discussions. Some Arabs will try to tell you otherwise, but don't believe them. This is because Arabs are trained throughout their education to look down on the colloquial speech, and taught that it is not 'pure' and has 'no grammar', which is nonsense!

Dialects all derive ultimately from the old Classical Arabic, and share many of the same structures. The chief divergences can basically be summed up as follows:

- Dropping the (in any case unwritten) so-called case and mood endings of the noun and verb.
- Using – for no apparent reason – different words from the huge Arabic lexicon for the same concept. For instance, the word used in this book for *to speak* is **yitkallam**, but in other parts of the Arab world **yiHkii** is used. Both are perfectly good Classical Arabic words.
- For historical reasons – often connected with the colonial powers – Arabic spoken dialects have absorbed foreign terms. These reflect historical and geographical influences. For instance Gulf Arabic uses many Persian and Indian words, such as **dariishah** (*window*, Persian), **siidah** (*straight ahead*, Indian). Colonial influence features most in the North African dialects, which have a huge number of French borrowings. Gulf Arabic shows some Portuguese influence (**maiz** *table*), and much English from the oil age (**fainri** *refinery*, **biTrool** in the sense of *crude oil*) and many more terms often connected with technology.

Spoken Arabic is not often written down, and there is no standard way of spelling it in the Arabic script. The main instances are cartoon captions in the newspapers and folk theatre, film and TV scripts. Even dialogue in novels tends to be rendered in Standard Arabic – which gives it a peculiar stilted flavour – though there have been attempts at compromise, often described as 'the third language'. In this book the spoken Arabic has been simply transcribed so that you can read it.

Introduction

The purpose of this book is to teach you how to speak and understand the spoken Arabic of the Gulf region. This is a group of closely related dialects, concentrated on the nations of the Arab Gulf from Kuwait down through Qatar, Bahrain, the United Arab Emirates and the Sultanate of Oman. Many of the dialects of the Kingdom of Saudi Arabia are closely related, as is that of (especially southern) Iraq.

It is not a manual of standard, or literary, Arabic, which is not a spoken language; for that use *Complete Arabic*, also published by *Teach Yourself*. However, so that you may have the added pleasure of being able to read road signs, shop names and other visual features of the Gulf environment, a simple account of the Arabic alphabet is given.

This book contains everything you need to know about basic Gulf Arabic. Work steadily at your own pace, and finish the course: don't hurry things or become disheartened after the first couple of chapters. This book introduces the language you really need: vocabulary and grammatical information have been limited to the necessities.

Of course, if you are living in the Gulf, you should seek help from native speakers at every opportunity. Here a slight word of warning: there exists in the Gulf a 'pidgin' variety of Arabic, used mainly between the Arabs and the huge numbers of expatriate workers, mostly from the Indian sub-continent. If your informants come up with something differing radically from what is given in this book (ignoring regional differences in pronunciation), check that you are not hearing 'pidgin'.

Arabs very much appreciate any attempt by a foreigner to learn their language, and your every effort will be greeted with amazement, then enthusiasm and offers of help. It is the key to a society of very friendly people which is often thought difficult to penetrate. Speaking even a little Arabic will enhance your social life and, in the business world, can open doors which would otherwise remain closed.

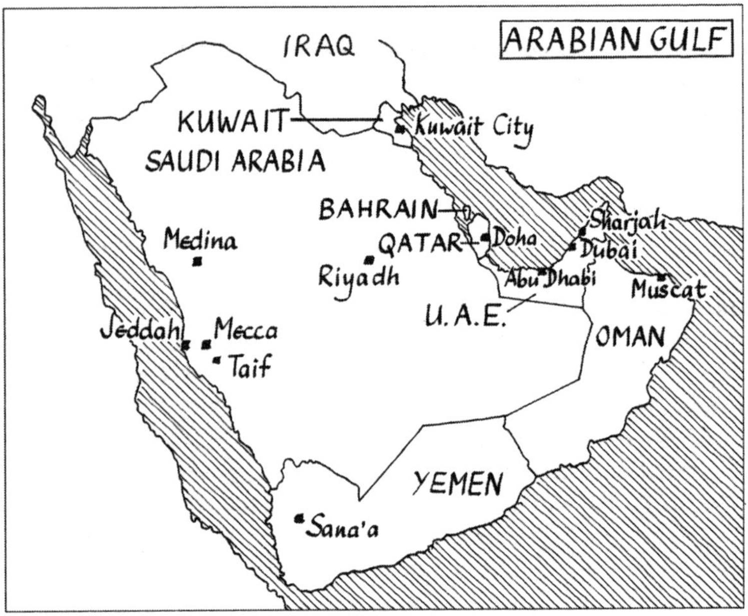

How to use this book

The book is divided into units, with all the important information that you need for good communication in Gulf Arabic given in the first ten units. The last four units refer to specific situations in which you might find yourself if you are visiting or resident in the region, and build on the words and grammar that you have learned.

At the beginning of each unit is a summary of the contents, which lists what you will be able to do after working through the unit.

Each unit contains several **Dialogues** (**Hiwáar**), which introduce the new language in a realistic context. In some instances you may find slight variants between the book and the recording. This is due to the regional differences in pronunciation. There are two or three questions to help you check your comprehension, and the answers to them and a translation of the dialogues are in the **Key to the exercises** at the end of the book.

Key words (Quick Vocab) are given after each dialogue in the order in which they appear. Then there are **Notes** (**mulaaHaDHáat**), which explain how the language works in the dialogue.

There are some **Cultural tips** (**ma:luumáat thaqaafíyyah**), which highlight some of the cultural aspects of life in the Arabian Gulf. There are also **Author insight** boxes, which give you helpful language tips based on the authors' experience.

If you have the recording, listen to it several times alone while reading the dialogue and practise repeating the dialogue to yourself to improve your pronunciation. Listening is the first step to learning a language; don't be disheartened if you don't always understand every word – picking out the gist of what is said is the key.

To sum up what you have learned in the dialogues, **Key phrases (ta:biiráat háammah)** will provide a valuable reference after you have worked through all the dialogues in the unit. These contain the main language elements and help you with the exercises.

This is followed by **Grammar points (núqaT naHwíyyah)**, where the constructions contained in the unit are explained and illustrated in sentences. Main grammatical concepts have often been grouped together for ease of reference, and they gradually build up to provide you with all the structures you need to understand and speak Gulf Arabic. These should be used for reference.

The next section, **Exercises (tamriináat)**, provides a variety of activities so that you can practise using the new words and structures. The answers are to be found at the end of the book, in the **Key to the exercises.** Some exercises are on the recording, and you may find it helps you to read the transcript of the recording at the back of the book.

The next section contains the **Arabic script (al-kháTT al-:árabi)**, which gradually takes you through the Arabic alphabet so that by the end you will easily be able to recognise simple words and notices, road signs and so on. There is then a short exercise for you to practise reading Arabic, and again the answers are in the **Key to the exercises.**

The final section of each unit is **Test yourself**, a self-assessment to help you monitor your progress before you attempt the next unit. The answers to these are also in the **Key to the exercises.**

After the **Key to the exercises** and the **Transcripts** of the recording, you will find a reference section. This contains a **Grammar summary** and a section on the **Arabic verbs**. Every verb you come across in the book can be matched in the verb tables with a verb which works in the same way. **Arabic–English** and **English–Arabic** glossaries are provided so that you can look up words alphabetically.

Pronunciation and transliteration

Transliteration means expressing a language which uses a different writing system (such as Arabic) in terms of symbols based on the Roman alphabet. There is no generally accepted system for doing this, and you will find that the English versions of, say, road signs, differ from what is given in this book.

The essential feature of a transliteration system is that it has an equivalent for every sound used in the target language. Instead of using a complicated system of accents and special symbols, this book is more or less restricted to the English alphabet, making use of capital letters to distinguish between Arabic sounds which seem related to us. For instance, Arabic has two sorts of *t* which are distinguished in this way: **'tiin'** means *figs*, and **'Tiin'** means *mud*. There is a full explanation of how to pronounce these sounds in the next section.

Consequently you will not find capital letters used in the book as they are conventionally used in English. An exception has, however, been made in the case of **'Allaah'** *Allah*, *God*.

The Arabic sounds

CD 1, TR 1, 0:50

Arabic has some sounds which are difficult for foreigners to pronounce. The following table is therefore divided into three parts:

1 Sounds that are more or less as in English.
2 Sounds which do not occur in English, but are found in other European languages.
3 Sounds which are peculiar to Arabic.

Group 1

b as in **baab** *door*

d as in **diinaar** *dinar*

th as in **ithnain** *two*, like *thank*, not like *this*, *that*, *father* etc.

dh as in **dhahab** *gold*. It is important not to mix this up with the sound written '*th*', as they convey different meanings in Arabic (**dhiyaab** *wolves*, **thiyaab** *garments*)

f as in **filfil** *pepper*

g as in **galam** *pen*

h as in **haadha** *this* but never omitted in speech as it very often is in English (e.g. Brahms). An exception is the common feminine ending **-ah**, and the word **fiih** *there is/are*. The final **-h** in these is there for a special reason and is not normally pronounced.

j as in **jisir** *bridge*

k as in **kabiir** *big*

l as in **laazim** *necessary*, which is mostly as *limp* but sometimes has a more hollow sound, roughly as in *alter*. This distinction is not meaningful in Arabic but depends on the surrounding consonants.

m as in **maay** *water*

n as in **naas** *people*

s as in **samak** *fish*

sh as in **shams** *sun*

t as in **tilifoon** *telephone*

w as in **walad** *boy*

y as in **yad** *hand*

z as in **zain** *good*

Group 2

r as in **riyaal** *riyal*. The Arabic **r** sound does not really occur in standard English, but is familiar in dialect pronunciation. It is the trilled *r* of Scottish *very*, and common in Italian and Spanish (*Parma*, *Barcelona*)

gh as in **gháali** *expensive*. This is near – but not quite the *r* of Parisian French. It is actually a more guttural scraping sound, and occurs in Dutch, e.g. *negen*. The Parisian *r* will do.

kh as in **khamsah** *five*. This is roughly the sound of *ch* in Scottish *loch* and *och aye*. Also familiar in German *Bach* and (written *j*) in Spanish *José*.

Group 3

S, T and **DH**	With the exception of **H** (see below), the capitalised consonants are pronounced in a roughly similar way to their small letter versions **s, t,** and **dh,** except that the tongue is depressed into a spoon shape, and the pressure of air from the lungs increased. This gives a forceful and hollow sound, often referred to as emphatic. These sounds have a marked effect on surrounding vowels, making them sound more hollow, e.g. **Saif** *summer,* **Taarig** *road,* **abu Dhabi** *Abu Dhabi.*
H and **:**	go together. To pronounce these sounds requires practice – and it is best to listen to native speakers – but they can be mastered.
:	We have a muscle in our throat which is never used except in vomiting. Think about that and pretend you are about to be sick. You will find that what is normally called in English *gagging* is actually a restriction in the deep part of the throat. If you begin to gag, and then release the airstream from the lungs, you will have produced a perfect **:** (called **:ain** in Arabic) ; e.g. **:umaan** *Oman.*
H	is pronounced in exactly the same way, except that, instead of completely closing the muscles, they are merely constricted and the air allowed to escape. The only time English speakers come near to a (weakish) **H** is when they breathe on their spectacle lenses prior to cleaning them, e.g. **kaif Haal-ak** *how are you.* Both of these letters should always be pronounced with the mouth fairly wide open (say *ah*).
'	This sound is fairly infrequent in Gulf Arabic. It occurs in English between words pronounced deliberately and emphatically (e.g. 'He [slight pause] *is* an idiot, isn't he'), but is probably more familiar as the Cockney or Glaswegian pronunciation of *t* or *tt* as in *bottle*. e.g. **yis'al** *he asks*

Unstable sounds in Gulf Arabic

Gulf Arabic is a collection of related but distinct dialects and is not governed by any strict pronunciation rules. Remember that, whatever any Arab tells you, the written or literary Arabic language is never spoken in everyday life. It exists only in the written form, and in formal speeches and religious language. What you will hear is dialect or vernacular Arabic.

As a rule, where a literary word is used in parts of the Gulf, this is given, as every educated Arab knows the literary language from school. If you are living in the Gulf, however, you should note and use local expressions.

Nevertheless, the regional pronunciations of some of the consonants can be confusing. These are explained below. The overall policy of this book has been to use the most common pronunciation throughout the area, and, where reasonable, to adopt the version closest to the literary language. Again, if a word is pronounced differently where you live or are visiting, use that pronunciation.

Common local variants

j	The official Arabic sound is identical to English *j* as in *jump*, but this letter is also pronounced as a *y* as in *yes* or, more rarely as a *g* as in *gone*.
DH	Not a problem with Gulf nationals, but many expatriates from the northern Arab world (e.g. Egypt, Palestine) pronounce this like an emphatic *z*, i.e. *z* pronounced with the same tongue position as **S** and **T** (see above). Northern Arabs also have an emphatic **D**. This is not used in Gulf Arabic, where it is replaced by **DH**.
gq	This is officially pronounced in Standard Arabic as a *k* produced far back in the throat. You hear this in parts of Oman and Iraq, and in some words borrowed from the literary language. In such cases, it has been transcribed as **q**. However, the overall common Gulf pronunciation is hard *g*, as in *get*, but it is also occasionally *j* as in *jet*.
kch	This is often heard as *ch* as in *church*. This pronunciation is obligatory in some contexts, where it is transcribed **ch**.

Vowels

CD 1, TR 1, 4:37

There are only five common vowels, three of which occur both long and short. These have been transcribed as follows:

aa as in **thaalith** *this*, an elongated emphatic *a* as in the word *and* in: 'Did he really eat a whole chicken?' 'Yes ... *and* he ate a steak as well.'

a as in **abadan** *never*, roughly as in *hat*
ii as in **kabiir** *big*, like *Eve*, and French *livre*
i as in **jibin** *cheese*, like *big*
uu as in **filuus** *money*, like *rude*, French *vous*, German *Schule*
u as in **buldaan** *countries*, like *put* (never as in *cup*)
oo as in **tilifoon** *telephone*, like *rose* as pronounced in Scotland, or French *beau*
ai as in **bait** *house*, like the sound in *wait*
The following diphthong also occurs occasionally:
ay as in *aye*. The place name Dubai is transcribed **dubay**.

Doubled consonants

CD 1, TR 1, 6:37

Doubled consonants (here written **bb, nn, ss** etc.) are important in Arabic, as they can change the meanings of words radically. They are only pronounced in English when they span two words, e.g. *But Tom, my brother. . .* In Arabic, however, they must always be pronounced carefully, wherever they occur, with a slight hesitation between them, e.g. **gaTar** is the place-name *Qatar*, **gaTTar** means *dripped, distilled*.

Stress

'Stress' refers to the syllable in a word which is pronounced more emphatically than the rest, e.g. *potato*, where the stress is on the second syllable *-ta-*. The stressed syllables of words have been marked with an acute accent: **á, áa,** etc. in the glossaries and the first six units so that you become used to where they occur. One simple rule, however, is that if a word contains a long vowel (*aa*, *uu*, etc.) the stress falls on this; and if there is more than one, the stress falls on the one nearest the end of the word.

The Arabic alphabet

There are several general points to be noted:

- Arabic is written from right to left – the opposite of English.
- Arabic script is always joined or cursive, i.e. there is no equivalent of the English text you are now reading, where all the letters have separate forms with spaces between them. There are no capital letters.
- In cursive writing letters are joined together by means of joining strokes (called ligatures). As a result, Arabic letters have slightly different forms, depending on whether they come at the beginning, middle, or end of a word.
- A few letters do not join to the following letter.
- Arabic writing looks complicated just because it is so different, but in fact it is not. Spelling in Arabic is easy, because, with a very few exceptions, all sounds are written as they are pronounced. There are no diphthongs, i.e. combinations of two letters to give a distinct sound, like *th*, *sh*, etc. in English.
- One thing you must get used to in the Arabic script is that short vowels, i.e. *a*, *i* or *u* (as opposed to the long vowels *aa*, *uu* and *ii*), are not shown in the script. For instance, the word **bank** (which Arabic has borrowed from English), is written **b-n-k**.

Because of the cursive nature of Arabic, it is necessary to give the *initial*, *medial* and *final* forms of each letter. Since some letters do not join to the one after them, a separate form has also been included. Although four forms of the non-joiners have been given, if you look carefully you will see that there are really only two shapes.

The Arabic alphabet is given below in its traditional order. Letters which do not join to the following one are marked with an asterisk.

Final is to be interpreted as final after a joining letter. If the preceding letter is a non-joiner, the separate form will be used. If you look closely, you can see that final and separate letters are usually elongated in form, or have a ‘flourish’ after them.

Also, in most cases, the initial form of the letter can be regarded as the basic or nucleus form. For example, if you look at **baa’** (the second letter in the following list), you will see that its basic (initial) form is a small left-facing hook with a single dot below it. The medial form is more or less the same, with a ligature coming in from the right (remember you are writing from right to left). The final form is the same as the medial, with a little flourish or elongation to the left (i.e. at the end of the word), and the separate form is the same as the initial, but again with the flourish to the left. Study the letters bearing these features in mind, as many of them follow the same principle. The ’ denotes a ‘glottal stop’ sound which is explained in the **pronunciation and transliteration** section. Fuller descriptions and other hints on deciphering will be given in the units.

Name	Initial	Medial	Final	Separate	Pronunciation
alif*	ا	ـا	ـا	ا	see below
baa’	بـ	ـبـ	ـب	ب	b
taa’	تـ	ـتـ	ـت	ت	t
thaa’	ثـ	ـثـ	ـث	ث	th
jiim	جـ	ـجـ	ـج	ج	j
Haa’	حـ	ـحـ	ـح	ح	H
khaa’	خـ	ـخـ	ـخ	خ	kh
daal*	د	ـد	ـد	د	d
dhaal*	ذ	ـذ	ـذ	ذ	dh
raa’*	ر	ـر	ـر	ر	r

zaay*	ز	ـز	ـز	ز	z
siin	سـ	ـسـ	ـس	س	s
shiin	شـ	ـشـ	ـش	ش	sh
Saad	صـ	ـصـ	ـص	ص	S
Daad[1]	ضـ	ـضـ	ـض	ض	D
Taa'	طـ	ـطـ	ـط	ط	T
DHaa'	ظـ	ـظـ	ـظ	ظ	DH
:ain	عـ	ـعـ	ـع	ع	:
ghain	غـ	ـغـ	ـغ	غ	gh
faa'	فـ	ـفـ	ـف	ف	f
qaaf[2]	قـ	ـقـ	ـق	ق	g
kaaf	كـ	ـكـ	ـك	ك	k
laam	لـ	ـلـ	ـل	ل	l
miim	مـ	ـمـ	ـم	م	m
nuun	نـ	ـنـ	ـن	ن	n
haa'	هـ	ـهـ	ـه	ه	h
waaw	و	ـو	ـو	و	w
yaa'	يـ	ـيـ	ـي	ي	y

[1]Daad:– This letter in Gulf Arabic is pronounced in exactly the same way as **DHaa'**.

[2]gaaf – This is normally pronounced like an English hard *g* (as in *gold*) in the Gulf. (See the section on transliteration.)

In addition to the above, there is one combination consonant **laam-alif**. This must be used when this series of letters occurs, and it is a non-joiner:

Name	Initial	Medial	Final	Separate
laam-alif	لا	ـلا	ـلا	لا

There is a letter which the Arabs call **taa' marbuuTah** and which is referred to in this book as the 'hidden *t*'. This is the Arabic feminine ending which only occurs at the end of words, so therefore it has only two forms: final (after joiners) and separate (after non-joiners). It is always preceded by a short 'a' vowel:

Final	Separate
ـة	ة

If you look carefully at this letter, you will see that it looks like a **haa'** with the two dots above of the **taa'** added, and this is exactly what it is. It is normally rendered in speech as a very weak *h*, but in certain combinations of words it is pronounced as *t*. It has therefore been transcribed as **h** and **t** accordingly.

There is one final item called the **hamza**. This is not regarded by the Arabs as a letter of the alphabet, but as the supplementary sign. Its official pronunciation is a glottal stop (as in cockney *bottle*) and it has been transliterated by means of an apostrophe ('). It is frequently omitted in speech, but it is common in written Arabic, where it occurs either on its own, or written over an **alif**, **waaw** or **yaa'**. (In the last case, the two dots under the **yaa'** are omitted.) It can also occur written below an **alif**, but this is less common. The actual **hamza** never joins to anything, but its 'supporting' letters take the form required by their position in the word:

Initial		Medial	Final	Separate
independent		ء in all cases.		
on **alif**	أ	ـأ	ـأ	أ
under **alif**	إ	does not occur		إ
on **waaw**	ـ	ـؤ	ـؤ	ؤ
on **yaa'**	ـ	ـئـ	ـئ	ئ

Note that, at the beginning of a word, ' is always written above or below **alif**.

Vowels

As already mentioned, in Arabic writing the short vowels are not usually marked except in children's school text books, the Holy Koran and ancient classical poetry.

The long vowels are expressed by the three letters **alif**, **waaw** and **yaa'**. **Alif** almost always expresses the vowel *aa*, but **waaw** and **yaa'** can also be consonantal *w* and *y* (as in English *wish* and *yes*).

However, **waaw** and **yaa'** can also express the (only) two Arabic diphthongs, usually pronounced *oo* (with **waaw**) and *ai* (with **yaa'**). The official pronunciation of these dipthongs is *ow* as in *down* and *ay* as in *aye* respectively, but these are heard in informal speech only in a few words.

All this is not as difficult as it sounds, as the real key to Arabic words is the long vowels. It will not usually cause serious misunderstanding if you pronounce a word with *a*, *u* or *i* (short vowels), but it is important to get the long vowels right.

One further note: the letter **yaa'** often occurs at the end of words. It is usually pronounced *-i*, or *-ii*, but sometimes also *-a*. In the former case, it is usually written with two dots under it (ي) and in the latter without them (ى), but this rule is not, unfortunately, always adhered to.

General

Since this book is intended to teach you to recognise the Arabic script, rather than to learn to write it, the above remarks should be sufficient for the purpose. As already mentioned, further information and tips will be given in the units.

Finally, it is better to think of the Arabic script as basically handwriting (since it is always cursive, no matter how produced: by hand, on a typewriter or computer). For this reason – and by dint of what the Arabs regard as the artistic nature of the script, calligraphy being a highly developed art in the Arab world – you are likely to see more variations of the form of the letters than you would in English.

The most important of these is that, very frequently, two dots above or below a letter are frequently combined into one dash, and three dots (which only occur above) into an inverted *v* like the French circumflex ^. Here is an example showing **taa'** and **thaa'**:
ت ث

There are many other variations, but the most important is the writing of س ش **siin** and **shiin** as simply long lines, ironing out their *spikes*, and often with a small hook below at the beginning. Arabic writing is fun. Look at it as an art form!

Credits

1

السلام عليكم
as-saláamu :alái-kum
Hello!

In this unit you will learn how to
- Say hello and goodbye
- Greet someone
- Give your name and ask for someone else's
- Say where you are from and ask someone where they are from

New words and phrases

CD 1, TR 2

Listen to the recording.

Hiwaar 1 (Dialogue 1) حوار ١

CD 1, TR 2, 0:57

Jim and Eleanor McDonald have arrived at the home of their friend Khaled in Muscat. Jim goes in to greet Khaled.

Jim	as-saláamu :alái-kum
Khaled	wa :alái-kum as-saláam
Jim	kaif Háal-ak?
Khaled	al-Hámdu li-l-láah bi-kháir, wa inta kaif Háal-ak?
Jim	bi-kháir, al-Hámdu li-l-láah, aish akhbáar-ak?
Khaled	al-Hámdu li-l-láah

Eleanor comes into the room.

Eleanor	as-saláamu :alái-kum
Khaled	wa :alái-kum as-saláam
Eleanor	kaif Háal-ak?
Khaled	al-Hámdu li-l-láah, wa ínti kaif Háal-ich?
Eleanor	al-Hámdu li-l-láah

QUICK VOCAB

as-saláamu :alái-kum	*Hello* (lit. *the peace [be] upon you*)
wa	*and*
:alái-kum as-saláam	*Hello* (reply to above)
kaif	*how*
Háal-ak/Háal-ich	*your condition* (to a man/woman)
al-Hámdu li-l-láah	*praise (be) to God*
bi-kháir	*well*
ínta/ínti	*you* (man/woman)
aish	*what (is)*
akhbáar-ak/akhbáar-ich	*your news* (to a man/woman)

---

mulaaHaDHáat (Notes) ملاحظات

1 as-saláamu :alái-kum

This set religious greeting is always addressed by the incomer to a group, and it and its reply always take the same form regardless of whom they are addressed to. The same expression can also be used for goodbye when taking one's leave. The **as-** at the beginning is a variant of **al-** *(the)*. This is explained in the Arabic script section at the end of this unit.

2 **kaif Háal-ak/Háal-ich**
No verb *to be* is necessary, so *How your condition* means *How (is) your condition*, i.e. 'How are you?' Similarly **aish akhbáar-ak/akhbáar-ich** means *What (is) your news?*

3 **Addressing people**
In Arabic you must distinguish between a man and a woman and more than one person when addressing people. The first part of the above dialogue is between two men, so you say **-ak** meaning *your* (to a man) in **Háal-ak** and **akhbáar-ak.**

When you are speaking to a woman, you must say **kaif Háal-ich** and **aish akhbáar-ich.**

Insight

This is the most common pronunciation in the Gulf, but you may also hear **-ish** or even **-ik**. It makes no difference whether you yourself are male or female, only who you are speaking to.

To speak to more than one person, called the plural form, say **kaif Háal-kum** and **aish akhbáar-kum** (see 1 above).

4 **al-Hámdu li-l-láah** *(thanks be to God)*
li-l-láah is a contraction of **li-** + **Al-láah** meaning *to God*. It is Arab etiquette to reply to any enquiry about your health with this phrase even if you have just broken both of your legs.

5 **bi-kháir**
This means literally *in well-being*, i.e. good health.

Hiwaar 2 (Dialogue 2) حوار ٢

🔊 CD 1, TR 2, 1:4

Khaled's brother Muhammad comes into the room and shakes hands with everyone.

Muhammad	SabáaH al-kháir
Khaled	SabáaH an-núur
Muhammad	áhlan wa sáhlan
Khaled	áhlan bii-k
Muhammad	kaif Háal-kum
Khaled & Jim	al-Hámdu li-l-láah
Muhammad	(*on leaving the room*) má:a s-saláamah
Khaled	fii amáan Al-láah

QUICK VOCAB

SabáaH	*morning*
SabáaH al-kháir	*good morning*
SabáaH an-núur	*reply to above*
áhlan wa sáhlan	*welcome, hello*
áhlan bii-k/bii-ch	*reply to above* (to a man/woman)
má:a s-saláamah	*goodbye*
fii amáan Al-láah:	*reply to above* (to a man or woman)

mulaaHaDHáat (Notes) ملاحظات

1 SabáaH al-kháir
This literally means *morning* (of the) *well-being*. (See note 5 above.) As **masáa'** means *afternoon*, *evening*, to say *good evening* you use **masáa' al-kháir**, and the reply is **masáa' an-núur**.

2 **áhlan wa sáhlan** is an age-old set phrase.
It can be translated in many ways into English (*welcome, hello,* etc.)

3 **bii-k** is a shortened form of **bi-ak**, literally *with/to you*.
Say **bii-k** to a man, and **bii-ch** to a woman. The plural form, for both men and women is **bíi-kum.**

4 **má:a s-saláamah** and its reply **fii amáan Al-láah.**
These remain the same whoever is addressed, man, woman or more than one person.

Hiwaar 3 (Dialogue 3) حوار ٣

CD 1, TR 2, 3:29

At a cultural evening at the university in Al Ain, Jack meets some of the students. First he meets Muhammad.

Jack	as-saláamu :alái-kum
Muhammad	wa :alái-kum as-saláam
Jack	aish ísm-ak?
Muhammad	ísm-i muHámmad. wa ínta?
Jack	ána ísm-i jaak
Muhammad	ínta min wain?
Jack	ána min ingiltérra. wa ínta?
Muhammad	ána min dubáy
Jack	áhlan wa sáhlan
Muhammad	áhlan bii-k

Then he meets Faridah with some of her friends.

Jack	masáa' al-kháir
Faridah	masáa' an-núur
Jack	aish ísm-ich?
Faridah	ísm-i faríidah. wa ínta?
Jack	ána ísm-i jaak. ínti min wain?
Faridah	ána min ábu DHábi. ínta min amríika?
Jack	laa, ána min ingiltérra
Faridah	áhlan wa sáhlan
Jack	áhlan bii-ch

(a) Where is Muhammad from?
(b) Where is Faridah from?
(c) Where does Faridah think Jack is from?

QUICK VOCAB

ism (or **is(i)m**)	*name*
ísm-ak/-ich	*your name* (man/woman)
ísm-i	*my name*
min	*from*
wain	*where*
ínta/ínti	*you* (man/woman)
ána	*I*
ána min . . .	*I (am) from . . .*
ingiltérra	*England*
dubáy	*Dubai*
ábu DHábi	*Abu Dhabi*
amríika	*America*
laa	*no*

---

mulaaHaDHáat (Notes) ملاحظات

1 **jaak** is of course the English name Jack, **muHámmad** is the common Arab name. In English it is spelled many different ways (*Mohamed, Mohammad,* etc.), the transliteration reflects how it should be pronounced in Arabic. **ingiltérra** is *England* (from the French *angleterre*).

Insight

Most names of Western Countries in Arabic are similar to the originals. The names of the Arab countries given here are in their familiar forms, stripped of 'Kingdom of . . .', 'State of . . .' and so on which feature in some of their official titles.

2 **ism/is(i)m** *name*.
The first form is the 'correct' one, but most Gulf dialects have an aversion to certain combinations of two consonants at the end of a word, and tend to add a 'helping' vowel to ease pronunciation.

These vowels have generally been inserted in this book (in brackets) to aid your listening comprehension, or when they are optional. When something is added to the word, they are generally left out:

ísm-ak *your name* (to a male)
ísm-ich *your name* (to a female)

3 The Gulf States
Here is a list of the rest of the Gulf states and the names of some other places. Notice the **al-** (*the*) in front of some of them.

lándan	*London*
iskutlánda	*Scotland*
ustráalya	*Australia*
al-baHráin	*Bahrain*
al-imaaráat	*The Emirates*
al-kuwáit	*Kuwait*
al-yáman	*Yemen*
ar-riyáaDH	*Riyadh*
as-sa:udíyyah	*Saudi Arabia*
ash-sháarjah	*Sharjah*
gáTar	*Qatar*
:umáan	*Oman*

Hiwaar 4 (Dialogue 4) حوار ٤

CD 1, TR 2, 4:58

Jack joins another group of students with his American colleague, Ken.

Jack	as-saláamu :alái-kum
Yasin	wa :alái-kum as-saláam. tá:raf :árabi?
Jack	ná:am, á:raf :árabi. íntu min wain?
Yasin	níHna min al-baHráin. íntu min amríika?
Jack	laa, ána min ingiltérra. húwwa min amríika
(*introducing Ken*)	
Yasin	áhlan wa sáhlan
Ken	áhlan bii-k

QUICK VOCAB

tá:raf/ta:rafíin	*you know* (to a man/woman)
:árabi	*Arabic* (language)
á:raf	*I know*
ná:am	*yes*
íntu	*you* (plural, both masc. and fem.)
níHna	*we*
húwwa	*he*

(a) What is the first question Yasin asks Jack?
(b) Where are Yasin and his friends from?
(c) Where does he think Jack and Ken are from?

---

mulaaHaDHáat (Notes) ملاحظات

1 Your first Arabic verb (or 'doing word'), **tá:raf** (*you know*) and **á:raf** (*I know*). The forms differ according to who is doing the action. To address a woman, use the form **ta:rafíin**. Notice that with Arabic verbs you do not have to use a pronoun, i.e. words for *I*, *you* etc.

Insight

In some dialects the final **-n** of the feminine form is omitted: **ta:ráfii**.

2 **tá:raf :árabi?** *do you know Arabic?*
When you ask someone a question like this in Arabic, you simply use the normal verb *you know . . . ?* without the '*do you . . .*'. The question is marked by a raising of the pitch of the voice at the end of the sentence.

---

ta:biiráat háammah (Key phrases) تعبيرات هامة

CD 1, TR 2, 6:08

How to say *hello*

as-saláamu :aláikum	*hello*
:alái-kum as-saláam	*hello* (in reply)

How to say *goodbye*

má:a s-saláamah	*goodbye*
fii amáan Al-Iáah	reply to above

How to greet someone

SabáaH al-kháir	*good morning*
SabáaH an-núur	*good morning* (in reply)
masáa' al-kháir	*good afternoon, evening*
masáa' an-núur	*good afternoon, evening* (in reply)
áhlan wa sáhlan	*welcome, hello*
áhlan bii-k/bii-ch	reply to above (man/woman)

How to say your name and ask someone else's

aish ísm-ak/ísm-ich?	*What is your name?* (man/woman)
ána ísmi jaak smart	*My name is Jack Smart.*

How to ask where someone is from, and say where you are from

ínta/ínti min wain?	*Where are you from?* (man/woman)
húwwa min wain?	*Where is he from?*
híyya min gáTar	*She is from Qatar.*
ána min amríika	*I am from America.*
níHna min ingiltérra	*We are from England.*

---

núqaT naHwíyyah (Grammar points) نقط نحوية

1 is/are

There is no word for *is/are* in Arabic:

ísm-i muHámmd	*My name is Mohammed.*
ínta min amríika?	*Are you from America?*

2 SabáaH al-kháir

Certain short words in Arabic are regarded as part of the word which follows them. As this often affects pronunciation, this book uses hyphens to mark it. The commonest example is **al-** *(the)* and its variants, but you also have **bi-** *(in)* as in **bi-khair** and **li-** *(to)* as in **al-Hamdu li-l-laah**, (lit. *the praise to God*).

3 Gender

Gender refers to whether a word is regarded as masculine (male) or feminine (female). In Arabic, words for human beings are obviously masculine for men and feminine for women. However, as in French, there is no neuter gender, and the things we refer to in English as *it* are either *he* or *she* in Arabic.

You must always be conscious of gender in Arabic as it affects other words such as pronouns (see below). Fortunately, the vast majority of feminine words in Arabic are marked by the ending **-ah**.

4 Pronouns

A pronoun is a kind of shorthand word which refers to a person or a thing, such as *he, him, his, it, me, my*.

ken min amríika	*Ken is from America.*
húwwa min amríika	*He is from America.*
al-bait kabíir	*The house is big.* (*house* is masculine)
húwwa kabíir	*It (he) is big.*
as-sayyáarah gháalyah	*The car is expensive.* (*car* is feminine)
híyya gháalyah	*It (she) is expensive.*

The Arabic pronouns

Singular		Plural	
ána	*I*	**níHna**	*we*
ínta	*you* (to a man)	**íntu**	*you* (both genders)

ínti	*you* (to a woman)	**húmma**	*they* (both genders)
húwwa	*he* (it)		
híyya	*she* (it)		

5 Possessives

Possessing or owning something, or something belonging, pertaining, or applying to you is expressed in Arabic by a series of endings, or suffixes. These will be dealt with in a later unit, but note for the moment those used in the dialogues in this unit:

ísm-i	*my name*
Háal-ak	*your condition* (to a man)
akhbáar-ak	*your news* (to a man)
Háal-ich	*your condition* (to a woman)
akhbáar-ich	*your news* (woman)

---

tamriináat (Exercises) تمرينات

1 Read each dialogue several times, listening to the recording if you have it, until you can remember both sides without looking.

2 Complete the sentences below using the words listed on the right. Use each word once only.

(a)	as-saláamu ____________	ísm-i
(b)	____________ li-l-láah bi-kháir	sáhlan
(c)	____________ akhbáar-ak	masáa
(d)	____________ sáarah	Háal-ak
(e)	____________ al-kháir	aish
(f)	kaif ____________	:alái-kum
(g)	áhlan wa ____________	min
(h)	ána ____________ amríika	al-Hámdu

3 Eleanor goes to greet Samirah, Khaled's wife. Complete the dialogue below, using **Dialogue 1** to help you. Check your answers with the key at the back of the book.

Eleanor	____________
Samirah	Wa :alái-kum as-saláam
Eleanor	____________?
Samirah	al-Hámdu li-l-láah bi-kháir, wa ínti kaif Haal-ich?
Eleanor	____________?
Samirah	al-Hámdu li-l-láah

4 Now complete the dialogue below where Eleanor greets and then takes her leave of Khaled's two sisters. Notice that it is later in the day. This time her side of the conversation is done for you. Use **Dialogue 2** as an example.

Eleanor	masáa' al-kháir
Maryam	____________
Eleanor	áhlan wa sáhlan
Maryam	____________
Eleanor	kaif Háal-kum
Maryam & Aishah	____________
Eleanor	(*leaving the room*) má:a s-saláamah
Maryam & Aishah	____________

5 Make up brief dialogues for the groups of people below, the person on the left speaking first. Remember the time of day and the number and gender of people being addressed. Suggested dialogues are given in the **Key to the exercises** at the back of the book.

(a) 5 pm (b) 8 pm (c) 11 am

6 Imagine you are talking to Nasir, and complete your side of the conversation.

Nasir	as-saláamu :alái-kum
ínta	(*say hello*)
Nasir	aish ísm-ak?
ínta	(*say your name, and ask his*)
Nasir	ana ísm-i-náaSir. ínta min wain?
ínta	(*say where you are from, and ask where he is from*)
Nasir	ána min :umáan
inta	(*reply appropriately*)
Nasir	áhlan bii-k

7 How would you translate the following sentences in Arabic?

(a) (*to two men*) Are you from Saudi Arabia?
(b) We are from Sharjah.
(c) Are they from London?
(d) No, he is from England. She is from Kuwait.
(e) (*to a woman*) Are you from the Emirates?
(f) Yes, I am from Abu Dhabi.

CD 1, TR 2, 5:31

8 Here is an interview with a woman student. If you have the recording, listen to it several times until you feel that you understand what is being said, or read the transcript at the end of the book. Then listen again and answer the questions below. First look at these new words:

titkállam / titkallamíin . . . ?	*Do you speak* (man/woman) . . . ?	**QV**
inglíizi	*English*	
atkállam inglíizi	*I speak English*	

(a) What is the first question the student is asked?
(b) Where does the interviewer guess she is from?
(c) What country is she from?
(d) What phrase is used to ask: *What is your name?*
(e) What phrase is used to ask: *Where are you from?*
(f) What is the last question which Jack asks?

al-khaTT al-:árabi (Arabic script) الخط العربي

al- *the*

Look at the dialogues in this unit, and you will notice that **al-** occurs frequently at the beginning of words. This is the Arabic word for *the*, which is always written the same, although it varies sometimes in pronunciation (see below). It is always attached to the following word and is written with two letters, **alif** ا and **laam** ل For obvious reasons it is a very common word in the language and a good one to start off with. It is easy to recognize as it always comes at the beginning of a word: ال

There is a special combination **laam-alif**, which is conventionally written لا. When preceded by the initial **alif** of the **al-** it looks like this: لا This combination is found in one place name on the map on page 34:

الامارات **al-imaaraat** *The (United Arab) Emirates*

You will find the other forms (middle, final etc.) of these letters in the alphabet table at the beginning of the book. Note that ***alif***, like another few letters, does not, by convention, join to the letter following it.

Pronunciation of **al-** *the*

Although it never changes in writing, **al-** has one peculiarity. If the word it is joined to begins with one of the following letters:

t, th, d, dh, r, z, s, sh, S, D, T, DH, l, n

the 'l' of **al-** is dropped in speech, and the first letter of the word *clearly* doubled. This is reflected in the transcription system used in this book, e.g. **al-kuwáit**, but **ar-riyáaDH** and **ash-sháarjah**. This is an important convention of pronunciation and you must pronounce the double versions of the letters listed above clearly.

Insight

If it helps, to begin with, leave a slight pause between them. It is much better to say **as- . . . saláamu :álai-kum** than **a-salaamu :alai-kum** (or, for that matter, **al-salaam :alai-kum** or **salaam :alai-kum**, the last very often heard from Europeans).

This photograph illustrates the unsystematic transliteration of Arabic found on public signs. Whatever you encounter, the official correct pronunciation is **as-suuq** (heard in some parts of Oman and Iraq), but elsewhere in the Gulf you usually hear **as-suug.**

Insight

An easy way to remember which letters this phenomenon occurs with is to pronounce them all from the above list and think what your tongue is doing as you say them. You will find that its tip always comes into contact with somewhere in the region bounded by the space between the top and bottom teeth (e.g. **th, dh**) and the inside front upper gum (**t, d**). Only **sh** is a slight exception, but none of the other letters get anywhere near this point of articulation (**b, f. k** etc.).

الكويت	Kuwait	قطر	Qatar
السعودية	Saudi Arabia	الامارات	the (United Arab Emirates)
أبو ظبي	Abu Dhabi	العراق	Iraq

دبي Dubai	عمان (Sultanate of) Oman
الشارقة Sharjah	اليمن Yemen
البحرين Bahrain	الخليج العربي The Arabian Gulf

Insight

Note the spelling of Sharjah. This reflects the local pronunciation of **g/q**, mentioned in the Pronunciation Guide.

Practice

As in English (e.g. Belgium, but *the* Netherlands) some countries in Arabic have **al-** before them, though this *the* is not usually preserved in the English versions of their names. Look at the map and make a list of those which do; practise saying the names as you go.

Now look through the unit again and look for all the Arabic words which have **al-** or its altered forms before them. e.g. **al-Haal, as-saláam(u)**.

Test yourself

This test covers the main vocabulary, phrases and language points given in Unit 1. If you are not sure about your answers, go back to the dialogues and exercises for some revision, before going on to Unit 2. For the answers, see the **Key to the exercises**.

Match the words or sentences appropriately:

1 as-saláamu :alái-kum	(a) ána min amríika
2 kaif Háal-ak?	(b) fii amáan Al-láah
3 SabáaH al-kháir	(c) ísm-i faríidah
4 aish ísm-ak?	(d) laa
5 ínta min wain?	(e) húwwa min dubáy
6 tá:raf :árabi?	(f) wa :alái-kum as-saláam
7 aish ísm-ich?	(g) ná:am, á:raf :árabi
8 Sáalim min wain?	(h) al-Hámdu li-l-láah bi-kháir
9 titkállam inglíizi?	(i) SabáaH an-núur
10 má:a s-saláamah	(j) ísm-i muHámmad

2

أين . . . ؟

wain . . .?

Where is . . .?

(Note: the written form of this word differs slightly from the spoken.)

In this unit you will learn how to
- Ask for places in a town
- Ask where places are
- Ask for and give directions

New words and phrases

CD 1, TR 3

Listen to the recording.

Hiwaar 1 (Dialogue 1) حوار ١

CD 1, TR 3, 0:53

Bill Stewart has arrived on business in Dubai and he asks the taxi-driver to take him to his hotel.

Bill	SabáaH al-kháir
sawwáag at-táksi	SabáaH an-núur
Bill	fúndug ash-sháiraTun min fáDHl-ak
sawwáag at-táksi	zain, in shaa' Al-láah
Bill	al-fúndug ba:íid :an al-maTáar?
sawwáag at-táksi	laa, húwwa garíib. :áshar dagáayig bass, muu ákthar
Bill	shúkran
sawwáag at-táksi	:áfwan

QUICK VOCAB

sawwáag	*driver*
sawwáag at-táksi	*taxi driver*
fúndug	*hotel*
fúndug ash-sháiraTun	*the Sheraton Hotel*
min fáDHl-ak	*please*
zain	*OK, good*
in shaa' Al-láah	*if God wills*
ba:íid :an	*far from*
maTáar	*airport*
garíib min	*near to* (lit. *near from*)
:áshar	*ten*
dagáayig	*minutes*
bass	*that's all, enough; only just*
muu ákthar	*not more*
shúkran	*thanks, thank you*
:áfwan	*you're welcome, don't mention it*

(a) Is this hotel far from the airport?
(b) How long will it take to get there?

---

mulaaHaDHáat (Notes) ملاحظات

1 sawwáag at-táksi
The word *taxi* has the *the* prefix, so literally it means *driver* (*of*) *the-taxi*. **fúndug ash-sháiraTun.** The English name here has been

Arabized and given the *the* prefix, so literally it says *hotel* (*of*) *the-Sheraton.*

2 **al-fúndug ba:íid :an al-maTáar.**
Just a reminder that there is no word in Arabic for *is* or *are* in such sentences.

---

ma:luumáat thaqaafíyyah (Cultural tips) معلومات ثقافية

in shaa' Al-láah This phrase is usually the first Arabic that Europeans pick up. Contrary to popular belief, it does not indicate an element of vague hope or possibility, but has (by the devout Muslim) to be prefixed to any reference to an action which has not yet taken place.

:áfwan In Arabic, as in most languages, one is expected to say something in reply to *thank you*. In the Gulf it can also be used for *excuse me* when asking someone politely to move out of the way.

Hiwaar 2 (dialogue 2) حوار ٢

CD 1, TR 3, 1:45

Bill needs to find a bank. He asks Mahmoud, the receptionist in the hotel.

Bill	SabáaH al-kháir
Mahmoud	SabáaH an-núur. Kaif Háal-ak?
Bill	bi-kháir, al-Hámdu li-lláah. wa ínta?
Mahmoud	al-Hámdu li-lláah
Bill	law samáHt, fiih bank garíib min hína?
Mahmoud	áywa fiih, al-bank al-wáTani. tá:raf sháari: ráashid?
Bill	laa:, maa á:raf

Mahmoud	zain. min al-báab wa liff yisáar, ba:dáin ruuH síidah wa khudh áwwal sháari: :ála l-yamíin. al-bank :ála l-yisáar
Bill	shúkran jazíilan
Mahmoud	:áfwan

QUICK VOCAB

law samáHt	*if you please*
fiih	*there is / is there?*
bank	*bank*
hína	*here*
áywa	*yes*
wáTani	*national*
sháari:	*street*
sháari: ráashid	*Rashid Street*
maa á:raf	*I don't know*
íTla:	*go out!*
baab	*door*
liff	*turn!*
yisáar	*left*
ba:dáin	*then, after, afterwards, after that*
ruuH	*go!*
síidah	*straight on, straight ahead*
khudh	*take!*
áwwal	*(the) first*
:ála	*on (sometimes shortened to* **:a** *before the definite article)*
yamíin	*right (direction)*
:ála l-yamíin	*on the right*
:ála l-yisáar	*on the left*
jazíilan	*copious, very much*

(a) What does Bill ask about a bank?
(b) Which way should he turn on leaving the hotel?
(c) Which street should he turn into?

mulaaHaDHáat (Notes) ملاحظات

1 **fiih bank . . .** is there a bank . . .
There is no word for *a*, *an* (called the indefinite article) in Arabic.

2 **áywa**
This is the most usual form of the word for *yes*. However, you have already encountered **ná:am** which is slightly more formal.

3 **áwwal sháari: :ála l-yamíin**
To help you find your way, here is a simple diagram:

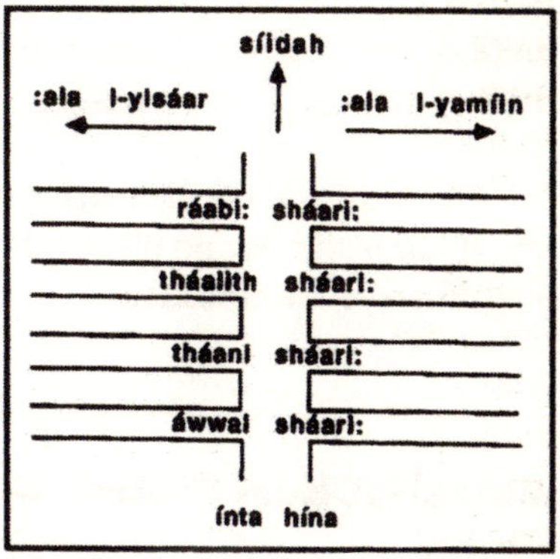

4 **shukran jazíilan**
The word **jazíilan** (*copious*, *abundant*) is rarely used in colloquial Arabic except with **shúkran** (*thanks*).

Hiwaar 3 (Dialogue 3) حوار ٣

CD 1, TR 3, 2:46

Bill takes a walk along the creek and asks a man the way.

Bill	law samáHt, as-súug min wain?
rajjáal	min hináak, :a l-yisáar
Bill	wa l-mátHaf min wain?
rajjáal	al-mátHaf fii dubáy muu hína. hína dáirah. ruuH síidah, liff yamíin, wa l-mátHaf ba:d al-jísir
Bill	shúkran
rajjáal	:áfwan

QUICK VOCAB

rajjáal	*man*
suug	*market*
hináak	*there*
min hináak	*over there, that way*
mátHaf	*museum*
muu	*not*
hína or **híni**	*here*
fii	*in*
dubáy	*Dubai (the old town)*
dáirah	*Deira (the commercial quarter of Dubai)*
ba:(a)d	*after (past)*
jís(i)r	*bridge*

(a) On which side is the market?
(b) What is the second place Bill asks about?
(c) Where is the museum?

---

mulaaHaDHáat (Notes) ملاحظات

min wain, min hinaak
It is better, though not essential, to put **min** before *where*, *here* and *there* when asking or giving directions. It implies *which way. . .*, *that way. . . .* It is, however, quite acceptable to say **wain as-suug?** (*where is the market?*)

Insight

:a l-yisáar
'Elision' means missing out or gliding over a vowel or letter, and it occurs a lot in Arabic, especially with **(a)l-** (*the*). Here **:ála + al-** has been reduced to **:a l-**. This is not a rule, but it is better to get used to hearing it.

wa l-mátHaf
This time the **wa** has elided with the **al-**. Sometimes **wa** sounds like a short English 'oo', usually when it comes before a consonant. In such cases it has been written **w:**
hína dáirah w hináak dubáy *Here is Deira and there is Dubai.*

Hiwaar 4 (Dialogue 4) حوار ٤

CD 1, TR 3, 3:32

Bill has hired a car and wants to get out of town to do some sightseeing. He stops to ask the way at a small shop.

Bill	masáa' al-kháir
SáaHib ad-dukkáan	masáa' an-núur
Bill	háadha Taríig raas al-kháimah?
SáaHib ad-dukkáan	ná:am. ruuH síida min hína, fáwwit al-mustáshfa, w ba:dáin liff yamíin :ind ad-duwwáar ath-tháani - laa, ad-duwwáar ath-tháalith, gábil al mádrasah. ba:dáin liff yisáar, w ba:dáin ruuH síidah
Bill	híyya ba:íidah :an dubáy?
SáaHib ad-dukkáan	wa-l-láahi . . . . tis:íin kíilo min hína tagríiban
Bill	n-záin. shúkran jazíilan. as-saláamu :alái-kum
SáaHib ad-dukkáan	má:a s-saláama

QUICK VOCAB

SáaHib	*master, owner*
dukkáan	*(small) shop*
SáaHib ad-dukkáan	*shopkeeper*
háadha	*this*
Taríig	*way, road*
raas al-kháimah	*Ras al-Khaimah*
fáwwit	*pass, go past!*
mustáshfa	*hospital*
:ind	*at, with*
duwwáar	*roundabout*
tháani	*second*
tháalith	*third*
gáb(i)l	*before*
mádrasah	*school*
híyya	*she, it*
wa-l-láahi	*by God*
tis:íin	*ninety*

kíilo, kiilomít(i)r	*kilometre(s)* (same for singular and plural)
tagríiban	*approximately*

(a) What time of day is it?
(b) In which direction is Bill told to go first?
(c) At which roundabout did the shopkeeper say Bill should turn right?

---

mulaaHaDHáat (Notes) ملاحظات

1 tis:íin kíilo
The (borrowed) word **kíilo(mít(i)r)** is often shortened to **kíilo** as here. The fact that it then coincides with **kiilo (ghráam)**, the measure of weight, doesn't seem to worry anybody.

2 n-záin
The word **zain** means *good*, *OK*, *fine*. It is common to prefix an **n-** to it when it stands on its own. The meaning is unchanged.

3 Map of Dubai
Look at the map and identify the following places:

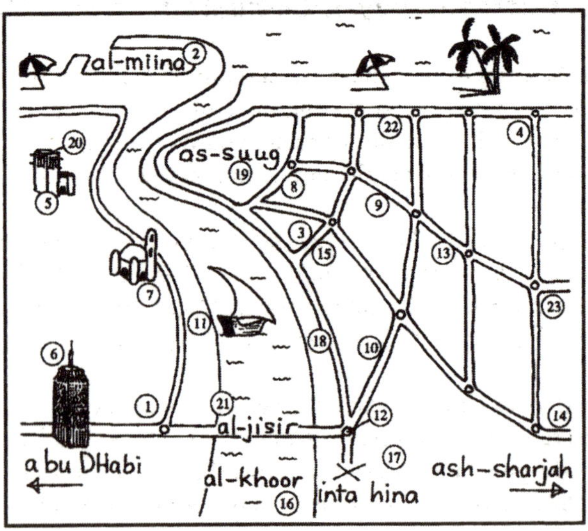

1 **máktab al-baríid** (*post office*)
2 **al-míina** (*the port, harbour*)
3 **al-bank** (*bank*)
4 **al-bustáan** (*garden, park*)
5 **al-HiSn** (*fort*)
6 **al-Jáami:ah** (*university*)
7 **al-jáami:** (*mosque*)
8 **maHáTTat al-baaS** (*bus station*)
9 **márkaz ash-shúrTah** (*police station*)
10 **al-márkaz at-tijáari** (*shopping centre*)
11 **al-máT:am** (*restaurant*)
12 **as-sáa:ah** (*clock (tower), watch*)
13 **aS-Saydalíyyah** (*chemist*)
14 **ash-shíishah** (*petrol station*)
15 **at-tilifóon** (*telephone*)
16 **al-khoor** (*creek*)
17 **al-maTáar** (*airport*)
18 **al-fúndug** (*hotel*)
19 **as-suug** (*market, souk*)
20 **al-mátHaf** (*museum*)
21 **al-jísir** (*bridge*)
22 **al-mustáshfa** (*hospital*)
23 **al-mádrasah** (*school*)
24 × **ínta hína** (*you are here*)

The word **jáami:** (*mosque*) refers to a large central mosque, used for the Friday prayers. A small mosque, such as can be seen at almost every corner, is called a **másjid**.

---

ma:luumáat thaqaafíyyah (Cultural tips) معلومات ثقافية

Most of the cities of the Gulf were laid out during the 70s and 80s, mainly as a result of the rocketing price of oil, and apart from the oldest parts or what remains of them, you find they are very spread out, because space is generally not at a premium.

The exceptions are where cities have grown up around natural features like the creeks of Dubai and Sharjah, and where the mountains around the Capital Area in Oman, for example, have forced development within a comparatively limited space.

A grid pattern of streets is usually linked by a number of roundabouts, which have such decorative features as fountains, clocks or even giant coffee-pots, and impressive flowerbeds and carefully tended lawns. The roundabouts themselves have become landmarks.

ta:biiráat háammah (Key phrases) تعبيرات هامة

CD 1, TR 3, 4:21

How to ask where a place is

fúndug ash-sháiraTun law samáHt	*The Sheraton Hotel, please*
fiih bank garíib min hína?	*Is there a bank near here?*
law samáHt, as-súug min wain?	*Excuse me, where is the market?*
háadha Taríig raas al-kháimah min fáDHI-ak?	*Is this the way to Ras al-Khaimah, please?*
al-fúndug ba:íid :an/garíib min hína?	*Is the hotel far from/near (to) here?*

How to tell someone where a place is

ruuH síidah	*go straight ahead*
liff yisáar/yamíin	*turn left/right*
khudh áwwal/tháani/tháalith sháari: :ála l-yisáar/l-yamíin	*take the first/second/ third street on the left/ on the right*
fáwwit al-mustáshfa	*go past the hospital*
al-mátHaf :ála l-yisáar/l-yamíin /síidah	*The museum is on the left/ right/ straight ahead*
húwwa garíib min/ba:íid :an hína	*It (the hotel) is near to/far from here*
húwwa :áshar dagáayig min hína	*It is ten minutes from here*
híyya garíibah min dubáy	*It (Sharjah) is near to Dubai*
fiih bank min hináak	*There is a bank over there, that way*
gábil al-mádrasa	*before the school*
ba:d al-mustáshfa	*after (past) the hospital*
:ind al-míina	*at the harbour*

núqaT naHwíyyah (Grammar points) نقط نحوية

1 How to say *please*

The most common way is to use the phrase **min fáDHl-ak** which means something like 'by your favour'. Like **kaif Háal-ak** (*How are you?*) in Unit I, the ending must change according to whom you are directing the request to:

min fáDHl-ak	*to a man*
min fáDHl-ich	*to a woman*
min fáDHl-kum	*to more than one person*

law samáHt (*if you permit*) is slightly more formal or polite. The endings again change, this time according to a different pattern. You must say:

law samáHt	*to a man*
law samáHti	*to a woman*
law samáHtu	*to more than one person*

2 *There is* and *there are*

These are expressed in Arabic by the word **fiih**. The *h* is silent, but it is convenient to write the word this way to distinguish it from fii meaning *in*. Remember there is no word for *a*, *an*.

fiih fúndug	*There is a hotel*
fiih fúndug fii dubáy	*There is a hotel in Dubai*

To make a question, just raise your voice at the end of the sentence

fiih fúndug?	*Is there a hotel?*

The negative (*there isn't/is no . . . there aren't/are no . . .* ,) is **maa fiih:**

maa fiih bank	*There isn't a bank, there is no bank*

Insight

Mainly in Bahrain you will hear the Persian borrowing **hast** used instead of **fiih**. In Kuwait and Iraq they say **áku**.

3 Telling people to do something

These forms of the verb (technically known as imperatives) are frequently used in giving directions. Those encountered in this unit are:

íTla:	*go out*
ruuH	*go*
liff	*turn*
fáwwit	*pass, go past*
khudh	*take*

These also have to be altered according to the person spoken to, and they take the same endings as **samaHt** (see above), so you have to say **íTla:i, rúuHi, líffi, fáwwiti** and **khúdhi** to a woman, and **iTlá:u, rúuHu, líffu** etc. to more than one person.

4 Numbers – *first, second, third* etc.

These are known as ordinal numbers, because they tell us the order things come in, and they are obviously common in giving directions.

áwwal	*first*
tháani	*second*
tháalith	*third*
ráabi:	*fourth*
áakhir	*last*

Unlike normal adjectives (see Note 5) these can sometimes come before the noun they describe, especially when giving directions:

khudh áwwal sháari: :ála l-yamíin *Take the first street on the right*

There is no need here for a word for *the*.

5 Noun/adjective phrases

Nouns refer to people, things and ideas; adjectives describe nouns. The correct use of noun/adjective phrases is fundamental to speaking Arabic.

With the sole exception of the ordinal numbers in the previous section the rules are as follows:

1 The adjective comes after the noun: **noun + adjective.**

2 It agrees with the noun in gender (masculine/feminine):

masc. noun + masc. adjective
fem. noun + fem. adjective

Nearly all Arabic adjectives form the feminine by adding the suffix (ending) **-ah.**

3 The use or omission of **al-** (*the*) has a powerful effect on the meaning of such phrases.

The absence of **al-** in the following is, for emphasis, marked with a triangle Δ. There are three basic phrase types:

(a) no **al-** on either word: Δ **noun** + Δ **adjective**

This produces an indefinite phrase:

maTáar kabíir	*a big airport* (masc.)
sayyáarah Saghíirah	*a small car* (fem.)

(Remember that Arabic does not have a word for *a* or *an*.)

(b) **al-** on both words: **al- noun + al- adjective**

This produces a definite phrase:

al-maTáar al-kabíir	*the big airport*
as-sayyáarah aS-Saghíirah	*the small car*

(c) **al-** on the noun, but not the adjective: **al- noun + Δ adjective**

This produces a sentence which, in English, would have the verb *is* or *are*, which as you already know is not used in Arabic:

al-maTáar kabíir	*The airport is big.*
as-sayyáarah Saghíirah	*The car is small.*

These three phrase types are fundamental to Arabic. Learn the examples above by heart and, as you progress, constantly construct similar phrases and sentences with the new words you learn. Here are some examples from this unit:

Type 1:

fiih bank garíib min hína?	*Is there a bank near here* (lit. *a near bank*)?

Type 2:

al-bank al-wáTani	*the National Bank*
al-márkaz at-tij áari	*the commercial centre*

Type 3:

al-fúndug ba:íid :an al-maTáar	*The hotel is far from the airport.*

In Type 3, a pronoun can substitute for the first noun, as in:

laa, húwwa garíib	*No, it's near.*

If you find that you can't take all this in at once, leave it and come back to it.

6 How to say *this is, these are*

In Arabic, the word **háadha** (*this*) is also a pronoun. It makes a verbless sentence if it is followed by a word without **al-**.

If the noun it refers to is feminine, use **háadhi**. and if it is plural, use **haadhóol** or **haadhéel**.

masc.	**háadha muHammad**	*This is Mohammad.*
fem.	**háadhi shíishah**	*This (is) a petrol station.*
plural	**haadhóol maSriyyíin**	*These (are) Egyptians.*

---

tamriináat (Exercises) تمرينات

1 Match up the Arabic sentences below with the correct diagrams on the opposite page.
   (a) fáwwit ash-shíishah
   (b) liff yisáar
   (c) khudh tháani sháari: :ála l-yamíin
   (d) al-bustáan :ála l-yamíin
   (e) al-márkaz at-tijáari min wain?

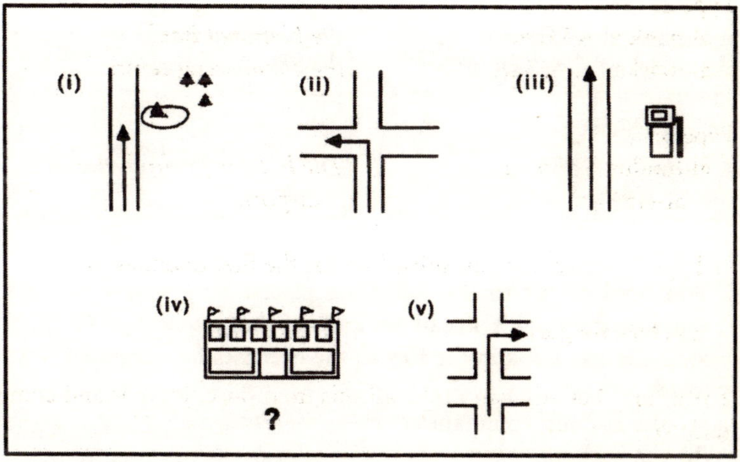

2 Which would you use here: **háadha, háadhi** or **haadhóol**? Fit the correct word into the sentence.
   (a) . . . míina
   (b) . . . kuwaitiyyíin

(c) . . . maTáar kabíir
(d) . . . mátHaf?
(e) laa, . . . jáami:ah

CD 1, TR 3, 5:02

3 Five people are asking the way round town. Listen to the recording, or read the transcript, and work out which place is being asked for and how they have to get there.

QV

kaif arúuh	*how do I go to . . . ?*
fúndug sii fyuu	*Sea View Hotel*
áakhir ash-sháari:	*at the end of the road* (lit. *the last of the road*)

4 Pick the correct verb from the box to put in the following sentences. You can only use each word once!

(a) . . . áwwal sháari: :ála l-yisáar	fáwwit
(b) . . . min hína	íTla
(c) . . . al-fúndug	liff
(d) . . . :ála l-yamíin	ruuH
(e) . . . síidah	khudh

5 You need to get to the following places: how would you ask someone the way? You can use **kaif arúuh** (*how do I go to . . . ?*) for a change. Look in the **Key to the exercises** for suggested ways to ask.
(a) the al-Bourj roundabout
(b) the harbour
(c) Abu Dhabi
(d) the Al-Khaleej restaurant

6 . . . and how would you give someone directions to get to the following places?

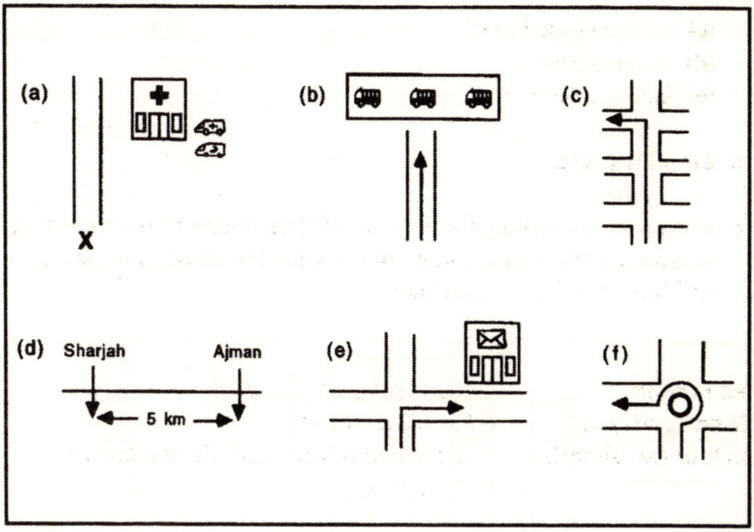

7 Using the map of Dubai on page 24, and the directions below, work out where you are being sent. Your position is marked **X** on the map, near the airport.

(a) ruuH síida, fáwwit ad-duwwáar wa khudh áwwal sháari: :ála l-yamíin, ba:d al-fúndug. ________ :ála l-yamíin.

(b) áwwal ruuh síidah, ba:dáin liff yisáar :ind ad-duwwáar, w-bá:d al-jísir, :ind ad-duwwáar, liff yamíin, wa ________ :ála l-yisáar, ba:d al-jáami:.

(c) ruuH síida, wa :ind ad-duwwáar, liff :ála l-yamíin, w-khudh tháani sháari: :ála l-yisáar, wa ________ :ála l-yisáar.

(d) ruuH síidah w-:ind ad-duwwáar liff :ála l-yisáar, w-ba:dáin ruuH síidah.

8 Lastly see how much new vocabulary you have learned! Find the Arabic for the places below and fit them into the puzzle.

Where would you go if you wanted:

Across

1 to go to the Friday prayers

6 to watch the container ships unload

Down

2 a children's learning centre

3 to get medical treatment

4 a centre for higher learning

8 public transport
10 to catch a plane
13 to do all your shopping under one roof
15 a place where traffic cirlulates
16 somewhere to stay
17 to know the time

5 to see an exhibition of old remains
7 something to eat
9 to buy a cold remedy
11 to cross the creek
12 to visit an ancient military building
14 to go to a traditional Arab shopping area

---

al-khaTT al-:árabi (Arabic script) الخط العربي

Since your main purpose in learning the script is to recognize Arabic, here are the next two most common letters:

m *miim* in Arabic. This letter occurs frequently because, apart from occurring internally and finally in words, it is a common prefix in Arabic. Like most Arabic letters, it has three forms, depending on whether it occurs at the beginning of a word, or in the middle or at the end.

Name	Initial	Medial	Final	Separate	Pronunciation
miim	مـ	ـمـ	ـم	م	m

When it follows **laam** – frequently after **al-** (*the*) الـ (**al-m . . .**).

Here, you will see that the **alif** has been moved to the left of the letter and the little circle has been filled in.

Insight

Remember that all Arabic letters join to the one before them (reading right to left). However some, by convention, do not join to the one after them (**álif** in the previous chapter was one of them). 'Beginning' (or 'initial'), 'middle' and 'final' letters should be interpreted in this context.

Practice

Try to distinguish the **miims** in the following words from this lesson and find out their meanings. The first word is the only one which begins and ends with **miim**. Can you work out which it is? The others are transliterated for you:

مطعم

مدرسة mádrasah

ميناء míina

المركز التجاري al-márkaz al-tijáari

محطة الباص maHáTTat al-baaS

Answer: the first word is **máT:am** (*restaurant*).

The other very common letter which you should learn to recognize is ة. This letter is easy to spot as it only occurs at the end of words, and actually marks the feminine ending **-ah**. Watch out for it on signs, place-names etc. Refer back to the place-names and map in Unit 1 and see how often it occurs.

Now look for it in some of the words you have learned in this unit:

مدرسة	mádrasah
شرطة	shúrTah
صيدلية	Saydalíyyah
ساعة	sáa:ah
راس الخيمة	raas al-kháimah
جامعة	jáami:ah

Test yourself

This test covers the main vocabulary, phrases and language points given in Unit 2. If you are not sure about your answers, go back to the dialogues and exercises for some revision, before going on to Unit 3. For the answers, see the **Key to the exercises.**

To assess your progress so far, pick an appropriate word from the list below to fit in the following sentences, using each word only once:

(a) háadha, (b) ruuH, (c) l-yamíin, (d) al-waTani, (e) min fáDHl-ak, (f) ákhir, (g) wain, (h) hináak, (i) garíib, (j) háadhi

1 maHáTTat al-baaS, . . .
2 fiih Saydalíyyah . . . min hína?
3 aywa, min . . .
4 law samáHt, al-mátHaf min . . . ?
5 . . . síidah
6 . . . máktab al-baríid?
7 laa, . . . mustáshfah
8 wain al-bank al-qaTari . . .?
9 huwwa :ála . . .
10 khudh . . . sháari: :ála l-yisáar

3

رقم التلفون . . .

rágam at-tilifóon . . .

The telephone number is . . .

In this unit you will learn

- The numbers
- How to ask for someone on the telephone
- How to ask for and give telephone numbers

New words and phrases

CD 1, TR 4

Listen to the recording.

Hiwaar 1 (Dialogue 1) حوار ١

CD 1, TR 4, 0:18

Bill is in his hotel room and needs to telephone a business contact. First he rings Directory Enquiries.

al-baddáalah	ayy rágam tiríid?
Bill	kam rágam tilifóon shárikat al-khalíij li t-tijáarah min fáDHl-ak?
al-baddáalah	ar-rágam ithnáin síttah árba:ah khámsah Sífir wáaHid.
Bill	shúkran
al-baddáalah	áfwan.

QUICK VOCAB

baddáalah	*(telephone) exchange*
ayy	*which*
rág(a)m/ráq(a)m	*number*
tiríid	*you want/do you want?*
kam	*what* (lit. *how many*)
rágam tilifóon	*telephone number*
shárikat al-khalíij li t-tijáarah	*Gulf Trading Company*
shárikah	*company*
al-khalíij	*the (Arab) Gulf*
li	*to, for*
tijáarah	*trade, trading*
ithnáin	*two*
síttah	*six*
árba:ah	*four*
khámsah	*five*
Síf(i)r	*zero*
wáaHid	*one*

(a) How does the operator ask which number is required?
(b) What number does the operator give Bill?

mulaaHaDHáat (Notes) ملاحظات

shárikat al-khalíij li t-tijáarah (*Gulf Trading Company*) This literally means 'The Company [of] the Gulf for the Trading'. This type of phrase is dealt with in Grammar point 1 later in this unit.

Insight

kam (in many parts of the Gulf pronounced **cham**). This means *how many?*, but it is also used when asking for phone numbers, where you would say *what*? (**aish** = what? is also used).

kam/aish rágam tilifóon . . . *what (is) the telephone number (of) . . . ?* No word for *of* is necessary.

Hiwaar 2 (Dialogue 2) حوار ٢

CD 1, TR 4, 0:56

Bill rings the number he has been given.

as-sikritáirah	SabáaH al-kháir, hína shárikat al-khalíij li t-tijáarah.
Bill	SabáaH an-núur, :abd al-:azíiz mawjúud min fáDHl-ich?
as-sikritáirah	min ism-ak, min fáDHl-ak?
Bill	ísm-i biil styuart.
as-sikritáirah	láHDHah law samáHt
(after a few moments:)	
Abdel Aziz	SabáaH al-khair, yaa biil. áhlan fii dubáy. kaif Háal-ak?
Bill	al-Hámdu li l-láah. aish akhbáar-ak?
Abdel Aziz	al-Hámdu li l-láah. kaif al-:áa'ilah?
Bill	bi-khair, al-Hámdu li l-láah. wa ínta, kaif al-:áa'ilah?
Abdel Aziz	bi-kháir, shukran. kaif mumkin asáa:id-ak?
Bill	múmkin ajíi-k fi l-máktab?
Abdel Aziz	Táb:an. a:Tíi-ni rágam tilifóon al-fúndug w attáSSil fii-k ba:d khams dagáayig

Bill	rágam al-fúndug ithnáin thamáaniyah wáaHid khámsah sáb:a thaláathah
Abdel Aziz	w rágam al-ghúrfah?
Bill	sáb:ah míyyah síttah wa :ishríin
Abdel Aziz	n-zain, attáSil fii-k ba:d shwayyah. Hayyáa-k Al-láah
Bill	fii amáan Alláah

QUICK VOCAB

sikritáirah	*secretary (female)*
mawjúud	*there, present*
láHDHah	*moment, a moment*
áhlan fii dubáy	*welcome to Dubai*
min or **man**	*who?*
yaa	*used before names when addressing people*
:áa'ilah or **:áayilah**	*family*
asáa:id-ak	*I help you / can I help you?*
ajíi-k	*I come to you*
máktab	*office*
Táb:an	*of course, naturally*
A:Tíi-ni	*give me*
attáSil fii-k	*I'll ring you*
thamáaniyah	*eight*
sáb:ah	*seven*
thaláathah	*three*
ghúrfah	*room*
míyyah	*hundred*
:ishríin	*twenty*
shwáyyah	*a little, some*
ba:d shwáyyah	*in a little while, later*
Hayyáa-k Al-láah	*goodbye*

(a) What is the telephone number of Bill's hotel?
(b) What is Bill's hotel room number?
(c) When is Abdel Aziz going to ring back?

mulaaHaDHáat (Notes) ملاحظات

1 **min** (*who?*) is exactly like the word for *from*.
The context will always make it clear which is meant. You also sometimes hear it pronounced **man**.

2 **yaa . . .**
It is obligatory when addressing someone to place this word before their name. It has no translation in English.

3 **fi l-máktab** (*in the office*)
This is short for **fii al-maktab**. This obligatory elision is pronounced **fil-**.

4 **khams dagáayig** (*five minutes*)
The Gulf Arabic numerals are given later in this unit.

5 **attáSil fii-k** (*I'll phone you*)
You can also use the phrase **asawwíi l-ak tilifóon**.

Insight

a: Tíi-ni (*give [to] me*). In certain parts of the Gulf you hear **:áT-ni** or even **nTíi-ni**.

ma:luumáat thaqaafíyyah (Cultural tips) معلومات ثقافية

kaif al-:áa'ilah (*how is the family?*) It is considered impolite to enquire too closely about an Arab family, especially the female element, unless you know that family very well. This phrase or the alternative **kaif al-áh(a)l** is the accepted way to do it. **áh(a)l** is another word for family, kinsfolk.

Hayyáa-k Al-láah (lit. *God give you life*) is another well-wishing phrase. It can mean *goodbye* as here, or even *thank you* depending on context.

Al-láah (*God, Allah*) has been spelled with a capital **A** in this book out of respect. It is actually composed of **al-** (*the*) plus **láah** which is a contraction of **iláah** (*a god*) , i.e. *the God*. Like all words beginning with **al-** the (in this case capital) **a** can be elided, as you have already seen in **al-Hámdu li l-láah** (*praise[be] to God*).

---

núqaT naHwíyyah (Grammar points) نقط نحوية

1 Possessives

Possessive constructions express the idea of belonging.
For example, in Unit 1 the endings or suffixes, applied to the words **Haal** (*condition*) and **akhbáar** (*news*) denote *your*:

kaif Háal-ak	*how (is) your condition* (to a man)
aish akhbáar-ich	*what (is) your news* (to a woman)

The same meaning of belonging can be expressed by placing two nouns together, the second one usually having **al-** (*the*) before it:

sawwáag at-táksi	*taxi driver* (lit. driver of the taxi)
SáaHib ad-dukkáan	*shopkeeper* (lit. owner of the shop)
rágam at-tilifóon	*phone number* (lit. number of the telephone)
shárikat al-khalíij li t-tijáarah	*Gulf Trading Company* (lit. company of the Gulf for the trading)

The last example illustrates the important rule that feminine nouns ending in **-ah** change this to **-at** when they are used as the first part of such constructions.

Note that the first word must never have **al-** placed before it. Instead it is placed before the second word. The indefinite equivalent of such phrases is **sawwáag táksi** and **SáaHib dukkáan** (*a taxi driver, a shopkeeper*).

2 Numbers

🔊 CD 1, TR 4, 2:24

Here are all the basic Arabic numbers. You should not try to learn them all at once, but use this list as a reference.

Using numbers to count things (e.g. six houses, three cars) will be dealt with in Unit 5. Here you'll find mainly telephone numbers, and 'abstract' numbers (e.g. in arithmetical calculations). Both of these use the independent form.

	Masculine/independent	Feminine
1	wáaHid	wáaHidah
2	ithnáin	thintáin
3	thaláathah	thaláath
4	árba:ah	árba:
5	khámsah	khám(a)s
6	síttah	sitt
7	sáb:ah	sab:
8	thamáan(i)yah	thamáan
9	tís(a):ah	tísa:
10	:ásharah	:áshar

Common gender (i.e. no distinction as above)

11	iHdá:shar
12	ithná:shar
13	thalaathtá:shar
14	arba:atá:shar
15	khamastá:shar
16	sittá:shar
17	sab:atá:shar
18	thamantá:shar
19	tis:atá:shar
20	:ishríin
21	wáaHid w-:ishríin

22	**ithnáin w-:ishríin**
23	**thaláathah w-:ishríin**

. . . and so on, using the masc. form of the unit

30	**thalaathíin**
40	**arba:íin**
50	**khamsíin**
60	**sittíin**
70	**sab:íin**
80	**thamaaníin**
90	**tis:íin**
100	**míyyah**
200	**miitáin**
300	**thaláath míyyah**
400	**árba: míyyah**
1000	**alf** (plural. **aaláaf**)
2000	**alfáin**
1000000	**milyóon** (plural. **malaayíin**)

Insight

Many speakers habitually leave out the final **–ar** on 11–19, and some speakers say **ímyah** for 100.

Making compound numbers

(a) When you say any number above 20, you are making a compound number, and the last two numbers always have **wa** (*and*) between them.

(b) The words are in the same order as in English, except that the units come before the tens.

(c) When you are talking about 200, you must use the special 'dual' form, **miitáin**, but for 300 or more use **míyyah**.

(d) When you are talking about 2000 you must also use the 'dual' plural, **alfáin**, but for three thousand or more use the normal plural, **aaláaf**.

(e) If the following word begins with a vowel, the **'h'** at the end of the masculine/independent number changes to a **'t'**.

36	**síttah w-thalaathíin**	six and thirty
120	**míyyah w-:ishríin**	one hundred and twenty
279	**miitáin tís:ah w-sab:íin**	two hundred, nine and seventy
1945	**alf tís:ah míyyah khámsah w-arba:íin**	one thousand, nine hundred, five and forty
2488	**alfáin árba: míyyah thamáaniyah w-thamaaníin**	two thousand, four hundred, eight and eighty
3075	**thaláathat aaláaf khámsah w-sab:íin**	three thousand, five and seventy

---

ma:luumaat thaqaafiyyah (Cultural tips) معلومات ثقافية

Here are two well-known Arabic story titles which include numbers:
alf láilah wa láilah *(a) thousand nights and (a) night*, (i.e *The Thousand and One Nights*, or *The Arabian Nights*)
:áli báaba wa l-arba:íin Haráami *Ali Baba and the Forty Thieves*

. . . and a proverb from Abu Dhabi!
al-bild sáb:ah wa l-báHar sáb:ah (lit. 'the line is seven and the sea is seven', used to express *just making ends meet*)
(**al-bild** is the plumbline used to test the depth of the sea in fathoms)

3 Telephone numbers

Telephone numbers in spoken Arabic are given in a straight series of digits - just like English, e.g. 123 456 (one two three, four five six). **Sífir** zero, is the origin of our English word *cipher*. The Arabs were responsible for getting Europe off the Roman numbering system (XVII etc.) in the Middle Ages, and introduced the zero into our numbering system.

We speak of Arabic (as opposed to Roman) numerals, but the Arabs actually borrowed them from the Indians. Hence the different forms.

4 Asking for people on the telephone

You simply say . . . (name of person) **mawjúud?**. This is the standard phrase for asking if someone is there or present. **mawjúud** is an adjective, describing a thing or person, so it has to agree in gender. If the person in question is a female, it becomes **mawjúudah**:

:abd al-:azíiz mawjúud?	*Is Abdel Aziz there?*
fáaTimah mawjúudah?	*Is Fatimah there?*
áywa, :abd al-:azíiz mawjúud	*Yes, Abdel Aziz is here.*
laa, fáaTimah muu mawjúudah	*No, Fatimah is not here.*

tamriináat (Exercises) تمرينات

CD 1, TR 4, 3:35

1 Listen to the recording and note down the football scores. If you don't have the recording, look in the transcript at the back.

CD 1, TR 4, 4:02

2 Here is a list of four hotel room numbers, and four telephone numbers.

Listen to the recording or read the transcript and jot down the numbers you hear. Some of them don't correspond with the ones below – which ones are wrong? Check your answers in the Key to the exercises at the back.

(a) 10	(c) 208	(e) 321–450	(g) 798–125
(b) 36	(d) 911	(f) 347–806	(h) 892–660

3 A visitor has come to see a hotel guest

záayir	aish rágam ghúrfat áHmad bin sá:ad min fáDHl-ak?
káatib	áHmad bin sá:ad fii ghúrfah rágam khams míyyah w :áshriin fi d-door al-kháamis.
záayir	shúkran

QUICK VOCAB

záa'ir or **záayir**	*visitor*
káatib	*clerk, receptionist*
door	*floor, storey*
al-kháamis	*the fifth*
ad-door al-kháamis	*the fifth floor*

Make up similar dialogues, using the information below and referring if necessary to the ordinal numbers in Unit 2.

Name	Room number	Floor
(a) Husáin :íisa	15	1
(b) múuna ábu Háidar	235	2
(c) ad-doktóor muHámmad al-wardáani	480	4

4 **Hisaab** (*Arithmetic*): The Arabs are proud of the fact that they invented modern arithmetic. Try the following sums in Arabic. Write the numbers and the answers in words. The main arithmetical expressions are as follows:

+ **wa** (*and*) (more formally **záayid** *increasing*)
– **náagiS** (*lacking*)
× **fii** (lit. *in*, more formally **DHarb** *multiplication*)
÷ **:ála** (lit. *on* **magsúumah :ala** *divided by*)
= **yisáawi** (*it equals, makes*)

(a) 2 + 5 = . . . (d) 1389 – 1260 = . . . (g) 1000 ÷ 50 = . . .
(b) 11 + 3 = . . . (e) 9 × 5 = . . . (h) 96 ÷ 12 = . . .
(c) 46 – 19 = . . . (f) 122 × 3 = . . .

al-khaTT al-:árabi (Arabic script) الخط العربي

In this Unit you'll take a rest from the Arabic alphabet and deal instead with the numbers.

Although the Arabic script is written from right to left, the numerals are written from left to right as in the West. This may seem bizarre, but it is a fact. As your eye scans a piece of Arabic, it has to reverse direction when numerals appear.

This problem is compounded in dates of day + month + year where the order of these elements is right to left, but the numbers expressing them go in the opposite direction. So where in English the 17th of December 2010 would be 17/12/2010, in an Arabic context it would be written 2010/12/17 – \٢٠١٠\١٢\١٧.

Some bilingual English/Arabic computer word processing packages even have a special way to accommodate this, so that you can keep typing in the same direction!

Nevertheless the numerals are fairly easy to learn. If you look at them closely and use a bit of imagination, you can often see a connection to the European version. Try turning them sideways; for instance, Arabic turned 90 degrees to the left and with the tail deleted is similar to our 3. The same applies to 7 and some others.

Since the computational system and direction of writing are the same as in the West, you have nothing more to learn.

1	١	6	٦
2	٢	7	٧
3	٣	8	٨
4	٤	9	٩
5	٥	0	٠

A few examples:

١٢	12
٥٦	56
٢٨٥	285
٢٠٠٦/٠٥/٢٣	7,942
٢٠٠٦/٠٥/٢٣	23/05/2006

(Watch the reading direction)

Insight

In handwriting, *3* is written like a printed *2* (i.e. with one concave curve at the top instead of two) and in such cases *2* is written with a convex (upward facing curve) at the top:

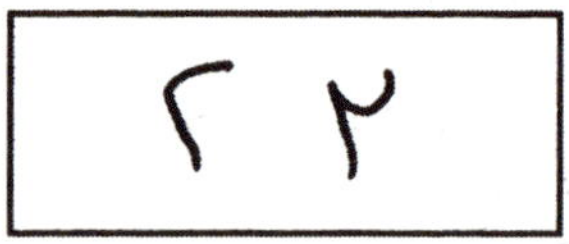

Some countries have adopted the western form of numerals. Look on this as a bonus!

Test yourself

This test covers the main vocabulary, phrases and language points given in Unit 3. If you are not sure about your answers, go back to the dialogues and exercises for some revision, before going on to Unit 4. For the answers, see the **Key to the exercises.**

How would you say the following sentences in Arabic?

1 What is the telephone number of the hotel?
2 The number is 264059.
3 Is Ibrahim al-Hussein there, please?
4 The room number is 310.

Write down the following numbers in English:

5 khamsatá:shar
6 sáb:ah wa-tis:íin
7 miitáin árba:ah wa-thalaathíin

Now write these numbers in Arabic:

8 12
9 54
10 681

4

السـاعة كم؟

as-sáa:ah kam?

What time is it?

In this unit you will learn

- How to ask and tell the time
- How to ask when things open and close
- The days of the week
- The times of day

New words and phrases

CD 1, TR 5

Listen to the recording.

Hiwaar 1 (Dialogue 1) حوار ١

CD 1, TR 5, 0:15

Bill's watch is still on London time, so he asks Mahmoud in reception what the time is.

Bill	as-sáa:ah kam law samáHt?
Mahmoud	al-Híin as-sáa:ah thamáanyah
Bill	as-sáa:ah thamáanyah bi DH-DHabT?
Mahmoud	ná:am, bi DH-DHabT
Bill	shúkran
Mahmoud	:áfwan

Another guests asks about the swimming pool.

DHaif	wain al-másbaH min fáDHl-ak?
Mahmoud	hináak :ála l-yisáar, láakin magfúul al-Hiin
DHaif	as-sáa:ah kam yíftaH?
Mahmoud	yíftaH as-sáa:ah tís:ah. ba:d nuSS sáa:ah
DHaif	ashkúr-ak
Mahmoud	áhlan wa sáhlan

Later that evening a guest asks when the hotel restaurant closes.

DHaif	al-máT:am yibánnid as-sáa:ah kam?
Mahmoud	as-sáa:ah iHdá:shar w nuSS
DHaif	shúkran
Mahmoud	:áfwan

(a) Bill's watch says 4 am. What is the time difference between London and Dubai?
(b) When does the swimming pool open?
(c) What phrase is used to ask when something opens?
(d) When does the restaurant close in the evening?

QUICK VOCAB

sáa:ah	*hour* (also *clock, watch*)
as-sáa:ah kam?	*What's the time/At what time . . . ?*
al-Híin	*now*
as-sáa:ah thamáanyah	*(the time is) eight o'clock*
bi DH-DHabT	*exactly*
DHaif	*guest*
másbaH	*swimming pool*
láakin	*but*
magfúul	*closed, shut*
yíftaH/tíftaH	*it (masc./fem.) opens*
ba:d nuSS sáa:ah	*in half an hour*

QUICK VOCAB

nuSS	*half*
nuSS sáa:ah	*half an hour*
ashkúr-ak	*thank you* (lit. *I thank you*)
yibánnid/tibánnid	*it (masc./fem.) closes*
as-sáa:ah iHdá:shar w nuSS	*(at) half past 11*

mulaaHaDHáat (Notes) ملاحظات

1 **as-sáa:ah kam?** (*What's the time / at what time . . . ?*)
This is the normal way to ask the time, but you may also hear **kam as-sáa:ah?** with the word order reversed.

2 **ba:d nuSS sáa:ah** *in* (lit. *after*) *half an hour.*
Where English says *in* half an hour, Arabic has **ba:d** (*after*).

Insight

ashkúr-ak is a slightly more formal variant of **shúkran** (*thank you*). Because this is a verb, meaning literally *I thank you*, the ending must change according to whom you are speaking to. So to a woman you say **ashkúr-ich**, and to several people, **ashkúr-kum** (the same endings you are familiar with from **kaif Háal-ak** etc.). **shúkran** never changes.

Hiwaar 2 (Dialogue 2) حوار ٢

CD 1, TR 5, 1:53

Abdel Aziz rings Bill in his hotel room.

Abdel Aziz	biil?
Bill	aywa :índ-ak. :abd al-azíiz?
Abdel Aziz	ná:am. kaif al-Háal?
Bill	bi-kháir, al-Hámdu li-lláah. wa Háal-ak ínta?

Abdel Aziz	al-Hámdu li-lláah. as-sáa:ah kam tííji l-máktab?
Bill	as-sáa:ah iHdá:shar zain?
Abdel Aziz	zain, láakin as-sáa:ah iHdá:shar w nuSS áHsan
Bill	zain. ídhan ashúuf-ak as-sáa:ah iHdá:shar w nuSS in sháa' Al-láah
Abdel Aziz	in sháa' Al-láah

QUICK VOCAB

:índ-ak	*with you (*i.e. *it's me speaking)*
tííji	*you come, will come*
áHsan	*better*
ídhan	*so, therefore*
ashúuf-ak	*I see you, I will see you*

(a) What does Bill wish to do?
(b) When does he suggest they meet?
(c) When do they agree to meet?

ma:luumáat thaqaafíyyah (Cultural tips) معلومات ثقافية

Arabs expect to go through a whole gamut of greetings each time they meet and it is considered rude to rush straight into your business, even if you were speaking o nly a few minutes ago. This goes slightly against the grain with us Westerners, but don't worry, just keep talking, even if your replies don't all exactly fit the questions. It is doubtful whether anyone actually listens.

ta:biiraat haammah (Key phrases) تعبيرات هامة

CD 1, TR 5, 2:43

Asking the time

kam as-sáa:ah min fáDHl-ak/ich? *What's the time please?*

Saying what time it is

as-sáa:ah khámsah	*It is five o'clock.*
as-sáa:ah árba:ah wa;rúba:	*Quarter past four.*
as-sáa:ah síttah wa-nuSS	*It is half past six.*
as-sáa:ah thaláathah ílla rúba:	*It is a quarter to three.*
as-sáa:ah thintáin ílla khams	*It is five to two.*

Saying whether something is open or closed

ad-dukkáan maftúuH	*The shop is open*
aS-Saydalíyyah magfúulah	*The pharmacy is closed*

Talking about opening and closing times

ad-dukkáan yíftaH as-sáa:ah tísa:ah	*The shop (masc.) opens (at) nine o'clock.*
aS-Saydalíyyah tíftaH as-sáa:ah tís:ah	*The pharmacy (fem.) opens at nine o'clock*
ad-dukkáan yíbánnid as-sáa:ah sáb:ah	*The shop (masc.) closes (at) seven o'clock.*
aS-Saydalíyyah tibánnid as-sáa:ah sáb:ah	*The pharmacy (fem.) closes at seven o'clock.*

---

núqaT naHwíyyah (Grammar points) نقط نحوية

1 Asking the time

The word **sáa:ah** means in English *hour*, *clock*, or *watch*. As the **-ah** ending tells us, it is feminine in gender. To ask the time, say:

kam as-sáa:ah? or **as-sáa:ah kam?**	*What (is) the time?*
kam as-sáa:ah min faDHI-ak/ich?	*What's the time, please?*

According to context, **as-saa:ah kam** (but not **kam as-saa:ah**) can also mean *at what time*:

as-sáa:ah kam tíiji?	*(at) what time will you come?*

2 Telling the time

Saying the time on the hour:

as-saa:ah waaHidah | **as-saa:ah thintain** | **as-saa:ah thalaathah**

as-sáa:ah iHdá:shar	*11 o'clock*
as-sáa:ah ithná:shar	*12 o'clock*

Note from the above that:
(a) *One* and *two o'clock* use the feminine form of the numeral
(b) *Three o' clock* to *ten o' clock* inclusive use the independent form
(c) For *eleven* and *twelve o' clock* there is only one possible form.

rúba:	*quarter*
thilth	*(third of an hour), 20 minutes*
nuSS	*half*

Where in English you say *past*, in Arabic you say **wa: as-sáa:ah** (current hour) **wa...** the hour is **x** plus...

For the English *to*, in Arabic use **ílla** (*except for, less*): **as-sáa:ah** (next hour) **ílla...** the hour is **x + 1** less...

as-saa:ah sittah wa khams | **as-saa:ah waaHidah wa nuSS** | **as-saa:ah arba:ah illa thilth**

as-sáa:ah iHdá:shar wa-rúba:	*quarter past eleven*
as-sáa:ah thaláathah ílla rúba:	*quarter to three*

Twenty-five past and *twenty-five to* the hour are expressed in Arabic as *the hour plus a half less five* and *the hour plus a half plus five* respectively:

as-sáa:ah khámsah wa-nuSS ílla khams	*25 past five*
as-sáa:ah khámsah wa-nuSS wa khams	*25 to six*

Note that in time expressions which end in *five* or *ten* (minutes) the numeral is in the feminine form.

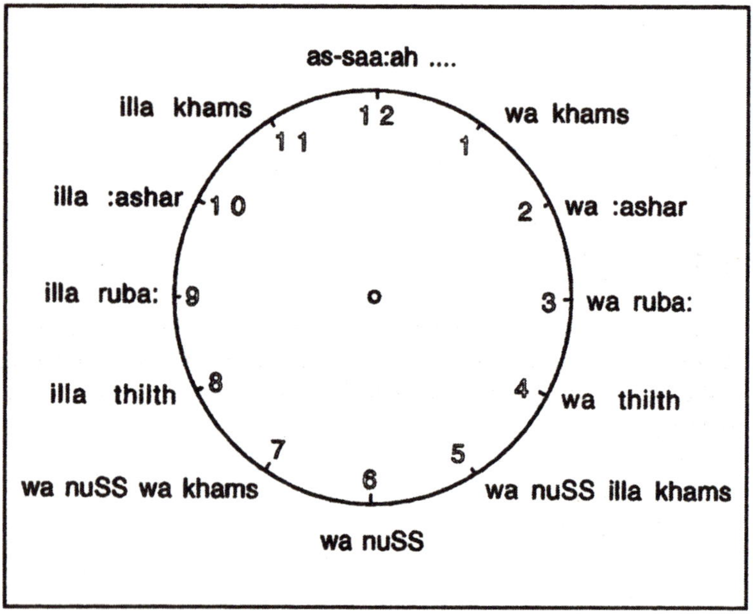

More formally (and less commonly) all times can be stated using the preceding hour plus the number of minutes:

as-sáa:ah :ásharah wa khamsah w arba:íin dagíigah	*10.45*

This is the method used by speaking clocks and other automats, and also sometimes on official radio and television announcements. These, however, usually use the literary Arabic forms of the numbers, which differ a lot (and are best avoided!).

3 Saying *at a particular time*

Arabic requires no additional word, so **as-saa:ah khamsah** can mean *(it is) five o'clock* or *at five o'clock:*

múmkin tíiji s-sáa:ah thaláathah ílla rúba:	*Can you come at quarter to three?*
wáSal as-sáa:ah iHdá:shar l-lail	*He arrived at eleven o'clock at night*

QV

wáSal	*he arrived*
al-lail, bi l-lail	*night, at night*

4 Times of day

If it is not clear from the context whether the hour referred to is before noon (am) or afternoon (pm), the Arabs have a set of words indicating parts of the day which may be placed after stating the time.

CD 1, TR 5, 3:04

QUICK VOCAB

aS-Súb(a)H	*morning, forenoon*
aDH-Dhúh(u)r	*around noon*
ba:d aDH-Dhúh(u)r	*afternoon*
al-:áS(i)r	*late afternoon (about four pm)*
al-mísȧ	*evening*
al-lail	*night*

as-sáa:ah sáb:ah aS-SúbaH	*seven o'clock (in) the morning*
as-sáa:ah tís:ah bi l-lail	*nine o'clock at* (lit. *in the*) *night*

This is by no means a complete list but will get you through the main sectors of the Muslim day. Some of these words refer to prayer times.

5 Asking about opening and closing times

To say whether somewhere is open or closed in Arabic, use the adjectives:

maftúuH	*open*
magfúul	*closed, shut*

Other local words are **mbánnad** for *closed* and **mbáTTal** for *open*, but these cannot be used in all contexts so it is better to stick to the first two given. In written Arabic you will see **múghlaq** (مغلق) but this is not used in speech.

ad-dukkáan maftúuH?	*Is the shop open?*
al-másbaH magfúul	*The swimming pool is closed.*

To speak about the time a place opens, use the verb **yíftaH/tíftaH** *it* (masc./fem.) *opens*:

máktab al-baríid yíftaH as-sáa:ah thamáanyah	*The post office (masc.) opens at eight o'clock.*
al-mádrasah tíftaH as-sáa:ah thamáanyah	*The school (fem.) opens at eight o'clock.*
íftaH yaa símsim!	*Open Sesame! (imperative form)*

And to say when it closes, use the verb **yibánnid/tibánnid** or **yígfil/tígfil** *it* (masc./fem.) *closes:*

máktab al-baríid yígfil as-sáa:ah árba:ah	*The post office closes at four o' clock.*
al-mádrasah tibánnid as-sáa:ah árba:ah	*The school closes at four o'clock.*

6 The days of the week

CD 1, TR 5, 3:52

QUICK VOCAB

yoom al-áHad	*Sunday*
yoom al-ithnáin	*Monday*
yoom ath-thaláathah	*Tuesday*
yoom al-árba:ah	*Wednesday*
yoom al-khamíis	*Thursday*
yoom al-júma:ah	*Friday*
yoom as-sabt	*Saturday*

You can see that five of these day names are related to the numbers (**áHad** is another form of **wáaHid**). The two exceptions are **yoom al-júma:ah** *Friday*, literally the day of congregation (i.e. for communal prayers in the mosque) and **as-sabt** which is the same word as our *sabbath*. The word **yoom** is sometimes omitted.

To say *on* Monday, Tuesday, etc., Arabic requires no extra word, as with the hours of the clock:

wáSal yoom al-khamíis	*He arrived on Thursday.*
áji yoom al-ithnain	*I'll come on Monday.*

7 Other expressions of time

QUICK VOCAB

al-yóom	*today*
báakir or **búkrah**	*tomorrow*
bá:d búkrah	*the day after tomorrow*
ams, ám(i)s	*yesterday*
áwwal ams	*the day before yesterday*

al-yoom yoom al-júma:ah w búkrah yoom as-sabt	*Today is Friday and tomorrow is Saturday.*
sa:íid wáSal áwwal ams	*Said arrived the day before yesterday.*
áji bá:d búkrah	*I'll come the day after tomorrow.*

:úgub is an alternative word for **bá:(a)d** *after* used in some parts of the Gulf.

---

ma:luumáat thaqaafíyyah (Cultural tips) معلومات ثقافية

The working day in the Gulf starts between seven and eight in the morning, and finishes between one and two in the afternoon. Most ministries and other government departments are then closed for the day, but the souk and most shopping centres open again at about four in the afternoon and stay open until eight or nine in the evening, when the temperature has cooled down. This is the time for families to go out shopping together, and you see groups of women choosing dress materials, families buying their food for the week, and everybody just enjoying the chance to get out for a walk. Some families even take picnics to eat on the grass verges, while the children play around them.

Friday is the Muslim day of prayer, and in the Gulf all offices and some large shops are closed on Thursday afternoon and all day Friday. For the souk and other small establishments, however, it is a seven day week.

tamriináat (Exercises) تمرينات

CD 1, TR 5, 4:50

1 Listen to the times of day on the recording or read the transcript, and look at the times below. Decide in each case what the correct time is.

(a) 1.15, 1.20 or 1.30?
(b) 6.25, 6.35 or 6.55?
(c) 10.15,10.30 or 10.45?
(d) 4.55, 5.00 or 5.05?
(e) 9.00 a.m. or 9.00 p.m.?

2 Ask what time it is, and say the time shown on the clock.
Example:
as-sáa:ah kam? as-sáa:ah thamáanyah
What time is it? It is eight o'clock.

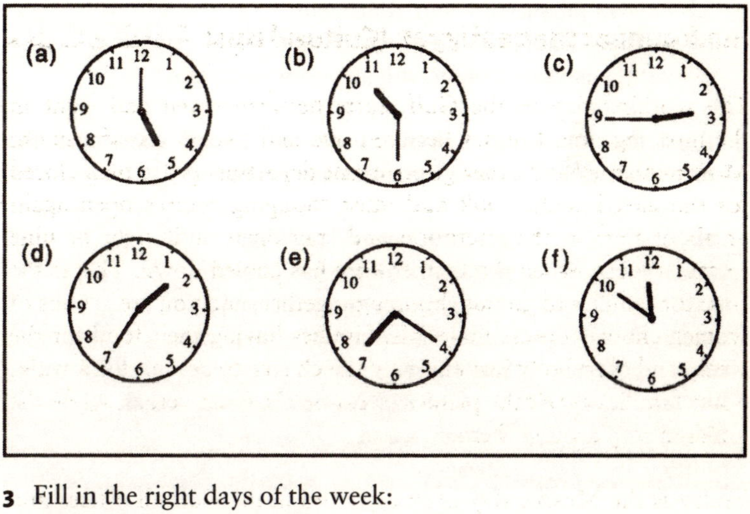

3 Fill in the right days of the week:
al-yóom yoom al-júma:ah

(a) :ams ______
(b) ______ yoom as-sabt
(c) bá:d búkrah ______
(d) ______ yoom al-árba:ah

4 Look at the working hours of the post office in Nizwa in Oman in the picture above. Are the following statements true or false?

(a) máktab al-baríid magfúul as-sáa:ah ithná:shar yoom al-khamíis
(b) húwwa maftúuH yoom al-júma:ah
(c) húwwa mbánnad yoom al-árba:ah
(d) yígfil as-sáa:h thintáin yoom as-sabt
(e) yíftaH as-sáa:ah thamáaniyah yoom al-ithnáin

5 Read the following dialogue between a hotel guest and the receptionist, and answer the questions below.

DHaif	as-sáa:ah kam min fáDHl-ak?
káatib	as-sáa:ah thamáaniyah ílla rúba:
DHaif	fiih Saydalíyyah garíibah min hína?
káatib	ná:am, fi l-márkaz at-tijáari :a l-yisáar
DHaif	tíftaH as-sáa:ah kam?
káatib	as-sáa:ah thamáaniyah, ba:d rúba: sáa:ah
DHaif	shúkran jazíilan
káatib	:áfwan

(a) What is the time?
(b) Where is the chemist's shop?
(c) When does it open?
(d) How long is it until it opens?

6 Today is your first day in Dubai, and you have some shopping to do, but you need to get cash, and you know that the banks will be closed. The receptionist tells you that the time is 3.30pm, that the nearest money changer is in the **souk** on the right, and that it opens at 4pm. Write a dialogue based on the one above.
(**Sarráaf** = *money changer*)

---

al-khaTT al-: árabi (Arabic script) الخط العربي

More practice in reading Arabic numerals

1 Write out the following dates in English in numerical fashion, e.g. 10/6/1989 (day/month/year). Watch the direction of writing!

١- ١٩٥٢/١٢/٣
٢- ٢٠١٣/١١/١٩
٣- ٢٠٠٠/١/١
٤- ١٩٩٠/٢/٢٨
٥- ١٨٨٠/٤/١٧

2 Write out the following times in words, using the 24 hour clock format, e.g.

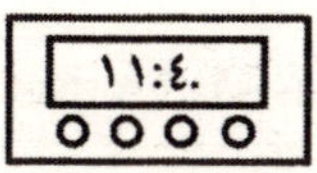

(as-sáa:ah)iHdá:shar wa arba:íin dagíigah
(**dagíigah** = *minute*; here also the plural *minutes*.

(a) ١٦:٣٥　　(c) ٠٩:٢٥

(b) ١٨:١٥　　(d) ٢٠:٥٥

(e) ٠٦:٤٥ (h) ١٤:٢٦

(f) ١٣:٢٠ (i) ٠١:١١

(g) ١٠:١٩ (j) ٢٣:٥٥

Test yourself

This test covers the main vocabulary, phrases and language points given in Unit 4. If you are not sure about your answers, go back to the dialogues and exercises for some revision, before going on to Unit 5. For the answers, see the **Key to the exercises.**

How would you say the following sentences in Arabic:

1 What's the time?
2 It is 4.30.
3 Is the bank open? No, it's closed.
4 Put the weekdays into the correct order:

yoom al-árba:ah, yoom as-sábt, yoom al-khamíis, yoom ath-thaláathah, yoom al-júm:ah, yoom al-ithnáin, yoom al-áHad

Next fill in the missing verbs, choosing one of the three below:

a tígfil, **b** yíftaH, **c** wáSal

5 al-márkaz at-tijáari. . . as-sáa:ah thamáanyah aS-SúbH
6 ibrahíim. . . ams
7 aS-Saydalíyyah. . . as-sáa:ah sáb:ah

Now do the same, but this time you fill in the correct verbs for the gaps in the sentences:

8 ad-dukkáan. . . as-sáa:ah tís:ah bi l-lail
9 . . . yoom al-khamíis ba:d aDH-Dhúhr
10 al-mádrasah. . . as-sáa:ah thamáanyah ílla rúba: aS-SúbH

5

بكم هذا؟

bi-kám háadha?

How much is this?

In this unit you will learn how to

- Ask whether things are available
- Ask what things are
- Ask how much they cost
- Do some simple bargaining
- Describe things

New words and phrases

CD 1, TR 6

Listen to the recording.

Hiwaar 1 (Dialogue 1) حوار ١

CD 1, TR 6, 0:18

Matthew Baker works in Qatar. He needs new batteries for his son's toy car, and goes to the small local shop.

Matthew	:índ-ak bayáatri, min faDHl-ak?
SáaHib ad-dukkáan	ná:am, fiih
Matthew	bi-kám háadha?
SáaHib ad-dukkáan	háadha bi-riyaaláin
Matthew	wa háadha?
SáaHib ad-dukkáan	háadha bi-riyáal wa nuSS
Matthew	a:Tíi-ni arba:ah min háadha sh-shakil
SáaHib ad-dukkáan	zain. tiríid shay tháani?
Matthew	laa, shúkran

Note: From this unit onwards, the plural of nouns and some adjectives will be given in the vocabulary in brackets after the singular.

QUICK VOCAB

:índ-ak	*you have, do you have*
báitri (bayáatri)	*battery/batteries*
bi-kám	*how much*
bi-riyaaláin	*for two riyals, costs two riyals*
a:Tíi-ni	*give me*
shák(i)l (ashkáal)	*kind, sort*
háadha sh-shákil	*this kind (often shortened to* **há sh-shákil***)*
tiríid	*you (masc.) want*
shay	*thing, anything*
tháani	*second, other, more*

(a) How much did the first battery cost?
(b) Since he bought the second batteries, how much did Matthew have to pay in total?

---

mulaaHaDHáat (Notes) ملاحظات

1 Gulf currency

Bahrain and Kuwait both have **diinéaars** (BD and KD), and they are divided into 1000 **fils**.

The Omani **riyáal** (RO) is divided into 1000 **baizah** (written **baisa.**) The Qatari **riyáal** (QR) is divided into 100 **dirhams,** and Saudi riyals (SR) into 100 **halala.**

The United Arab Emirates has **dirhams** (Dh), divided into 100 **fils.**

The words for all the units of currency change when you talk about them in the plural:

báizah (baizáat)
diináar (danaaníir)
dirham (daráahim)
fils (filúus)
riyáal (riyaaláat)

There is a complete explanation of the use of numbers with money in the grammar notes at the end of the unit.

2 riyaaláin

When you talk about *two* of anything in Arabic, you use a special dual form which adds **-áin** to the end of the word. You then don't need to use the word **ithnáin/thintáin** (*two*).

Hiwaar 2 (Dialogue 2) حوار ٢

CD 1, TR 6, 0:59

Peter and Sally are on holiday in the Emirates. They spend a morning in the souk in Sharjah looking for souvenirs. They have found a shop selling local crafts and antiques, and go in to have a look around.

Peter & Sally	as-saláamu :alái-kum
SáaHib ad-dukkáan	wa :alái-kum as-saláam. kaif Háal-kum?
Peter	Tayyibíin, al-Hámdu li-lláh
SáaHib ad-dukkáan	aish tiríiduun?
Peter	naríid nashúuf bass

They look around the shop for a while.

Sally	(*pointing to a dagger*) háadha aish ísm-uh bi-l-:árabi min fáDHl-ak?
SáaHib ad-dukkáan	háadha ísm-uh khánjar

Peter	haadha min faDHDHah?
SáaHib ad-dukkáan	na:am faDHDHah, faDHDHah gadíimah.
Sally	(*pointing to an incense burner*) wa háadha aish ísm-uh?
SáaHib ad-dukkáan	háadha ísm-uh míjmar.
Sally	háadha aS-Saghíir bi-kám?
SáaHib ad-dukkáan	sáb:a daráahim
Sally	w al-kabíir?
SáaHib ad-dukkáan	iHdá:shar dírham. tiríidiin al-kabíir?
Sally	ná:am . . . láakin gháali.
SáaHib ad-dukkáan	laa, muu gháali! rakhíiS! . . . n-zain, tís:ah daráahim
Sally	zain, áakhudh háadha bi-tís:ah daráahim.

QUICK VOCAB

Táyyib	*good, well, fine, OK*
tiríiduun	*you (plural) want*
naríid	*we want*
nashúuf	*we look, are looking*
naríid nashúuf	*we want to look*
aish ísm-uh bi-l-:árabi	*What is this called in Arabic?* (lit. *what [is] its name in Arabic?*)
khánjar (khanáajir)	*dagger*
min	*of, made from*
fáDHDHah	*silver*
gadíim	*old*
míjmar (majáamir)	*incense burner*
aS-Saghíir	*the small one*
al-kabíir	*the big one*
tiriidíin	*you (fem.) want*
gháali	*expensive*
rakhíiS	*cheap*
áakhudh	*I (will) take*

(a) What does Peter tell the shopkeeper they want to do?
(b) What is the first thing Sally asks about?
(c) What is the price of the small incense burner?

mulaaHaDHáat (notes) ملاحظات

1 Tayyibíin Note the plural, implying '**we**' are well.

2 **naríid nashúuf** (lit. *we-want we-look*).
Arabic has no way to say *to look*, and instead puts two verbs together. This will be explained in more detail in a later unit.

3 **bass** This useful word means *that is all* in this context.
It means *enough* when you are being offered food or drink.

4 **háadha aish ísm-uh bi-l-:árabi** (*what is this called in Arabic?*)

5 **háadha ism-uh khánjar** *This is called a dagger* (lit. *this-one his-name* [is] *khanjar*)
If the item you are asking about is feminine, the answer will be:
háadhi ísm-ha zoolíyyah *This is called a carpet* (lit. *this-one her-name* [is] *carpet*)

6 **Saying what things are made of**

In Arabic you use **min** (of):

húwwa min dháhab	*It* (masc.) (*is*) *gold.*
híyya min gúTun	*It* (fem.) (*is*) *cotton.*

ma:luumáat thaqaafíyyah (Cultural tips) معلومات ثقافية

The Gulf Arabs (both male and female) are fond of perfumes. Every home in the Gulf has at least one **mijmar** (*incense burner*), and these take many forms, depending on fashion and location. They are usually made of earthenware, although nowadays people often have electric ones.

A few live coals are put into the burner, and a sweet-smelling substance is dropped on the coals. This could be sandalwood (the most expensive if it is of good quality), frankincense (a dried resin from Oman or Yemen), or a homemade mixture of resins and woods mixed with sugar, all of which are sold in the souk either loose or in small metal tins.

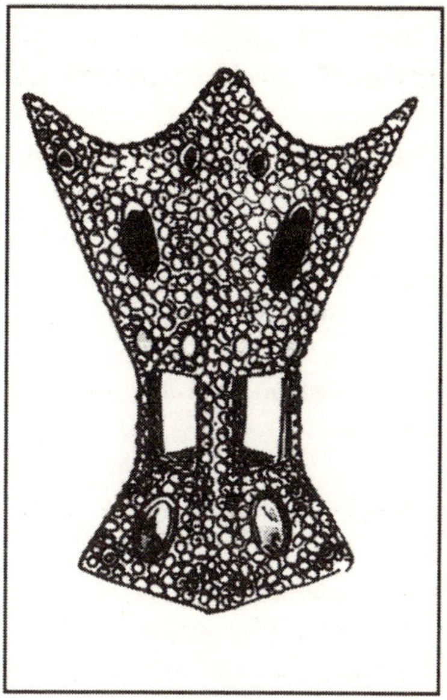

Clouds of perfumed smoke then rise into the room for half an hour or so. The **mijmar** is placed in the sitting room for guests, or brought out at the end of a visit and passed around the company, so that the smoke can be wafted into their clothes before they depart.

Hiwaar 3 (Dialogue 3) حوار ٣

CD 1, TR 6, 2:24

Sally wants to buy a gold chain, and she has been looking in the shop-windows of the gold souk in Dubai. She sees one she likes, and goes into the shop to enquire.

Sally	bi-kám háadhi s-sílsilah?
SáaHib ad-dukkáan	háadhi hína?
Sally	laa, haadhíik hináak.

The shopkeeper takes the chain out of the window but Sally sees that it is too short.

Sally	háadhi gaSíirah. fiih :índ-ak wáaHidah áTwal?

SáaHib ad-dukkáan	(*selecting a different chain*) ná:am. háadhi áTwal shwáyyah.
Sally	háadhi áHsan. bi-kam?
SáaHib ad-dukkáan	lálHDHah min fáDHl-ich . . . . (*he weighs it*) háadhi bi-miitáin wa-thalaathíin dírham
Sally	kathíir!
SáaHib ad-dukkáan	háadha dháhab ithnáin wa-:ishríin qiiráaT. miitáin dirham zain?
Sally	laa, kathíir. khallíi-ha bi-míyyah wa thamaaníin.
SáaHib ad-dukkáan	laa, ma:a l-ásaf, muu múmkin. a:Tíi-ni míyyah wa tis:íin.
Sally	zain. míyyah wa tis:íin dírham. (*handing him the money*) tfáDHDHal

QUICK VOCAB

sílsilah (saláasil)	*chain*
haadhíik	*that one*
gaSíir	*short*
áTwal	*longer*
áHsan	*better*
láHDHah (laHaDHáat)	*moment*
kathíir	*a lot, too much*
dháhab	*gold*
qiiráaT	*carat*
khallíi-ha	*leave it, let it be*
má:a l-ásaf	*I am sorry*
muu	*not*
múmkin	*possible*
t(a)fáDHDHal	*welcome, here you are*

(a) What is the price the shopkeeper first gives Sally?
(b) What reason does he give her for the high price?
(c) What price do they agree on?

---

mulaaHaDHaat (Notes) ملاحظات

1 **khallíi-ha** (*leave it*)
This is another imperative verb. You also hear the shortened form **khall** for the masculine in many places. **shuuf** (**-i**) (*look*), **and khudh** (**-i**), (*take*) are two more imperative verbs which are very common.

2 **ma:a l-ásaf** (*sorry*)
This literally means *with* (*the*) *regret*, and does not change no matter who it refers to.

3 **t(a)fáDHDHal**
This is a very common expression. It is used when politely offering someone something, to take a seat, accept food or (as here) money, enter a room, car etc. It is actually an imperative verb, so it takes the ending **-i** when addressed to a woman, and **-u** when addressed to more than one person. The first **a** is often omitted in normal speech.

---

ma:luumáat thaqaafíyyah (Cultural tips) معلومات ثقافية

One of the most amazing sights in any town in the Gulf is that of the gold souk, where dozens of small shops blaze with light and the glitter of gold. Generally the gold is either 18 or 22ct., and it looks yellower than the 9ct. gold usually sold in the West.

Jewellery is always sold by weight, and craftsmanship doesn't much affect the price. Arab ladies often sell back their older pieces of jewellery to be melted down and made into new pieces, so that they can keep abreast of fashion. Nobody is interested in second-hand jewellery, although old silver is collected by tourists. The shopkeeper will always expect to bargain with you, and you should never accept his first price.

ta:biiráat háammah (Key phrases) تعبيرات هامة

🔊 **CD 1, TR 6, 3:40**

Asking for something in a shop

aríid ashtári zoolíyyah	*I want to buy a carpet.*
aríid ashúuf bass	*I just want to look.*
fiih :índ-ak khánjar	*Do you have a dagger?*

Asking how much things cost

húwwa/híyya bi-kám?	*How much is it?*
bi-kám háadha l-khánjar?	*How much is this dagger? (masc.)*
bi-kám háadhii d-dállah?	*How much is this coffee pot? (fem.)*
bi-kám háadhool	*How much are these? (plural)*
kam tiríid?	*How much do you want?, What do I owe you?*

Saying what things cost

húwwa bi-riyáal/. . . -áat	*It (masc.) costs a riyal/ . . . riyals.*
híyya bi-diináar/. . . danaaníir	*It (fem.) costs a dinar/. . . dinars.*
haadhóol bi-dírham/. . . daráahim	*These cost a dirham/. . . dirhams.*

al-film bi-kam? húwwa bi-riyáal *How much is the film? It costs one riyal.*

bi-kám al-míjmar? húwwa bi-sába:ah daráahim *How much is the incense burner? It is seven dirhams.*

az-zoolíyyah bi-kám? híyya bi-síttah míiyyat dírham *How much is the carpet? It costs 600 dirhams.*

bi-kám ash-shánTah? híyya bi-khámsah danaaníir *How much is the suitcase? It is 5 dinars.*

Talking about what things are called

háadha aish ísm-uh bi-l-:árabi min fáDHl-ak? *What is this called in Arabic please?*
ísm-uh khánjar *It (masc.) is called a dagger.*
ísm-ha sílsilah *It (fem.) is called a chain.*

Describing things

húwwa	**gadíim/jadíid**	*It is old/new (masc.)*
híyya	**gadíimah/jadíidah?**	*Is it old/new? (fem.)*
	fáDHDHah?	*silver?*
	dháhab?	*gold?*
	Suuf?	*wool?*
	gúTun?	*cotton?*
	min :umáan?	*from Oman?*
	min iiráan?	*from Persia?*
	min bakistáan?	*from Pakistan?*
húwwa/híyya (wáajid) zain		*It is (very) good, nice.*
	muu zain	*not good.*
	gháali/gháalyah	*expensive.*
	rakhíiS/-ah	*cheap.*
	kabíir/-ah	*big.*
	Saghíir/-ah	*small.*
háadha muu gháali		*That's not expensive.*
háadha wáajid ghaali		*That's very expensive.*
háadha kathíir		*That's a lot.*

Comparing things

háadha ákbar min haadháak	*This is bigger than that one.*
:índ-ak wáaHid árkhaS?	*Do you have a cheaper one?*

Saying you will take something

áakhudh háadha	*I will take this (one).*

núqaT naHwíyyah (Grammar points) نقط نحوية

1 How to say *have*

There is no verb *to have* in Arabic. Instead Arabs use a preposition, **:ind**, meaning something like *with*, *in the possession of* and a pronoun suffix.

It is common but not essential to state the subject or the person before **:ind:**

ána :índ-i sayyáarah *I have a car* (lit. with me [is] a car).
muHámmad :índ-uh marsáidis? *Does Mohammad have a Mercedes?*
laa, :índ-uh toyóota *No, he has a Toyota.*

(ána) :índ-i	*I have*
(ínta) :índ-ak	*you have (masc.)*
(ínti) :índ-ich	*you have (fem.)*
(húwwa) :índ-uh	*he (it) has*
(híyya) :índ-haa	*she (it) has*
(níHna) :índ-na	*we have*
(íntu) :índ-kum	*you have*
(húmma) :índ-hum	*they have*

Insight

You sometimes hear **:ind** shortened to **:id**, especially before suffixes beginning with a consonant, e.g. **:id-na** (*we have*).

2 *That, those*

These are not used so frequently as in English, and are usually restricted to emphatic or contrastive situations. The three forms are:

haadháak (masc. sing.) **haadhíik** (fem. sing.) **haadhooláak** (plural)

háadha maHáll kabíir	*This (is) a big shop (masc.).*
wa haadháak Saghíir	*And that (one) is small.*

háadhi zoolíyya iraaníyya	*This is a Persian rug (fem.).*
wa haadhíik zoolíyya baakistaaníyya	*And that (one) is a Pakistani rug.*

3 How to say prices and numbers of things

Use this section for reference, and you will find that with practice it becomes second nature to you!

(a) To say *one* of anything in Arabic use the singular noun followed by **WáaHid** (masc.) or **wáaH(i)dah** (fem.)

riyáal wáaHid	*one riyal* (masc.)
sayyáarah wáaHidah	*one car* (fem.)

(b) To say *two* of anything, Arabic uses a special form called the dual. To form this, add **-áin** to the singular.

riyaaláin	*two riyals* (masc.)
sayyaar(a)táin	*two cars* (fem.) (the **a** in brackets is often omitted in pronunciation)

The word *two* is only used for special emphasis, after the noun:

waladáin ithnáin	*two boys*
bintáin thintáin	*two girls*

Insight

The stress moves to the end of the word. If the word has the feminine ending **-ah**, this changes to **-at**.

(c) Between three and ten of anything, use the number (agreeing in gender with the noun) followed by the noun in its plural form:

thaláathah daráahim	*three dirhams*
thaláath sayyaaráat	*three cars*

(d) For 11 and above, use the independent gender (i.e. unchanging) number and *singular* noun:

iHdá:shar dirham *11 dirhams*
iHdá:shar sayyáarah *11 cars*

For quick reference, use the table below:

1	2	3–10	11+	English
dírham	dirhamáin	daráahim	dírham	dirham
riyáal	riyaaláin	riyaaláat	riyáal	riyal
diináar	diinaaráin	danaaníir	diináar	dinar
wálad	waladáin	awláad	wálad	boy
sayyáarah	sayyaaratáin	sayyaaráat	sayyáarah	car

4 Describing things

In Arabic a describing word, or adjective, comes after a noun and has to agree with it. Nearly all adjectives form their feminine by adding **-ah**. The same feminine ending is also used when describing plural things (as opposed to people).

míjmar kabíir *a big incense burner* (masc. noun)
sílsilah rakhíiSah *a cheap chain* (fem. noun)
bayáatri Saghíirah *small batteries* (plural of things)

A few adjectives, mostly referring to the main colours, have irregular feminine forms, e.g.

ábyaDH/báiDHa *white* (masc./fem.)
áswad/sóoda *black*
ákhDHar/kháDHra *green*
áHmar/Hámra *red*

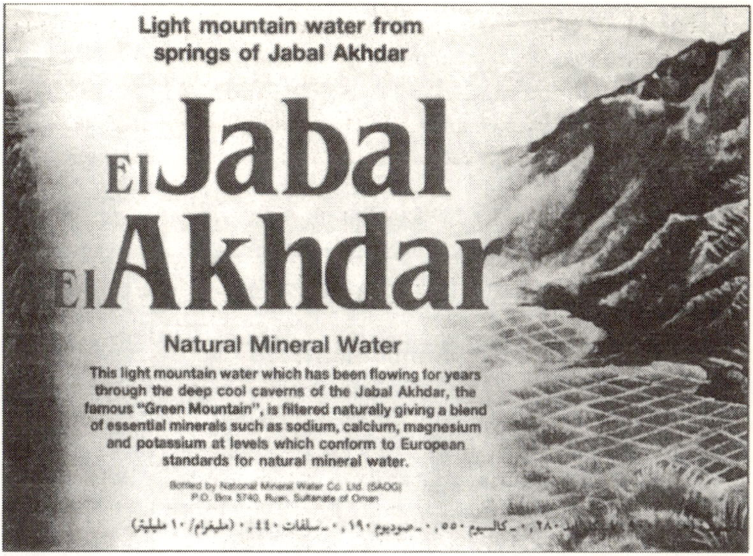

áSfar/Sáfra	*yellow*
ázrag/zárga	*blue*
al-jábal al-ákhDHar	*the green mountain*
sayyáarah Hámra	*a red car*

5 Comparing things

When you say that something is bigger or taller than something else, you are using a comparative adjective. English usually forms this comparative by adding **-er**, but Arabic makes changes in the word, and the forms will be given as they occur.

These adjectives are the same for both masculine and feminine, and the word for *than* is **min**.

zain	*good*	**áHsan**	*better*
rakhíis	*cheap*	**árkhaS**	*cheaper*
kabíir	*big*	**ákbar**	*bigger*
Saghíir	*small*	**áSghar**	*smaller*

wáaHid áHsan	*a better one*
dállah árkhaS	*a cheaper coffee pot*
sáalim ákbar min ráashid	*Salim is older than Rashid.*
fáaTimah áSghar min máryam	*Fatimah is younger than Mariam.*

Insight

When applied to people, **kabíir** and **Saghíir** mean *old* and *young*.

The same formation is used for the superlative (ending in **-est** in English).

(a) **al-** noun followed by **al-** comparative:

al-fúndug al-ákbar	*the biggest hotel*
aT-Táyyaarah al-ásra:	*the fastest aeroplane*

Note that there is no change for gender.

(b) comparative without **-al** followed by noun without **-al:**

ákbar fúndug	*the biggest hotel*
ásra: Tayyáarah	*the fastest aeroplane*
áTwal wálad	*the tallest boy*
áSghar sayyáarah	*the smallest car*

The second construction (b) is more common in practice.

6 The words for *not*

muu or **muub** is used with nouns and adjectives, and **maa** with verbs and all other words.

aDH-DHahráan muu ba:íidah :an al-baHráin	*Dhahran is not far from Bahrain.*
háadha muub zain	*This is not good.*
ána maa min ingiltérra	*I am not from England.*
maa :índ-na dállah rakhíiSah	*We do not have a cheap coffee pot.*
ána maa aríid ashtári dháhab	*I don't want to buy gold.*

tamriináat (Exercises) تمرينات

CD 1, TR 6, 4:32

1 With a little practice, you will soon get used to understanding numbers in Arabic. Listen to the recording or read the transcript and note down the five prices you hear.

2 How would you say the following prices in Arabic?
(a) 60 dirhams (Dh)
(b) 750 baiza
(c) 10 riyals
(d) 2 dinars
(e) 1 dinar 50 fils
(f) half a riyal
(g) 18 dinars
(h) 5 Dh

3 You are looking for souvenirs but you are not sure what these objects are called. How would you ask what they are, using the correct form of **háadha, háadhi** and **ism-uh, ism-ha**?

(a) **zoolíyyah** (*carpet*)
(b) **dállah** (*coffee pot*)
(c) **Hálag** (*earrings*)
(d) **bánjari** (*bracelet*)
(e) **mákHalah** (pronounced **mák-Halah**) (*kohl pot*)

Now ask how much each one costs, using the correct pronoun **huwwa, hiyya.**

4 You are working in Abu Dhabi and need to do some shopping. Look first at the new words below then play your part in the conversation.

ínta	*Ask if he has any pens*
SáaHib ad-dukkáan	ná:am hína. ayy loon tiríid?
ínta	*Say you'll have a black one and a red one.*
SáaHib ad-dukkáan	tiríid shay tháani?
ínta	*Say you want a packet of aspirins.*
SáaHib ad-dukkáan	maal árba:ah w :ishríin aw síttah w thalaathíin Hábbah?
ínta	*Say* 36.
SáaHib ad-dukkáan	shay tháani?
ínta	*Ask how much the sunglasses over there are.*
SáaHib ad-dukkáan	khámsah w khamsíin dírham
ínta	*Say no, that's too much and ask how much you. owe him*
SáaHib ad-dukkáan	khámsah wa :ishríin dirham

QUICK VOCAB

maal	*belonging to, pertaining to, applying to, for, etc.* (placed between two nouns, it implies any kind of connection between them)
gálam (agláam)	*pen*
loon (alwáan)	*colour*
:ílbat asbríin	*packet of aspirins*
Hábbah	*pills*
aw	*or*
naDHDHáarah (naDHDHaaráat)	*(pair of) glasses*
shams	*sun*
naDHDHáarah maal shams	*pair of sun-glasses* (lit. *glasses for sun*)

5 Write out these sentences using the correct form of the adjective given in brackets:

(a) *Faridah is hungry*. (**joo:áan**)
(b) *I* (male) *am thirsty*. (**:aTsháan**)
(c) *Are you* (female) *tired?* (**ta:báan**)
(d) *Arabic is not difficult*. (**Sa:b**)
(e) *The Mercedes is a good car*. (**jáyyid**)
(f) *Aisha is a beautiful girl*. (**jamíil**)

al-lúghah al-:arabíyyah	*Arabic, the Arabic language*
jáyyid	*good (quality)*

---

al-khaTT al-:árabi (Arabic script) الخط العربي

In this unit you will learn to read banknotes. There are several new letters involved, but they will be repeated and explained more fully in future units. At least, if you are solvent, you will have a ready-made crib in English on the back of the note!

The values are generally printed in the middle of the Arabic side of the note at the bottom, and the writing is usually quite clear, although some countries use decorative calligraphy which is more difficult to read. The number of units is written before the currency name, except for **waaHid** according to the rules given in this lesson, so look carefully to see where the currency name begins.

Wherever you are in the Arabian peninsula, your local currency will be either riyals, dirhams or dinars. Here is the full set of these currencies, phonetically-transcribed and in Arabic:

riyáal ريال	riyaaláat ريالات
dírham درهم	daráahim دراهم
diinááar دينار	danaaníir دنانير

These forms reflect the Arabic spelling more accurately than the English equivalents printed on the notes. Remember again that, in

Arabic, the short vowels are not usually written, so for instance, **dirham** is written simply **d-r-h-m**. The long vowels (doubled in our transcription: **aa, ii, uu**) are, however, represented in the script (so **riyáal is r-y-aa-l**).

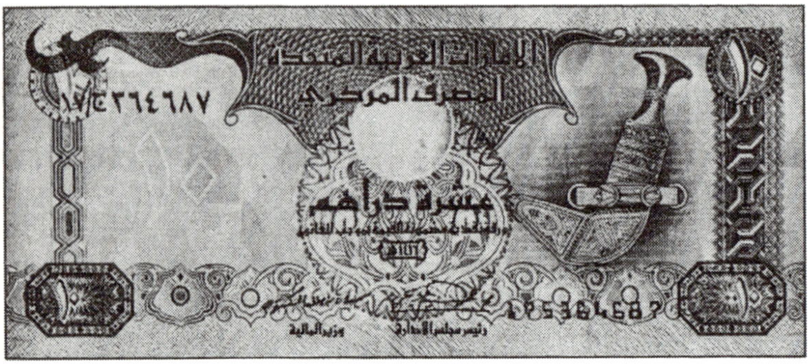

The consonants involved in the money words are:

Name	Initial	Medial	Final	Separate	Pronunciation
alif	ا	ـا	ـا	ا	(see below)
taa	تـ	ـتـ	ـت	ت	t
daal	د	ـد	ـد	د	d
raa'	ر	ـر	ـر	ر	r
miim	مـ	ـمـ	ـم	م	m
nuun	نـ	ـنـ	ـن	ن	n
haa'	هـ	ـهـ	ـه	ه	h
yaa'	يـ	ـيـ	ـي	ي	y

You met the letter *alif* in Unit 1 as the first letter of the word **al-** (ال) *the*. In that word it represents a short '**a**', but in the middle of words it usually represents a *long a* (**aa**) in the transcription. There is a long *a* in **riyáal** and in **diinàar**. The singular **dírham** does not have one, but its plural **daráahim** does. (Remember that the plural in Arabic is only used after the numerals 3–10, so expect it only on 5 and 10 unit notes.)

r Look for the initial form in **riyáal** ريال and **dírham** درهم, and the final in (plural) **danaaníir** دنانير.

y is used to mark the long **ii** vowels in **diináar** دينار and its plural **danaaníir** دنانير.

l occurs at the end of **riyáal** ريال.

t occurs at the end of **riyaaláat** ريالات where it has its independent form after the non-joiner **alif** (here in its combination form **laam-alif**, see alphabet table).

d in its initial form occurs at the beginning of **dírham** درهم and **diináar** دينار and their respective plurals.

h occurs in **dírham** درهم and its plural (in both cases in its initial form after the non-joiners **r** and **alif** repectively).

m It occurs here as the final letter of **dírham** درهم and its plural **daráahim** دراهم.

Practise recognising these words on your own bank notes or the photographs in this unit and make note of the individual letters for future use.

Insight

On the 20 and 50 unit notes, an **alif** is added to the singular of the currency name. This is a rule of written Arabic, and does not alter the pronunciation.

Test yourself

This test covers the main vocabulary, phrases and language points given in Unit 5. If you are not sure about your answers, go back to the dialogues and exercises for some revision, before going on to Unit 6. For the answers, see the **Key to the exercises.**

You are on holiday in Dubai and you want to buy some old silver as a souvenir of your holiday. Play your part in the following conversation:

The shopkeeper greets you.

1. *Tell the shopkeeper you just want to look around.*
2. *Ask if he has any daggers.*
   [He shows you some, and offers you one but you prefer another]
3. *Say No, this one here.*
4. *Say it's not a good one, and ask if he has got a better one.*
5. *Ask him if it is old.*
6. *Ask how much it costs.*
   [*The shopkeeper asks for 300 riyals.*]
7. *Tell him that's very expensive.*
8. *Offer him 200 riyals.*
9. *Say you're sorry but you have only got 250.*
10. *Tell him OK, you'll take this one.*

6

انت جوعان؟

inta joo:áan?

Are you hungry?

In this unit you will learn how to
- Buy snacks and drinks
- Express your wants and preferences
- Say what you like and dislike

New words and phrases

🔊 **CD 1, TR 7**

Listen to the recording.

Hiwaar 1 (Dialogue 1) حوار ١

🔊 **CD 1, TR 7, 0:16**

In Mattrah Jim and Eleanor are shopping with Khaled. He suggests that they stop at one of the drink stalls in the souk.

Khaled	tiHíbb tíshrab aish?
Jim	fiih aish :índ-hum?
Khaled	(*asking the shopkeeper*) aish :índ-kum min mashruubáat?
SaaHib ad-dukkaan	:índ-na shaay, gáhwah wa :aSíir burtugáal w-laimóon
Jim	ána áakhudh gáhwah bi-dúun Halíib ídha kaan múmkin
Khaled	wa ínti, aish tiriidíin tishrabíin?
Eleanor	ána afáDHDHal :aSíir laimóon
SaaHib ad-dukkaan	laimóon bi-shíkar?
Eleanor	na:am
Khaled	wa-ána áakhudh shaay
SaaHib ad-dukkaan	zain. wáaHid shaay, wáaHid gáhwah w-wáaHid :aSíir laimóon.

QUICK VOCAB

tiHíbb/-íin	*you like, would you like?*
tíshrab/-íin	*you drink*
fiih aish . . . ?	*what is there . . . ?*
mashruubáat	*drinks*
shaay, chaay	*tea*
gáhwah	*coffee*
:aSíir	*juice*
burtugáal	*orange*
laimóon	*lemon, lime*
áakhudh	*I take, I'll have*
bi-dúun	*without*
Halíib	*milk*
ídha kaan	*if*
tiríid/ -íin	*you want, wish*
afáDHDHal	*I prefer*
bi	*with*
shíkar	*sugar*

True or false?

(a) The stall sells two kinds of fruit juice.

(b) Eleanor chooses lime juice without sugar.

(c) Jim and Khaled both have tea.

mulaaHaDHáat (Notes) ملاحظات

1 **fiih aish :índ-hum** (*What do they have?*, lit. *there is what with them?*) and **aish :índ-kum min mashruubáat** (*What do you have* (in the way) *of drinks.*)

The use of **fiih** in this kind of sentence is optional.

2 wáaHid shaay
When you are buying drinks or dishes in a restaurant, use the singular form of the drink and the masculine (independent) number. In this kind of context, **wáaHid** and **ithnáin** usually come before the noun, for emphasis.

Hiwaar 2 (Dialogue 2) حوار ٢

CD 1, TR 7, 1:21

Mike Smith is a surveyor working in Abu Dhabi. He and Salim ar-Rumaihi, an associate in his firm, are driving to Al-Ain, having made an early start.

Salim wa l-láaHi, ána joo:áan!
Mike ána kamáan. khallíi-na nóogaf fii háadhi sh-shíishah w- nashtári shwayyat akil. múmkin fiih :índ-hum sandwiicháat.

They stop at a petrol station which has a small shop selling drinks and snacks.

Salim fiih aish :índ-kum min ákil min fáDHl-ak?
SáaHib ad-dukkáan :índ-na sandwiicháat w-baiDH w-kaik w-shibs
Salim fiih aish min sandwiicháat :índ-kum?
SáaHib ad-dukkáan :ind-na dajáaj w-láHam w-baiDH má:a SálaTah
Salim tiríid táakul aish yaa maayk?

Mike	ana áakhudh sandwíich dajáaj. múmkin tisawwíi-li sandwíich baiDH bi-dúun SálaTah min fáDHl-ak?
SáaHib ad-dukkáan	Táb:an. wa l-akh?
Salim	ána áakhudh sandwiicháin maal láHam
SáaHib ad-dukkáan	shay ghair?
Salim	ná:am a:Tíi-ni shwáyyat kaik kamáan.
SáaHib ad-dukkáan	zain. wáaHid sandwíich maal dajáaj, ithnáin maal láHam wa wáaHid baiDH bi-dúun SálaTah, w kaik wáaHid. nasawwíi-ha l-Híin.

QUICK VOCAB

joo:áan	*hungry*
kamáan	*also, as well*
khallíi-na	*leave us, let us*
nóogaf	*we stop*
nashtári	*we buy*
ák(i)l	*food*
shwáyyat ákil	*a little food, something to eat*
sand(a)wíich (-aat)	*sandwich*
báiDHah (baiDH)	*egg*
kaik	*pastry, cake*
shibs	*crisps, chips*
dajáajah (dajáaj)	*chicken*
sandwíich maal dajáaj	*chicken sandwich*
láH(a)m	*meat (excluding poultry)*
má:a	*with, along with, together with*
SálaTah	*salad*
táakul/íin	*you eat* (masc./fem.)
tisáwwi	*you make, do*
tisawwíi-li	lit. *you make for me*
Táb:an	*of course, naturally*
al-akh	lit. *the brother, here a polite reference to the other person*
ghair	*other than, else*
nasáwwi	*we do, make; will do, will make*
al-Híin	*now, right away*

(a) What words mean *we'll buy a little food?*
(b) What kind of food is available apart from sandwiches?
(c) What extra thing does Salim order?

"Coca-Cola" is a registered trademark of The Coca-Cola Company

---

mulaaHaDHáat (Notes) ملاحظات

1 kamáan (*also*)
This is a popular borrowed word from northern (i.e. Egyptian, Jordanian, etc.) Arabic. The true Gulf Arabic is **ba:d**, or the more formal **áyDHan**.

2 sandwíich maal dajáaj (*chicken sandwich*)
An example of the word **maal** associating two things with each other. The simple possessive **sandwíich dajáaj** can also be used.

3 má:a, bi-
Both mean *with*, but **má:a** always means *along with, together with*, while **bi-** also means *by means of*, as in **bi-sikkíin** *with a knife*.

Hiwaar 3 (Dialogue 3) حوار ٣

CD 1, TR 7, 2:51

Mike and Salim have been waiting for the food to be prepared.

SáaHib ad-dukkáan	as-sandawiicháat jáahizah. tiriidúun tishrabúun shay?
Salim	fiih aish :índ-kum báarid?
SáaHib ad-dukkáan	fiih Halíib, :aSíir, sóodah, kóola, sávan-aap w maay masáafi.
Salim	aish tiríid tíshrab ya maayk?
Mike	ayy shay - láakin maa aHíbb al-Halíib. fiih aish :índ-kum min :aSíir?
SáaHib ad-dukkáan	:índ-na burtugáal, laimóon, ámbah, ananáas, mooz.
Salim	múmkin ta:Tíi-na tashkíil bi :ásharah daráahim?
SáaHib ad-dukkáan	na:am, zain.
Salim	háadha kúll-uh kám?
SáaHib ad-dukkáan	háadha yisáawi :ásharah záayid síttah záayid tís:ah wa nuSS. khámsah wa-:ashríin wa nuSS
Salim	(*handing him the money*) tfáDHDHal

QUICK VOCAB

jáahiz	*ready*
báarid	*cold (of things)*
maay	*water*
maay masáafi	*Masafi water (mineral water of the UAE)*
ayy shay	*anything*
maa	*not (before verbs)*
maa aHíbb	*I don't like*
ámbah, hámbah	*mango*
ananáas	*pineapple*
mooz	*bananas*
ta:Tíi-na	*you give us*

tashkíil (tashkiiláat)	*selection, variety*
kúll-uh	*altogether, lit. all of it*
yisáawi	*equals, makes (of money)*
yá:ni	*I mean, that is to say*

QUICK VOCAB

(a) What drink does Mike not like?
(b) What does Salim suggest they have to drink?
(c) How much were they charged for the food?

mulaaHaDHáat (Notes) ملاحظات

1 **fiih aish :índ-kum báarid?**
Where we would say in English *What do you have that is cold*, in Arabic it is sufficient to say *What do you have cold.*

2 **ayy shay** (*anything*)
ayy can mean *any* or *which?* according to the context and tone of voice.

Insight

yá:ni lit. *it means.* This is perhaps the most over-used word in Arabic (all dialects). Depending on the tone of voice, it has a thousand meanings, the most common being '*I am having a pause to think*' (Eng. '*um*, *er*'). Start listening for it and practise using it right away!

ma:luumáat thaqaafíyyah (Cultural tips) معلومات ثقافية

Everywhere in the Gulf you see little stalls set up in the markets where fresh fruits are squeezed for juice. The most common are orange and lime or lemon. Restaurants often have a colourful row of containers of fruit juices in the window.

Fresh fruit is widely available, as orange and lemon trees fruit in the Gulf in the winter, and mangoes and papayas and other exotic fruits ripen during the summer. Small shops selling snacks and drinks may just have a fridge full of cartons and cans of drinks costing only a few fils or baiza each. People drink a lot of mineral water and all the Gulf countries have 'branded' and bottled spring water.

---

ta:biiráat háammah (Key phrases) تعبيرات هامة

CD 1, TR 7, 3:44

How to ask someone what they'd like to eat or drink

aish tiHíbb tíshrab?	*What would you like to drink?*
aish tiríid táakul?	*What do you want to eat?*

How to ask about food and drink

aish :índ-kum min mashruubáat?	*What (sort) of drinks do you have?*
aish :índ-kum min ákil?	*What (sort) of food do you have?*
fiih aish min sandwiicháat :índ-kum?	*What (kinds) of sandwiches do you have?*
fiih aish :índ-kum báarid?	*What do you have that is cold? (lit. What is with you of cold (drinks)?*

How to order food and drink

(ána) áakhudh :aSíir laimóon bi-shíkar	*I'll take lemon juice with sugar*
(ána) áakhudh sandwíich maal dajáaj bi-dúun SálSat fílfil áHmar	*I'll take a chicken sandwich without red pepper sauce.*
a:Tíi-ni shwáyyat kaik	*Give me some cake.*

How to express your likes and dislikes

ána aHíbb ash-shaay	*I like tea.*
maa aHíbb al-Halíib.	*I don't like milk.*

How to express your wants and preferences

(ínta) tiríid gáhwah?	*Do you want coffee?*
laa, maa aríid gáhwah	*No, I don't want coffee.*
tifáDHDHal shaay?	*Do you prefer tea?*
na:am, afáDHDHal shaay	*Yes, I prefer tea.*

How to ask someone to do something for you

múmkin tisawwíi-li sandwíich baiDH min faDHl-ak?	*Could you make [for] me an egg sandwich, please?*
múmkin ta:Tíi-na tashkíil bi :ásharah daráahim?	*Could you give us a selection for 10Dh?*

How to ask what it all comes to

háadha kúll-uh kám?	*How much is all of that?*

---

núqaT naHwíyyah (Grammar points) نقط نحوية

1 Verbs in the present tense

There are only two tenses in Arabic, the present tense and the past tense. The present tense is used for all actions which are not yet complete, and the past for all actions which have been completed.

All Arabic verbs are formed from a basic stem; both tenses are formed by adding prefixes and/or suffixes to the stem.

The present tense stem for the word *to drink is* **-shrab**, so here is the verb with its prefixes and suffixes, separated by hyphens for clarity.

The same prefixes and suffixes are used for virtually all verbs in the present tense, although the stem may change in certain verbs. However, the vowels of the prefixes are often modified to help pronunciation. In this unit, for example, you have **áakul** (*I eat*), **yáakul** (*he eats*), **táakul** (*she eats*), and **nóogaf** (*we stop*), **yóogaf, tóogaf**. See the appendix for both of these types of verbs, and for present or past stems.

Singular	
á-shrab	*I drink, am drinking*
tí-shrab	*you (masc.) drink, are drinking*
ti-shrab-íin	*you (fem.) drink, etc.*
yí-shrab	*he drinks*
tí-shrab	*she drinks*
Plural	
ná-shrab	*we drink*
ti-shrab-úun	*you (plural) drink*
yi-shráb-uun	*they drink*

Insight

The pronouns are not used unless necessary for clarity. **tíshrab** and **inta tíshrab** equally mean *you drink, you are drinking* (masc.).

2 Saying what you want or don't want

yiríid = *he wants*: The present tense stem is **-ríid,** so you need to add the prefix (and suffix if required):

(ínta) tiríid gáhwah?	*Do you want coffee?*
laa, maa aríid gáhwah	*No, I don't want coffee.*

Often you can use this verb with a second one as in *I want to drink ...* and where you would use the word *to* in English, Arabic uses a second present tense verb. This kind of construction is called a verb string.

aish tiriidíin tishrabíin	*What do you (fem.) want to drink?* (lit. *what [do] you-want you-drink?)*
tiriidúun tishrabúun shay?	*Do you (plural) want to drink anything?*
naríid nashúuf bass	*We just want to look.*
aríid ashtári khánjar	*I want to buy a dagger.*

3 Saying that you prefer something

yifáDHDHal (*to prefer*): The present tense stem is **faDHDHal.**

tifáDHDHal shaay aw gáhwah?	*Do you prefer tea or coffee?*
afáDHDHal shaay	*I prefer tea.*

Insight

Do not confuse this with **tfaDHDHal** used when offering something to someone, where the 't' is part of the stem.

4 Saying that you like or dislike things

If you are talking of something your feelings don't change about, use the verb **yiHíbb** (*to like, love*).

Note that what you are talking about must be definite; that is, it must have **al-** (*the*) before it, as in French 'j'aime le chocolat':

(ínta) tiHibb ar-riyáaDHah?	*Do you like sport?*
laa, maa aHíbb ar-riyáaDHah	*No, I don't like sport.*
(ínti) maa tiHibbíin al-láHam?	*Don't you (fem.) like meat?*
ána aHíbb al-mooz	*I like bananas.*

5 Saying you might be able to do something

In Arabic you put the word **múmkin** before the verb to express the possibility of doing something:

múmkin tisawwíi-li sandwíich baiDH bi-dúun SálaTah?	*Could you make [for] me an egg sandwich without salad?*

Note that the verb must agree with the person (potentially) doing the action, but **múmkin** never changes.

6 *Me/my, you/your, him/his, etc.*

These words belong to the class of pronouns. The independent pronouns (**ana, inta,** etc.) introduced in Unit 1 are used when the person referred to is doing something.

However, there is another set of pronouns, in the form of suffixes, in such phrases as:

aish akhbaar-ak	*What is your news?*
ism-i saalim	*My name is Salim.*

When used with nouns they express possession (*my*, *his*, *our*, etc.), but in Arabic they are also used after verbs and other words to express the equivalent of English *me, him, it, us,* etc:

nasawwíi-ha	*we will make her (*i.e. *it)*

You have already seen these pronouns at work with **:ind-** the Arabic equivalent of *to have*, but literally meaning *with me, with you,* etc. (see Unit 5).

In this book they are separated from the words they join on to by hyphens for the sake of clarity.

Singular	
-i (-ni with verbs)	*me, my* (This is the only one which has two distinct forms.)
-ak	*you* (masc.), *your*
-ich	*you* (fem.), *your*
-uh	*him, his, it, its*
-ha	*her, it, its*
Plural	
-na	*us, our*
-kum	*you, your*
-hum	*them, their*

Here are a few examples:

(a) with a noun to show possession of a thing:

ism-i	*my name*
ákh-i	*my brother*
ism-ak	*your name*
ism-uh	*his name, its name*

(b) with a verb, where the pronoun is the object of the verb (i.e. the action is done to it):

ashkúr-ak	*I thank you*
ashúuf-ak	*I (will) see you*
khallíi-na nóogaf	*let us stop (*lit. *let-us we-stop)*

(c) with a preposition:

aish :índ-kum min akil?	*What kind of food do you have? (*lit. *What with you from food?)*
tisawwíi-li	(*you*) *make for me (***li** *'for'* + **-i** *'me')*

Note the following points:

(a) When a noun ends in **-ah**, the 'hidden t' appears and the **-ah** changes to **-at** before the suffix:

as-sayyáarah	*the car*
sayyáarat-ak	*your (masc.) car*
sayyáarat muHámmad	*Muhammad's car*

(b) No word for *the* is used when a pronoun suffix is added.

(c) To say *my*, *me*, use **-i** with nouns or prepositions, and **-ni** with verbs. All the other suffixes are the same whatever type of word they are used with:

Sadíig-i	*my friend*
jamb-uh	*next to him*

múmkin asáa:id-ak	*can I help you?*
a:Tíi-ni	*give [to] me*

(d) If a word ends in a vowel, this becomes long and stressed, and if the suffix begins with a vowel, this vowel is omitted:

ma:áa-ha (má:a+-ha)	*with her*
khallíi-na (khálli+-na)	*let us*
aish fii-k? (fii+-ak)	*what's the matter with you?* (lit. *what [is] in you?)*
nashtaríi-h (nashtári+-uh)	*we buy it (him)*

Most prepositions take a suffix without difficulty, but some have to be modified, and we will point them out to you as you meet them.

Insight

A popular saying demonstrating traditional Arab hospitality: **bait-na báit-kum** *our house [is] your house*, or as we would say, *make yourself at home!*)

---

tamriináat (Exercises) تمرينات

CD 1, TR 7, 4:17

1 Five Kuwaitis are buying drinks. Listen to the recording or read the transcript and write down what they are ordering.

qv

chakláit	*chocolate*
lában	*yoghurt drink*

2 Which of the following words is the odd one out?

(a) shaay, Halíib, láHam, gáhwah

(b) burtugáal, laimóon, ámbah, shíkar

(c) aríid, áshrab, áakul

(d) báiDHah, akh, dajáaj, sálaTah

3 Match the questions below with their correct answers

(a) aish tiríid tíshrab?	1 :índ-na baiDH w-kaik w-shibs
(b) aish :índ-kum min mashruubáat?	2 laa, maa aHíbb al-Halíib
(c) háadha kúll-uh kám?	3 háadha :ishríin dírham
(d) aish :índ-kum min akil?	4 :índ-na shaay, gáhwah w-:aSíir burtugáal
(e) tiHíbb al-Halíib?	5 ayy shay!

4 Look at the juice menu below and answer the questions in Arabic.

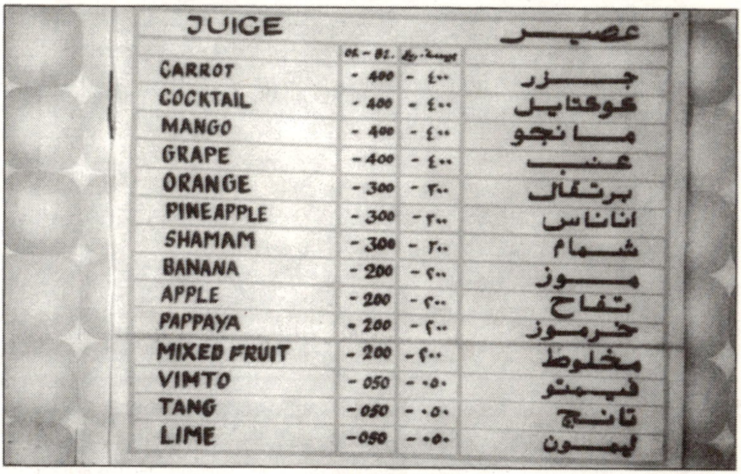

(a) :aSíir al-ámbah húwwa al-ághla aw al-árkhaS?
(b) bi-kám :aSíir at-tuffáaH?
(c) aish fiih bi thaláath míyyat báizah?
(d) wáaHid mooz wa wáaHid jázar yisáawi kam?
(e) aish árkhaS shay?

QV

tuffáaH	*apples*
jázar	*carrots*
ághla	*more/most expensive*

Insight

The word for *mango* is written **maanju** on the menu. However in spoken Gulf Arabic it is always **ámbah** or **hámbah.**

CD 1, TR 7, 4:43

5 Listen to these five people in a fast food restaurant in Kuwait choosing something to eat and drink, or read the transcript. First look at the new words below, then listen to the recording and write down the orders.

QV

ayskriím	*ice cream*
baTáaTas	*chips, potatoes*
dajáaj má:a baTáaTas	*chicken and chips*

sámak	*fish*
bárgar sámak	*fishburger*
háambargar	*hamburger*
jíb(i)n	*cheese*
bárgar bi l-jíbin	*cheeseburger*

QUICK VOCAB

6 You and your friend Julie are in the Al-Khaleej Cafe in Doha. This time you want to buy something to eat. Play your own part and help out your friend Julie who doesn't know any Arabic.

ínta	Ask what they have to eat.
SáaHib ad-dukkáan	:índ-na baiDH, dajáaj, shawármah, sandwiicháat, kaik w shibs
ínta	Ask Julie what she would like
júuli	Help her to ask what kind of sandwiches they have
SáaHib ad-dukkáan	:índ-na láHam, jíbin, faláafil w baiDH
júuli	She says she doesn't like meat. She'll have a falafel sandwich
ínta	Say you prefer meat. Order one falafel and one meat sandwich
SáaHib ad-dukkáan	tiríiduun Sálsat fílfil áHmar?
ínta	Ask Julie if she likes it. She says no, so say no thank you, you don't want it
júuli	Asks the shopkeeper to give you cake and crisps as well
SáaHib ad-dukkáan	zain.
ínta	Ask how much that costs altogether
SáaHib ad-dukkáan	háadha......sítta wa árba:a w-ithnain......yá:ni......ithná:shar riyaal
ínta	Offer him the money

shawármah	*thin slices of roast lamb cut from a rotating spit*
faláafil	*fried bean patties*
Sálsah	*sauce*
fílfil	*pepper*
Sálsat fílfil áHmar	*red pepper sauce*

QUICK VOCAB

Insight

shawármah is called doner kebab in the West, and slices are carved off the spit and served with pitta bread and salad. **faláafil** is also known as **Ta:amíyya**. Both of these snacks are originally Lebanese, and, like much other food from Lebanon and Syria, have been adopted in the Gulf as Arab food.

(a) What food could you eat if you were a vegetarian?
(b) What does the man offer you that you don't want?
(c) You gave the shopkeeper a 20 riyal note. How much change does he give you?

CD 1, TR 7, 6:11

7 You are talking about coffee with some friends from Abu Dhabi.
(a) Tell them you like it.
(b) Tell them you prefer it with milk.
(c) Say you don't like coffee with sugar.
(d) Thank them and say you don't want one now.

8 Your friend Ahmed is visiting you.
(a) Ask him if he wants anything to eat.
(b) Ask him if he'd like chicken or meat.
(c) Say you'll make a chicken sandwich for him.
(d) Ask him if he wants red pepper sauce.

---

al-khaTT al-:árabi (Arabic script) الخط العربي

Vowels in Arabic

As you know, short vowels are not normally represented in everyday Arabic script, but only in children's text books, the Holy Koran and classical texts used by scholars, where they are indicated by small marks above and below the consonants like this:

بِسمِ اللّٰهِ الرَّحْمٰنِ الرَّحِيم

This way of writing is possible in Arabic is because the language uses a restricted number of word patterns. For example, if C represents any consonant, there is no native (written) Arabic word which can look like CiCuC, while CuCi (and CaCaC, CaCiC and others) are common. Frankly, much is left to guesswork. **Hamad** (a man's name) and the word **Hamd** *praise* as in **al-Hamdu li-llaah** are written identically in the Arabic script. It was once said 'In other languages one has to read to be able to understand: in Arabic one has to understand in order to read'. This, as far as reading aloud is concerned, is not far from the truth. As your knowledge of the language grows, 'providing' the short vowels becomes much easier, as the context usually makes it clear which possible combination is meant. At this stage, reading road signs and notices and so on, you will learn what to expect as your vocabulary increases, and this is the only way to tackle the problem.

However, long vowels are much more important than short ones, and are consistently shown except in a very few common words. To identify word structures you should look for these long vowels. There are only three long vowels recognized in Arabic. These are **aa, uu**, and **ii**. The other two used in this book, **oo** and **ai**, are regarded as variants of **uu** and **ii** respectively, and are written identically to them. **aa** is always written with an **alif** (except in one or two common exceptions), and this letter has no other sound in the language.

At the beginning of a word **alif** usually represents a short **a**, as in ال **al-** *the* (see Unit 1). **ii** The word دينار *dinar* illustrates the use of the Arabic letter **yaa'** to mark the long **ii** in the first syllable. It is easily recognized as it is the only Arabic letter with two dots under it. This same letter can mark the sound **ai** as in **bait** *house*.

uu The third long vowel marker is the letter **waaw**. It has only two forms و and ـو as it does not join to the following letter. It is easy to recognize, as it looks like a large comma with a hollow top. It also marks the vowel **oo**.

Pick out the long vowels in this well-known name.

Remember that **alif** almost always represents **aa**, except at the beginning of a word, but **waaw** and **yaa'** in any position can also have the consonantal values of **w** as in 'went' and **y** as in 'yes'. In practice, though, they are more often long vowels. Long vowels in Arabic are also important to pronunciation. A lot of 'pairs' of Arabic first names differ only in the distribution of their vowels - but to the Arabs they are as different as Jules and Jim.

In the following exercise, try to spot which name is which. This is not an exercise in reading, as you don't know all the letters yet, but practice in picking out the all-important long vowels. Remember that if a word has a long vowel, the stress goes on that vowel. If it has more than one long vowel, the stress goes on the one nearest the end of the word.

1 (a) سالم (b) سليم — **sáalim** and **salíim**

(answer: (a) is **sáalim** because it has an **alif** for long **aa**. (b) is **salíim** by elimination and because it has **yaa'** for long **ii**.)

2 (a) محمد (b) محمود — **muHámmad, maHmúud**

3 (a) سعيد (b) سعد (c) سعاد (d) سعود — **su:áad, sá:ad, sa:úud, sa:íid**

4 (a) حمد (b) حامد (c) حميد — **Hamíid, Hamad, Háamid**

5 (a) رشيد (b) راشد — **ráashid, rashíid**

6	(a) زيد	(b) زايد		záayid, zaid
7	(a) ابو ظبي	(b) عمان	(c) الشارقة	:umáan (Oman), abu DHábi, ash-sháarigah (Sharjah)
8	(a) عزيز	(b) عزة		:azíiz, :ázzah
9	(a) قطر	(b) البحرين	(c) العراق	gáTar (Qatar), al-:iráaq, al-baHráin
10	(a) جدة	(b) الرياض	(c) الفجيرة	ar-riyáaDH, jaddah (Jeddah), al-fujáirah

Test yourself

This test covers the main vocabulary, phrases and language points given in Unit 6. If you are not sure about your answers, go back to the dialogues and exercises for some revision, before going on to Unit 7. For the answers, see the **Key to the exercises.**

Complete the following sentences. You fill in the missing pronoun suffixes:

1 ism- (*her*) fariidah
2 khallii-(*us*) nashuuf al-mashruubaat
3 a:Tii-(*me*) nuSS kiiloo mooz
4 bait-(*his*) gariib min hina

In the next exercises we have given you the present stem of the verbs, and you need to fill in the prefixes and/or suffixes.

5 -riid- (*you masc. pl.*) shaay aw gahwah?
6 -riid- (*you fem. sing.*) shay ghair?
7 -faDHDHal (*you masc. sing.*) dajaaj aw jubnah?
8 -sawwi (*I*) la-k sandawiitsh maal laHam
9 -riid (*she*) tishtari shay?
10 -Hibb (*we*) -shrab :aSiir laimoon

7

العائلة

al-:aa'ilah

The family

In this unit you will learn how to

- Talk about your family
- Talk about more than one person or thing
- Talk about people's occupations
- Say what you do every day

Note: Until this unit, the stress has been marked on every word so that you could become accustomed to pronouncing words correctly. By now you will be getting a feel for the language, so the stress is only given when a word appears for the first time in the vocabulary.

New words and phrases

CD 2, TR 1

Listen to the recording.

Hiwaar 1 (Dialogue 1) حوار ١

CD 2, TR 1, 0:12

In Muscat, Samira is asking Eleanor about her children.

Samira	kaif al-awlaad?
Eleanor	bi-khair, al-Hamdu li l-laah
Samira	kam jaahil :ind-ich al-Hiin?
Eleanor	thalaathah, walad w bintain
Samira	(*laughing*) thalaathah bass?
Eleanor	(*laughing with her*) aywa, w inti?
Samira	niHna :ind-na sab:ah, thalaathah awlaad w arba: banaat
Eleanor	maa shaa' allaah!
Samira	al-awlaad kam :umr-hum?
Eleanor	al-walad :umr-uh ithna:shar sanah, wa l-bint al-akbar :asharah, wa l-bint aS-Saghiirah sab: sanawaat
Samira	humma wain?
Eleanor	humma saakiniin ma:a l-waalidah, :ala shaan laazim yiruuHuun al-madrasah
Samira	al-marrah al-gaadimah, laazim tijiibiin-hum li :umaan
Eleanor	in shaa' allaah

QUICK VOCAB

wálad (awláad)	*boy, son*
jáahil (jiháal)	*child*
bint (banáat)	*girl, daughter*
maa sháa' alláah!	*good heavens!*
:úm(u)r	*life, age*
sánah (sanawáat or **siníin)**	*year*
sáakin (saakiníin)	*staying, resident*
wáalidah	*mother*
má:a	*with, together with, along with*
:ála shaan	*because; in order to*
láazim	*(it is) necessary*
láazim yiruuHúun	*they have to go*
mádrasah (madáaris)	*school*
márrah (marráat)	*time, occasion*
gáadim	*next, coming*
yijíib	*to bring*

True or false?

(a) Eleanor has three children.
(b) Samira has eight children altogether.
(c) Eleanor's son is twelve years old.

---

mulaaHaDHaat (Notes) ملاحظات

1 **kam jáahil?** (*how many children do you have?*)
Remember, **kam** always takes the singular where English uses the plural. **awlaad** (lit. *boys, sons*) is also commonly used to mean *children*.

2 **bintáin**
You have already encountered the dual ending **-áin,** meaning *two* people or things.

3 **kam :umr-hum?** (lit. *how many [years] their life*)
It is equally possible to say **:umr-hum kam sanah?** (lit. *their-life how many years?*).

Hiwaar 2 (Dialogue 2) حوار ٢

CD 2, TR 1, 1:19

Abdel Aziz's son Mohammad is a student at Al-Ain University, and he is being interviewed for a student survey.

Interviewer	al-akh min wain?
Mohammad	ana min ash-shu:aib, laakin :aa'ilat-i saakiniin fii dubay
Interviewer	aishgadd Saar la-k tiskun fi l-:ain?
Mohammad	Saar lii thalathta:shar shahar al-Hiin
Interviewer	ta:jib-ak al-:ain?
Mohammad	na:am ta:jib-ni kathiir

Now the interviewer asks him about his family.

Interviewer	wa waalid-ak aish yishtaghal?
Mohammad	waalid-i mudiir sharikah fii dubay. waalidat-i maa tishtaghal
Interviewer	khabbir-na :an :aa'ilat-ak shwayyah
Mohammad	:ind-i thalaathah ikhwaan w ukhtain. akhuu-ya al-akbar mitzawwaj w yishtaghal :ind abuu-ya. akhuu-ya kariim DHaabiT fi l-jaish, w akhuu-ya l-aSghar maa zaal yidrus. hum muu mitzawwajiin.
Interviewer	w akhwaat-ak?
Mohammad	hum th-thintain mudarrisaat. naadya saakinah :ind-na fi l-bait fii dubay. jamiilah mitzawwajah w tiskun fii abu DHabi. zooj-ha muwaDHDHaf fii wizaarat al-i:laam. :ind-hum thalaathah awlaad.
Interviewer	shukran yaa muHammad

QUICK VOCAB

aishgádd	*how long . . .*
Saar	*it happened*
Saar la-k, li	*it happened to you, me*
aishgádd Saar la-k	*how long have you . . . (been somewhere, lived somewhere)*
sháh(a)r (shuhúur)	*month*
yá:jib	*to please*
ta:jíb-ak	*if (fem.) pleases you*
wáalid	*father*
yishtághal	*to work*
mudíir (múdara)	*manager*
khábbir	*tell (imperative)*
akh (ikhwáan)	*brother*
ukht (akhawáat)	*sister*
mitzáwwaj	*married*
:ind	*with*
ab	*father*
DHáabiT (DHubbáaT)	*officer*
jaish (juyúush)	*army*

QUICK VOCAB

áSghar	*smallest,youngest*
maa záal	*still*
yídrus	*to study*
al-ithnáin, fem. **ath-thintáin**	*both* (lit. *the two)*
mudárris (mudarrisíin)	*teacher (male)*
mudárrisah (mudarrisáat)	*teacher (female)*
:índ-na fi l-bait	*at home with us*
yískun	*to live, reside*
tískun	*you live, she lives*
zooj	*husband*
muwáDHDHaf (muwaDHDHafíin)	*official*
wizáarah (wizaaráat)	*ministry*
wizáarat al-i:láam	*Ministry of Information*

(a) How long has Mohammad been studying in Al-Ain?
(b) How many brothers and sisters does he have?
(c) Who is a teacher?
(d) What is his brother-in-law's occupation?

Insight

hum *they* is an alternative to **humma.**

mulaaHaDHaat (Notes) ملاحظات

1 :aa'ilah (*family*)

The apostrophe represents a glottal stop (see Pronunciation guide at the beginning of the book). This is not a common sound in the middle of words in Gulf Arabic where it often changes to 'y' (**:aayilah**).

:aa'ilat-i (*my family*) is the feminine possessive where the **-ah** has changed to **-at**, and the suffix ending is **-i** (*my*).

2 **aishgádd Saar la-k** (*how long have you...?*) done something, lived somewhere, etc.
Saar never changes, but the suffix pronoun after **l(i)-** *to, for* and the main verb (always present tense) have to be altered to suit the person referred to.

3 **aishgádd** (*how long, for what period/extent?*)
This can be replaced with a **kam** (*how many*) expression followed by (the singular) of a time word (day, week, year etc.)

aishgádd Saar l-ak tískun hina?	*How long have you lived here? (to a man)*
Saar l-i thalaath sanawaat askun hina	*I have lived here three years*
aishgádd Saar l-ich tidrusiin :arabi?	*How long have you been studying Arabic? (to a woman)*
Saar l-i thalaathah shuhuur/ sanatain adrus :arabi	*I have been studying Arabic for three months/two years.*

Here are some more expressions of time:

QUICK VOCAB

:áadatan	*usually, generally*
kathíir	*often, frequently*
aHyáanan	*sometimes*
min Hiin íla Hiin	*now and then, occasionally*
dáayman	*always*
ábadan	*never*
yoom (or **ayyáam) al-júm:ah**	*on Fridays, every Friday*
áakhir al-usbúu:	*at the weekend (*lit. *at the end [of] the week)*

4 **akhúu-ya** (*my brother*)
The **-ya** here is a variation of **-i** (*my*), because of the special form of **akh** brother used before the suffix pronouns. You sometimes also hear **ákh-i, akhúu-i.**

Insight

The word **ab** (*father*) behaves in the same way, but here you have an alternative; you may find it simpler to use **waalid** (see below) instead.

---

ma:luumaat thaqaafiyyah (Cultural tips) معلومات ثقافية

It was mentioned in Unit 3 that it is better not to enquire too closely about an Arab family. However, once you get to know an Arab well, he will welcome you into his family and show a real interest in yours, particularly in any children. Arabs take great pleasure in their children, and are very indulgent towards them!

Men should nevertheless be careful about mentioning an Arab's womenfolk. Of course some families are more liberal than others, but it is safest not to mention the female members of the family directly or (if you are a man) to expect to see them when you go on a visit or for a meal.

Arab families (and extended families) are much more close-knit than ours in the West, so you need to learn the relationship words (men bearing in mind the warning above about asking after womenfolk). There are a couple of relationships which we do not distinguish in English. Paternal uncle or aunt means your father's brother or sister, while maternal refers to the same relationship on your mother's side. The distinction extends to a cousin, who is merely the son or daughter of a paternal or maternal uncle or aunt. There are no separate words for nephew or niece, who are son or daughter of brother or sister.

wáalid or **ab**	*father*
wáalidah or **umm**	*mother*
akh (ikhwáan)	*brother*
ukht (akhawáat)	*sister*
:amm	*paternal uncle*
khaal	*maternal uncle*

:ámmah	*paternal aunt*
kháalah	*maternal aunt*
ibn/bint :amm	*male/female cousin (on father's side)*
ibn/bint khaal	*male/female cousin (on mother's side)*
jadd	*grandfather*
jáddah	*grandmother*
waalidáin	*parents*
ajdáad	*grandparents, forefathers*
zooj	*husband*
zóojah	*wife*

ab and **akh** usually become **abu** and **akhu** with possessive nouns and pronouns (see above). In the Gulf countries, it is common once you know people well to refer to a man as **abu** plus the name of his eldest child, and his wife as **umm** plus the same:

abu SáaliH lit. father of Salih
umm háashim mother of Hashim

abu is also used of humans and inanimates to indicate some attribute:

abu líHyah	*a man with a beard* (lit. *father of a beard)*
abu DHabi	*(Abu Dhabi)* lit. *father of gazelle (in which it presumably once abounded)*

umm is occasionally used in the same way.

akhi (lit. my brother) is a term of address used between males of approximately equal status.

The more formal **al-akh** (the brother) is used as a polite way of addressing a stranger.

If an Arab is addressing an older person he does not know, he might say **yaa :amm-i** (lit. *my uncle*).

The word **ibn** (*son*) is mostly used with the suffix pronouns, for example, **ibn-i** (*my son*). It has an alternative form **bin** used in proper names which, in the Gulf, often take the form of: first name + **bin** + father's first name + **al-** tribal name (usually ending in **-i**):

yuusif bin aHmad al-qaasimi Youssef bin Ahmed al-Qasimi.

This means a man called Youssef, whose father's first name was Ahmed and who belongs to the tribe of the Qasimis.

muHammad bin maHmuud al-kindi Mohammed bin Mahmoud al-Kindi (Muhammed son of Mahmoud of the Kindi family/tribe).

Two proverbs

wálad al-kalb, kalb míthl-uh	*The son of a dog is a dog like it.*
bint al-báTTah :awwáamah	*The daughter of a duck is a (good) swimmer.*

An equivalent proverb in English would be: *Like father, like son.*

kalb (kiláab)	*dog*
míthl-uh	*like him, it*
báTTah (baTT)	*duck*
:awwáam (-ah)	*a (good, better than average) swimmer*

Hiwaar 3 (Dialogue 3) حوار ٣

CD 2, TR 1, 2:48

Bill Stewart is having coffee with Abdel Aziz's son Salim in the office in Dubai.

Bill	aishgádd Saar l-ak tishtaghal hina fi l-maktab ma:a waalid-ak yaa saliim?
Salim	Saar l-i sanah al-Hiin
Bill	inta tiskun :ind al-waalid?

Salim	laa, naskun fii shaggah gariibah min hina. bait al-waalid ba:iid :an al-maktab. :ala shaan ana adaawim min aS-SubH badri, w aHyaanan laazim ashtaghal bi l-lail
Bill	wa t(i)shuuf al-:aa'ilah kathiir?
Salim	na:am, aruuH :ind-hum kull yoom.
Bill	wa t(i)shuuf-hum yoom al-jum:ah?
Salim	na:am, :aadatan naruuH - al-:aa'ilah kull-ha ya:ni - nazuur jadd-i w jaddat-i yoom al-jum:ah
Bill	hum saakiniin wain?
Salim	fi sh-shu:aib. :amm-i w :ammat-i yiskunuun wiyyáa-hum fii nafs al-bait

QUICK VOCAB

máktab (makáatib)	*office*
shággah or **shíggah (shígag)**	*flat, apartment*
bait (buyúut)	*house*
yidáawim	*to keep office hours*
bádri	*early*
kull	*every, all, whole*
kull yoom	*every day*
yirúuH	*to go*
yizúur	*to visit*
wiyya	*with, along with*
wiyyáa-hum	*with them.*
yoom al-júm(a):ah	*on Friday,* i.e. *at the weekend*
nafs	*self, same*

(a) Why does Salim not live at home?
(b) When does he go to visit his grandparents?
(c) Where do his uncle and aunt live?

---

mulaaHaDHaat (Notes) ملاحظات

1 yidaawim

You hear this verb a lot in the Gulf. It expresses the working hours one keeps; when one will be in one's office, at one's desk.

2 **bait al-waalid** (*father's house*)
Just as you add pronoun suffixes to nouns to express possession, you can also add another noun. In this type of construction (as here) the second noun usually has the **al-** (*the*) unless it is someone's name. The first noun never has it. If the first noun has the **-ah** ending, the 'hidden t' appears, as in **wizaarat al-i:laam** *[the] ministry of information*, from **wizaarah.**

3 **al-:aa'ilah kull-ha ya:ni** *the whole family, I mean.*
Here **kull-ha** refers to the family (feminine).

4 **nafs**
This word followed by a noun with **al-** means *the same*:

nafs ai-bait	*the same house*
nafs ash-shay	*the same thing*

You can also use the pronoun suffixes:

nafs-i/-ak/-uh/-ha, etc. (*myself, yourself, himself, herself*)

---

ta:biiraat haammah (Key phrases) تعبيرات هامة

CD 2, TR 1, 3:44

How to talk about the family

:ind-i akh waaHid w thalaath akhawaat *I have a brother and three sisters.*
maa :ind-i laa ikhwaan wala akhawaat *I have no brothers or sisters (***laa . . .wála** *neither . . .nor).*
haadha akhuu-ya saliim *This is my brother Salim.*
haadhi ukht-i jamiilah *This is my sister Jamilah.*

Talking about how old people are

maHmuud :umr-uh kam sanah? :umr-uh ithna:shar sanah *How old is Mahmoud? He is 12 years old.*

awlaad-ak kam :umr-hum? waaHid:ind-uh khamasta:shar sanah w waaHid :ind-uh arba:ata:shar (sanah) *How old are your children? They are 15 and 14 years old (*lit. *one is....).*

How to talk about where you live and your occupation

wain tiskun? *Where do you live?*
askun fi l-baHrain *I live in Bahrain.*

The adjective **saakin** *living, residing* can be used:

inta saakin wain? ana saakin fi l-baHrain wain tishtaghal? *Where do you work?*
ashtaghal fii maktab/bank/mustashfa/sharikah *I work in an office/bank/hospital/company.*
aish shughl-ak? *What is your work?*
ana muhándis/mudárris/mudiir sharikah *I am an engineer/a teacher/a company director.*

How to talk about your daily routine

as-saa:ah kam tiguum (min an-noom)? *When do you get up (from sleep)?*
aguum as-saa:ah sittah aS-SubaH *I get up at 6 a.m.*
tiruuH ash-shughul as-saa:ah kam? *What time do you go to work?*
aruuH al-maktab as-saa:ah sab:ah, w adaawim min as-saa:ah thamaanyah li-ghaayat as-saa:ah ithnain *I go to the office at 7a.m. and work from 8 a.m. to 2 p.m.*
as-saa:ah kam taakul ar-riyuug/al-ghada? *When do you eat breakfast/lunch?*
aakul ar-riyuug/al-ghada as-saa:ah sittah/thintain wa nuSS *I have breakfast/lunch at 6 a.m./2.30 p.m.*
as-saa:ah kam tiruuH tinaam? *When do you go to bed (*lit. *to sleep)?*
aruuH anaam as-saa:ah iHda:shar w nuSS *I go to bed at 11.30 p. m.*

QUICK VOCAB

yiguum	*to rise, get up (from sleep)*
li-ghaayat	*up to, until*
riyúug	*breakfast*
gháda	*lunch*
yináam	*to sleep*

núqaT naHwíyyah (Grammar points) نقط نحوية

1 Saying *you have to, must do* something

This is done by using the word **laazim** [*it is*] *necessary* [*that*]. . . before the (present) verb:

laazim ashtaghal yoom as-sabt	*I have to work on Saturday.*
laazim aruuH al-kuwait baakir	*I have to go to Kuwait tomorrow.*
laazim titkallam :arabi	*You must speak Arabic.*

2 Saying *you like* something

In the previous unit you learnt to use the verb **yiHibb** to express a permanent like or dislike, as of tea or chocolate.

If you are talking about something which just strikes you as good, or pleasing, use the verb **ya:jib** (*to please*) and add the suffix ending according to who is being pleased.

ya:jib-ni (*it pleases me*) is identical to the French '*il me plait*'. Remember that places are usually feminine, so the verb prefix must be feminine:

ta:jib-ak al-:ain?	*Do you like Al-Ain? (*lit. *it [fem.] pleases you Al-Ain?)*
na:am ta:jib-ni kathiir	*Yes, I like it a lot.* (lit. *it pleases me a lot)*
háadhi S-Súurah maa ta:jib-ni	*I don't like this picture.* (lit. *this picture does not please me)*

3 Talking about more than two people or things

Arabic plurals are formed in one of three ways, depending on the word:
(a) by changing the internal shape of the word
(b) by adding **-iin** to the singular word
(c) by adding **-aat** to the singular word.

(a) Many commonly-used nouns (and some adjectives) have 'broken' plurals, formed by changing or 'breaking up' the internal structure of the word itself, like English *mouse → mice, foot → feet*. This type of plural, where it exists, is used for both human beings and things:

wálad → awláad (*boy*)
bait → buyúut (*house*)

Insight

In general, it is 'shorter' nouns, i.e. those with fewer letters, which take broken plurals. Broken plurals can be formed from foreign borrowings if they meet the 'length' criterion. Compare the examples above with the two following types of plurals:

film → afláam (*film*)
bank → bunúuk (*bank*)

With a few exceptions, nouns have only one plural form. The two categories of plurals which follow do not have a broken plural. They are not alternatives.

(b) Words which do not have a broken plural and which signify male human beings usually add the ending **-íin** to the noun.

muhándis → muhandisíin (*engineer*)
mudárris → mudarrisíin (*teacher – male*)
kuwáiti → kuwaitiyyíin (*Kuwaiti*)

Note that words which end in **-i** in the singular, add a 'helping' y or yy before this ending.

A few common foreign words for males use the ending **-iyya:**

dráiwil → draiwilíyya (*driver*)
kúuli → kuulíyya (*coolie, labourer*)

(c) Words which do not have a broken plural and which signify female human beings or inanimates drop the ending **-ah** if present and add **-aat**:

> **mudárrisah → mudarrisáat** (*teacher – fem.*)
> **sayyáarah → sayyaaráat** (*car*)
> **baaS → baaSáat** (*bus*)

Note: A relatively few very common nouns denoting female members of the family take irregular or hybrid plurals:

> **umm → ummaháat** (*mother*)
> **ukht → akhawáat** (*sister*)
> **bint → banáat** (*girl, daughter*)

sanah (*year*) has two plurals, **sanawáat** and **siníin** (the latter being the only common exception to the 'men only' rule for the **-iin** suffix).

In the end, you just have to learn the plurals along with the singulars. They are given in brackets after the noun in the vocabulary, in full if they are broken, or with **-íin** or **-áat**.

4 Plural adjectives

Adjectives have plurals just like nouns, which must be used when you are talking about people. For things you use the feminine singular **-ah**.

humma saakiniin wain?	*Where are they living?*
al-banaat al-kuwaitiyyaat	*the Kuwaiti girls*
sayyaaraat kathiirah	*many cars*

A few common adjectives have broken plurals, and these will be given in the vocabulary in the same way as the plural of nouns. If no plural is given for an adjective, assume that it takes **-iin**.

tamriinaat (Exercises) تمرينات

CD 2, TR 1, 4:55

1 Listen to these six people saying what their occupations are or where they work, or look at the transcript. Make a note of what they tell you, and check your answers in the key.

Tabíib (aTibba)	*doctor*
Táalibah (-aat)	*student (female)*
ta:líim	*education*

qv

2 Which questions would be appropriate to ask each of these people, and which replies belong to which person?

(a) tishtaghal aish?
(b) aishgádd Saar l-ich tishtaghaliin hinaak?
(c) ana muhandisah
(d) tiHibbiin shughl-ich?
(e) ana mudiir sharikah
(f) aish shughl-ich?
(g) tiHibb ash-shughul hinaak?
(h) aishgádd Saar l-ak tiskun hinaak?

3 Complete the following Arabic sentences using the new words given below. Remember the rules for using the plural as explained in Unit 5.

(a) kam (*houses*) fiih fi sh-sháari:?
(b) fiih sáb: (*emirates*) fi-l-imaaráat al-:arabiyyah al-muttaHidah
(c) al-baHrain fii-ha thalaathah wa-thalaathiin (*islands*)
(d) ana :ind-i thalaathah (*brothers*) wa arba: (*sisters*)

(e) fiih mushkilah - :ind-na iHda:shar (*people*) laakin :asharah (*chairs*)
(f) fi l-madrasah khamasta:shar (*men teachers*) wa thalaath (*women teachers*).
(g) fiih kam (*rooms*) fi l-fundug?
(h) fii (*2 roundabouts*) gabil al-maTaar.

QUICK VOCAB

imáarah (-áat)	*emirate*
al-imaaráat al-:arabíyyah al-muttáHidah	*the UAE*
jazíirah (jazáayir or **júzur)**	*island*
mushkílah (masháakil)	*problem*
shakhS (ashkháaS)	*person, individual*
kúrsi (karáasi)	*chair*
mudárrisah (-áat)	*teacher (f.)*
ghúrfah (ghúraf)	*room*
duwwáar (-áat)	*roundabout*

4 Mohammad, from Qatar, shows you his family tree below. Answer the questions about his relatives in Arabic. The first question is answered for you.

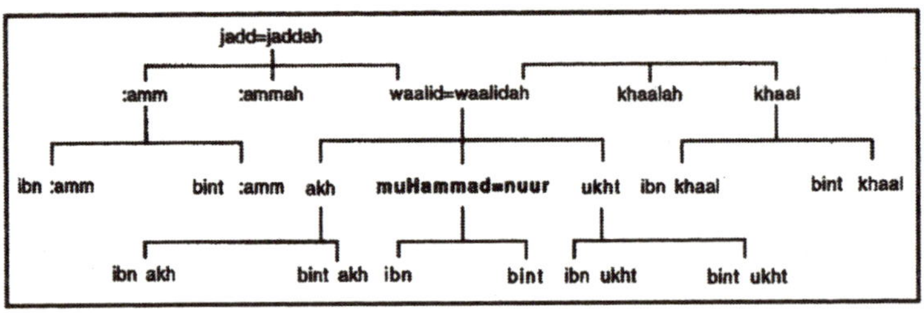

(a) man zoojat waalid muHammad? (answer: **wáalidat-uh**)
(b) khaal-uh akh man?
(c) man ibn akhuu-h?
(d) man waalidat bint ukht-uh?
(e) man waalidat ibn-uh?
(f) man ibn :amm-uh?
(g) man akh bint-uh?
(h) man waalidat abuu-h?

5 You are on a short visit to Bahrain and have been invited to a party, where you meet Munir and his wife Nadia

inta	*Ask them where they come from.*
Munir	niHna min al-kuwait. inta min wain?
inta	*Tell them where you are from. Ask them if they live in Bahrain.*
Munir	laa, niHna saakiniin fi l-kuwait, laakin akhuu-ya yiskun hina. yishtaghal fi s-sifaarah al- kuwaitiyyah, w naaji hina nazuur-uh kathiir. inta aishgádd Saar l-ak tiskun fi l-baHrain?
inta	*Say you have only been there three days. Ask them what they do.*
Nadia	zooj-i muhandis w ana ashtaghal fii bank. ayy shughul tishtaghal inta?
inta	*Tell them what you do and where you work.*
Nadia	ta:jib-ak al-baHrain?
inta	*Tell them you like it very much.*

QV

sifáarah (-aat) *embassy*
náaji *we come*

🔊 **CD 2, TR 1, 5:20**

6 Listen to the recording or read the transcript on Ahmad talking about his life in Abu Dhabi. Look at the new words given below, and check your comprehension by answering the questions.

QUICK VOCAB

noom *sleep* (noun)
yiwáSSil *to take someone, give them a lift*
bi-sayyaarát-ha *in her car*
yitghádda *to lunch, eat lunch*
yishúuf at-tilifizyóon *to watch television*

(a) When does Ahmad get up?
(b) Where does his wife go?
(c) When does he finish work?
(d) What does he do after lunch?
(e) When do they usually go to bed?

al-khaTT al-:árabi (Arabic script) الخط العربي

Originally (believe it or not!) the ancient Arabic language was written with far fewer letters, many of them having several different pronunciations. To remedy the confusion which this defective alphabet caused, dots were added to some of the letters to distinguish between these varying pronunciations. The 'dot system' in Modern Arabic uses the following combinations:

(a) one, two or three dots above the letter

(b) one or two (but not three) dots below the letter

Of course some letters are not dotted at all.

The dotting phenomenon enables us to divide the Arabic alphabet into groups or sets of letters for convenience of learning.

The largest group contains the letters **b, t, th, n** and **y**. Three of these have been mentioned in earlier units, but now you have the full set. You know by now that, as with most of the Arabic letters, there is a 'nucleus' form, to which are added joining strokes or ligatures for the other forms. In addition, the final form used at the end of words frequently undergoes some elongation or embellishment.

Apart from the number and placement of dots, the letters in the following list are all identical except for variations in the final and separate forms of two of them. This series of letters is written small in height, and the 'nucleus' form is no more than a small hook placed on the line. They all join to both preceding and following letters.

Name	Initial	Medial	Final	Separate	Pronunciation
baa'	بـ	ـبـ	ـب	ب	b
taa'	تـ	ـتـ	ـت	ت	t
thaa'	ثـ	ـثـ	ـث	ث	th
nuun	نـ	ـنـ	ـن	ن	n
yaa'	يـ	ـيـ	ـي	ى	y

A look at the above table will show that the letters are identical, except for the final and separate forms of '**n**' and '**y**'. The former extends below the line, and is an incomplete 'egg-on-end' shape, while the latter is a double curve, again below the line. Notice that the dots of the initial and medial forms of the above letters are centred above or below the upward pointing tooth of the letter. In the final and separate forms, the dots are centred above or below the flourish. There are no difficulties of pronunciation in this group, but remember that '**y**' sometimes represents a long **ii** or **ai** as described in Unit 6. Now try to recognize the following words, which incorporate some of these new letters. Remember to supply the short vowels.

Insight

Write down the consonants with a hyphen between them, and see what they suggest. For example, the first word below, which uses three letters from this group, is: **b-n-t**, i.e. **bint**. We have provided clues to help you.

	١. بنت
(usually after **shay**: this is really something else!)	٢. ثاني
(the second letter is ':'; not feeling too bright?)	٣. تعبان
(pronounce the first letter as 'i': a pronoun)	٤. إنت
(a present from Arabia)	٥. مَن
(one syllable; middle vowel is '**ai**' written with Arabic '**y**': there's no place like it)	٦. بيت
(remember long vowels: delicious squeezed...)	٧. ليمون
(written with a hyphen after the first letter in our transcription: no sugar thanks)	٨. بدون
(second letter is ':' again: most useful word in Arabic)	٩. يعني
(cool, creamy and delicious)	١٠. لبن

Test yourself

This test covers the main vocabulary, phrases and language points given in Unit 7. If you are not sure about your answers, go back to the dialogues and exercises for some revision, before going on to Unit 8. For the answers, see the **Key to the exercises.**

1 Match these professions or people with their corresponding places of work, and indicate whether they are male or female:

(a) mudíir	(i) mádrasah
(b) Tabíib	(ii) máktab
(c) mudárrisah	(ii) mustáshfa
(d) Táalibah	(iv) jáami:ah

2 How well do you remember the names for the members of the family? Give the corresponding male or female to the ones below.

(a) ukht	(d) bint
(b) waalid *or* ab	(e) zooj
(c) :amm	

3 Give the plurals for the following words:

(a) walad	(c) sayyaarah kabiirah
(b) bank	(d) muhandis kuwaiti

4 Arrange these expressions of time in order of frequency, with the most frequent first:
(a) abadan, (b) kathiir, (c) daayman, (d) aHyaanan

How would you answer the following questions in Arabic?

5 aishgadd Saar l-ak tiskun hina?
6 as-saa:ah kam tiguum min an-noom?
7 laazim tirúuH ash-shughl as-saa:ah kam?
8 as-saa:ah kam taakul al-ghada?
9 tiHibb tishúuf at-tilifizyóon?
10 as-saa:ah kam tiruuH tinaam?

8

في الفندق

fi l-fundug

In the hotel

In this unit you will learn how to

- Reserve and ask for a room
- Ask about the services
- Ask about mealtimes
- Make a complaint

New words and phrases

CD 2, TR 2

Listen to the recording.

Hiwaar 1 (Dialogue 1) حوار ١

CD 2, TR 2, 0:15

Tony is in Saudi Arabia on business, and he has driven from Jeddah to visit Taif. He goes into the Centre Hotel.

Kaatib	ahlan wa sahlan, marHab
Tony	ahlan bii-k. :ind-ak ghurfah min faDHI-ak?
Kaatib	ghurfah li shakhS waaHid aw shakhSain?
Tony	shakhS waaHid, bi Hammaam
Kaatib	li muddah aish?
Tony	lailatain.
Kaatib	dagiigah min faDHI-al . . . . . na:am, fiih ghurfah
Tony	hiyya bi-kam, min faDHI-ak?
Kaatib	miyyah w :ishriin riyaal bi l-khidmah
Tony	zain. aakhudh-ha.
Kaatib	imla haadha l-kart min faDHI-ak. mumkin ta:Tii-ni jawaaz as-safar law samaHt?
Tony	tfaDHDHal. al-fuTuur as-saa:ah kam min faDHI-ak?
Kaatib	al-fuTuur min as-saa:ah sittah w nuSS fi l-maT:am, aw mumkin tiTlub-uh fi l-ghurfah.
Tony	zain
Kaatib	ghurfah ragam khams miyyah w arba:ata:shar. haadha huwwa l-miftaaH. (*calls the porter*) ta:aal yaa :abdallah. huwwa yisaa:id-ak bi sh-shúnuT

QUICK VOCAB

káatib (kuttáab)	*clerk*
márHab	*welcome, hello*
ghúrfah li shakhS wáaHid	*single room*
aw	*or*
ghúrfah li shakhSáin	*double room*
Hammáam (-aat)	*bathroom*
li múddah aish	*for how long*
láilah (layáali)	*night*
khídmah (khadamáat)	*service*
ímla	*fill in (imperative)*
yímla	*to fill (in)*
kart (kurúut)	*card*
jawáaz as-sáfar	*passport*
fuTúur	*breakfast*
yíTlub	*to order (something), ask for*
miftáaH (mafatíiH)	*key*

ta:áal	*come* (imperative)
yisáa:id	*to help*
shánTah (shúnuT)	*bag, suitcase*

(a) What kind of room does Tony want?
(b) How long does he want to stay?
(c) What does the receptionist ask Tony to give him?

---

mulaaHaDHaat (Notes) ملاحظات

1 marHab
This is a common alternative to **ahlan wa sahlan.**

2 aw *or*
Both **aw** and **wálla** are commonly used.

3 **li muddah aish?** (*for how long?*)
This is comprised of three elements: **li-** (*to, for*) + **muddah** (*period of time*), (sometimes showing the hidden '**t**') + **aish** (*what*).

4 **lail(a)tain** (*for two nights*)
This is the dual of **lailah** (*night*). **li** (*for*) can sometimes (as here) be omitted.

5 **shanTah** (*suitcase*)
This is often pronounced **janTah.**

---

ma:luumaat thaqaafiyyah (Cultural tips) معلومات ثقافية

al-fuTuur (also called, less formally **ar-riyuug**) (breakfast) is often just fresh fruit, or bread with cheese.

For most people the main meal of the day is **al-ghada** (*lunch*), when everyone comes home from work and school, and various hot fish, meat or poultry curries are served with rice, vegetables and salads.

In the evening people tend to have simpler food, like sandwiches or take-away meals, although of course in the hotels and restaurants people would eat a more substantial dinner, **al-:asha**.

Breakfast	**الفطور**
Fresh fruit juice	عصير الفواكه الطازجة
Assorted fruit	فواكه مشكّلة
Arabic breakfast (dates, ful mudammas, labnah, salad and bread)	الفطور العربي (تمر، فول مدمّس، لبنة، سلطة وخبز)
American breakfast (eggs, tomatoes, sausages, toast)	الفطور الأمريكي (بيض، طماطم، سجوق وتوست)
Tea	شاي
Coffee (Turkish or American)	قهوة (تركية او أمريكية)
K.D. 3.00	٣ دنانير كويتية

Hiwaar 2 (Dialogue 2) حوار ٢

CD 2, TR 2, 1:27

Youssef, an Iraqi, has business in Kuwait, and he telephones the Gulf Pearl Hotel to reserve a room.

Youssef	SabaaH al-khair. ana baaji l-kuwait ash-shahar al-gaadim, w ariid aHjiz ghurfah min faDHl-ak.
kaatib	zain. fii ayy taarikh in shaa'allaah?
Youssef	ariid ghurfah li shakhS waaHid, min as-sabt thamaanyah fibraayir li ghaayat iHda:shar fibraayir
kaatib	laHDHah . . . . ya:ni arba:at ayyaam?

Youssef	aywa, SaHiiH.
kaatib	na:am, zain. as-saa:ah kam tooSal in shaa' allaah?
Youssef	in sha'allah ooSal yoom thamaanyah ba:ad aDH-DHuhur. yimkin yikuun fiih bard fi l-kuwait fi sh-shita. al-ghurfah fii-ha tadfi'ah?
kaatib	maa fiih mushkilah. al-ghuraf kull-ha fiih tadfi' ah, wa takyiif w tilifizyoon mulawwan.

QUICK VOCAB

yíijii	*to come*
báaji	*I will be coming*
gáadim	*next*
yíHjiz	*reserve*
taaríikh	*date*
fibráayir	*February*
yoom (ayyáam)	*day*
SaHíiH	*correct, right*
yóoSal	*to arrive*
aDH-DHúh(u)r	*(the) noon*
yímkin	*maybe*
yikúun fiih	*there will be*
bard	*cold (noun)*
ash-shíta	*(the) winter*
tádfi'ah	*heating*
takyíif	*air-conditioning*
muláwwan	*coloured*

(a) Does Youssef ask for a single or a double room?
(b) When is he hoping to arrive?
(c) What is he worried about?

---

mulaaHaDHaat (Notes) ملاحظات

1 baaji
This is simply **aaji** (*I come*) prefixed with a **b-** to make it in the future tense, *I will come.*

Insight

Note that this is the true Gulf Arabic usage. Northern dialects prefix an **H-** for the future, and use **b-** for other purposes. You may hear this, as all Gulf Arabs are familiar with Egyptian Arabic from the television, and it is influencing their speech habits.

2 tooSal (*you will arrive*)
As in English, the future need not be marked if it is obvious from the context ('He's arriving on Tuesday').

3

QUICK VOCAB

shuhúur as-sánah	*the months of the year*
yanáayir	*January*
fibráayir	*February*
mars	*March*
abríil	*April*
máayo	*May*
yúunyo	*June*
yúulyo	*July*
aghúsTos	*August*
sabtámbar	*September*
októobar	*October*
nufámbar	*November*
disámbar	*December*
min maayo li sabtambar	*from May to September*
fii yanaayir	*in January*

Instead of naming the month, it is also common to say just the day and number of the month:

baaji l-kuwait shahr fibraayir	*I am coming to Kuwait in February.*
baaji l-kuwait shahr ithnain	*I am coming to Kuwait in February (month two).*

Insight

The old Arab months, the best-known in the West being **ramaDHáan** *Ramadan*, are based on the Islamic calendar which starts from 16th July 622 AD. Converting dates from this is not merely a matter of subtracting 622. Since the year consists of 12 lunar months it is about ten days shorter. For instance, 1st January 2000 = 24th Ramadan 1420.

There is a third set of month names which begins the year with the month **kaanúun ath-tháani** (*Kanun the Second*). Stick to the European months.

4 To say *on* such and such a date use **fii** (*i n*) or simply nothing at all:

fii tis:ah yuunyo	*on the 9th of June*
:asharah :asharah	*on the 10th of October*

Insight

The ordinary numbers are used for dates, not the ordinals (7th, 20th etc.) as in English.

5 **yímkin** (lit. *it is possible*)
This verbal form is more or less interchangeable with the adjective **mumkin.**

6 **yikúun fiih** (*there will be*)
This is the future of **fiih** (*there is*).
yikuun fiih bard (*it will be cold* lit. *there will be coldness*).

ma:luumaat thaqaafiyyah (Cultural tips) معلومات ثقافية

takyíif (*air-conditioning*) in cars and buildings is an essential part of modern life in the Gulf. This is the formal word for it, but you will frequently hear the adapted English **kandáishan.**

Although the Gulf is famed for the intense heat of its summers, in the northern Gulf in the winter months it can be bitterly cold. Even the smallest hotels will have air-conditioning units in the rooms, which are needed all year in the southern Gulf, but you might wish to confirm that there is heating if you are going to the north in winter.

aS-Saif	*summer*
ash-shíta	*winter*
fi S-Saif	*in summer*
fi sh-shíta	*in winter*

Hiwaar 3 (Dialogue 3) حوار ٣

CD 2, TR 2, 2:34

Tony is in his room but he has a problem and calls reception.

Tony	haalo. hina ghurfah ragam khams miyyah w arba:ata:shar. fiih mushkilah
kaatib	aish hiyya l-mushkilah? in shaa' allaah nasaa:id-ak
Tony	aHtaaj ila fuwaT ziyaadah fi l-Hamaam, w at-takyiif kharbaan, maa yishtaghal
kaatib	muta' assifiin jiddan. attaSil fii khidmáat al-fundug w yiTarrishuun Had fawran yiSalliH-uh w yijiib fuwaT
Tony	zain. shukran

QUICK VOCAB

múshkilah, masháakil	*problem*
yiHtáaj ila	*to need*
ziyáadah	*more*
fúuTah (fúwaT)	*towel*
kharbáan	*broken*
mut(a)'ássif (-iin)	*sorry*
jíddan	*very*
khidmáat al-fundug	*hotel services*
yiTárrish	*to send*
Had	*someone*
fáwran	*immediately*
yiSálliH	*to mend, fix, repair*
yijíib	*to bring*

(a) What is the problem?
(b) What does the receptionist promise to do?

---

mulaaHaDHaat (Notes) ملاحظات

1 yiHtaaj ila (*to need*)
In English you say *I need something*, but the Arabic verb requires ila (lit. to, towards) after it.

2 ziyaadah (*more*)
This is not actually an adjective, but a noun meaning literally *an increase*, so it does not change for gender.

---

ta:biiraat haammah (Key phrases) تعبيرات هامة

CD 2, TR 2, 3:27

Booking a room

ariid aHjiz *I want to reserve, make a reservation.*
:ind-ak ghurfah li shakhS waaHid/shakhSain? *Do you have a room for one person/for two people?*
ariid ghurfah li shakhS waaHid/shakhSain) *I want a single/double room.*
afaDHDHil ghurfah bi Hammaam *I prefer a room with a bathroom.*
(al-ghurfah) fii-ha takyiif? *Does it (the room) have air-conditioning?*
tilifizyóon? *television?*
tilifóon *a telephone?*
thalláajah *a fridge?*
al-ghurfah bi kam? *How much is the room?*
haadha bi l-khidmah? *Is the service (charge) included?*

Saying how long you want to stay

kam lailah? *How many nights?*

li muddat aish? *For how long?*
(li) lailah waaHidah *For one night.*
lailatain *two nights.*
thalaathat ayyaam *three days.*
usbuu: *a week.*

Saying when you will arrive

mata tooSal? *When will you arrive?*
ooSal baakir *I will arrive tomorrow.*
lailat al-arba:a *on Wednesday night*
al-khamiis al-gaadim *next Thursday*
thalaathah oktoobar (thalaathah :asharah) *on the 3rd of October/ the 10th (month)*
Hawaali s-saa:ah sab:ah *At about 7.00 p.m.*
al-mísa *In the evening.*

Checking in

mumkin timla haadha l-kart min faDHl-ak?. *Can you fill in this card please?*
mumkin tiwaggi: hina? *Can you sign here?*
mumkin ta:Tii-ni jawaz as-safar/al-buTaagah sh-shakhSiyyah? *Can you give me your passport/identity card?*

qv

yiwággi:	*to sign*
buTáagah shakhSíyyah	*identity card*

Asking about meals

al-fuTuur as-saa:ah kam? *What time is breakfast?*
min as-saa:ah sittah li ghaayat as-saa:ah :asharah *From 6 am. until 10 am.*
wain naakhudh al-fuTuur/al-ghada/al-:asha? *Where is breakfast/ lunch/dinner served? (*lit. *where do we take . . .).*
fi l-maT:am/al-koofii shoob *In the restaurant/coffee shop*
mumkin tiTlub-uh fi l-ghurfah *You can order it in your room (*lit. *in the room).*

Making a complaint

ana fii ghurfah khams miyyah w khamsah. fiih mushkilah *I am in room number 505; there is a problem.*
min faDHl-ak jiib fúwaT/Saabúun/thalj ziyáadah *please bring more towels/soap/ice.*
at-takyiif/ad-dushsh kharbaan/maa yishtaghal *The air-conditioning/ shower is broken/does not work.*
maa fiih Saabuun/fuuTah/maay saakhin *There is no soap/towel/ hot water.*
al-ghurfah waajid Saghiirah/baaridah/was(i)khah *The room is very small/cold/dirty.*

In Arabic there is no word for *too*; use **waajid** or **jiddan** *very*

ariid ghurfah naDHíifah/háadyah *I want a clean/quiet room.*
aHtaaj ila makháddah/barnúuS/shárshaf/fúuTah thaani/yah *I need an other pillow/blanket/Sheet/towel.*

---

núqaT naHwíyyah (Grammar points) نقط نحوية

1 Talking about the future

The future tense (English *I shall*) in Gulf Arabic is formed by the relevant part of the present tense prefixed with **b-**. Before consonants, this acquires a helping vowel, usually **-i**, and the vowels of the verbal prefixes **t(i)-**, **y(i)-** and **n(a)-** are omitted to smooth out pronunciation. (These are merely habits of speech, so do not worry about them unduly.) Here is the verb **yisawwi** (*to do, make*) in full in both the present and the future:

Present		Future	
asawwi	*I do*	**basawwi**	*I shall/will do*
tisawwi	*you (masc.) do*	**bitsawwi**	*you will do*
tisawwiin	*you (fem.) do*	**bitsawwiin**	*you will do*
yisawwi	*he does*	**biysawwi** (or **byisawwi**)	*he will do*

tisawwi	*she does*	**bitsawwi**	*she will do*
nasawwi	*we do*	**binsawwt**	*we will do*
tisawwuun	*you (plural) do*	**bitsawwuun**	*you will do*
yisawwuun	*they do*	**biysawwuun** (or **byisawwuun)**	*they will do*

Insight

In most parts of the Gulf, verbs like **yisawwi** whose present stem ends in -i drop this before the suffixes **-iin**, and **-uun**.

As in English, if the time sequence is obvious from the context, the simple present can be used:

aish bitsawwi fi S-Saif?	*What are you doing in the summer?*
aruuH ingilterra	*I am going to England.*
mata btooSal?	*When will you arrive?*
ooSal yoom as-sabt al-gaadim	*I will arrive next Saturday.*

2 More verb strings

In Unit 6 you learnt how to use two verbs together:

nariid nashuuf	*We want to look (*lit. *we-want we-look).*
aish tiriidiin tishribiin?	*What do you want to drink?*

In both the above cases the person doing the 'wanting' is the same person or people doing the 'looking' or 'drinking', and so the form of the verb is the same in both cases.

If there are different people doing each action, the forms of the verbs have to agree accordingly:

yiTarrishuun Had yiSalliH-uh	*They will send someone to mend it (*lit. *they [will]-send someone he [will]-mend-it.)*

nariid-ak tiSalliH-uh *We want you to mend it* (lit. *we-want-you you-mend-it.)*

---

tamriinaat (Exercises) تمرينات

CD 2, TR 2, 4:07

1 Listen to these four people booking a room or read the transcript. Look at the options they have, and mark which ones they choose (with reservation)/(without reservation).

(a) :ind-hum Hajz — maa :ind-hum Hajz

(b) ghurfah li shakhS waaHid — li shakhSain

(c) lailah waaHidah — lailatain — thalaath layaali

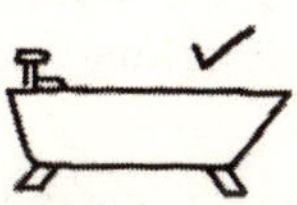 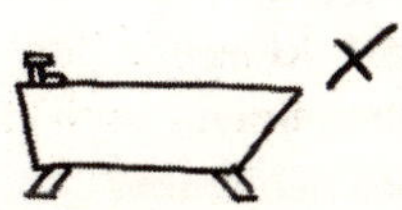

(d) bi Hammaam — bi-duun Hammaam

2 You overhear a new guest in the hotel asking the receptionist some questions. What does he want to know? Look at the new words, and answer the questions below.

DHaif	fiih thallaajah fi l-ghurfah?
kaatib	na:am. fiih miini baar
DHaif	ayy yoom :asha s-samak?
kaatib	yoom al-arba:a min as-saa:ah sittah w nuSS
DHaif	mumkin tiguul li-i, fiih tilifoon fi l-loobi?
kaatib	na:am. hinaak jamb al-maSaa:id.

(a) Is he asking if the room has (i) air-conditioning (ii) satellite TV (iii) a fridge?
(b) Does he want to know about (i) breakfast (ii) lunch or (iii) dinner?
(c) Is he asking for (i) the lift (ii) a telephone (iii) the coffee shop?

V Q

sámak	*fish, seafood*
lóobi	*lobby*
jamb	*beside*
míS:ad (maSáa:id)	*lift*

3 You hear three people booking a room. What dates do they want a room for?
  (a) min ithnain w :ishriin li arba:ah w :ishriin shahar :asharah
  (b) min thalaathta:shar li tis:ata:shar maayoo
  (c) min :asharah li sab:ata:shar shahar ithna:shar

4 Now it's your turn to book ahead. Write down what you would say in (transliterated) Arabic, and check your answers in the **Key to the exercises.**
  (a) 2nd to 5th March
  (b) 9th to 16th July
  (c) 1st to 8th September

5 Mealtimes. How would you ask the following?
  (a) when dinner is served?
  (b) when the restaurant opens?
  (c) whether you can order lunch in your room?
  (d) where the lift is?

6 Put the replies in this dialogue into the correct order.
SabaaH al-khair. mumkin asaa:id-ak?
—bi-dushsh
na:am. li shakhS waaHid aw li shakhSain?
—al-ghurfah bi-kam min faDHl-ak?
bi Hammaam aw bi-dushsh?
—al-ghurfah wain min faDHl-ak?
li kam lailah?
—SabaaH an-nuur. :ind-ak ghurfah min faDHl-ak?
akiid
—thalaath layaali
al-lailah bi khamsah w :ishriin diinaar
—shukran jaziilan. fii amaan Al-laah
hiyya fi T-Taabag ath-thaani, ghurfah ragam sab:ah w :ishriin. haadha huwwa l-miftaaH
—li shakhS waaHid

akíid	*certain(ly)*
Táabag (Tawáabig)	*floor, storey*

CD 2, TR 2, 4:50

7 You have asked your friend Youssef to tell you something about the hotel he stayed in, and he reads aloud to you from the brochure. Listen to the recording or read the transcript, and answer the questions below to check your comprehension.

Look at the new words given below first, but don't worry about understanding every word that is said; concentrate on trying to get the gist of what he says.
(a) How many rooms are there?
(b) What facilities do they have besides bathroom?
(c) What types of cuisine do the restaurants offer?
(d) When is the coffee-shop open?
(e) Where do they serve a drink or snack outside?
(f) What is the function room used for?

lu'lú'at ash-sharg	*Pearl of the East*
káamil	*complete*
jináaH (ájniHah)	*suite, wing*
al-ittiSáal al-mubáashir li-l-kháarij	*direct dialling abroad*
máT:am (maTáa:im)	*restaurant*
áwwal dárajah	*first-class*
Tabíikh	*cuisine*
máqha	*café*
qáa:ah	*hall, large room*
iHtifáal (-aat)	*celebration, party, function*
mu'támar (-aat)	*conference, convention*
tijáari	*business (adjective), commercial*
a:máal	*affairs*
wagt al-faráagh	*leisure*
yisúdd	*to meet, fulfil*
Háajah (-aat)	*need (noun)*

---

al-khaTT al-:árabi (Arabic script) الخط العربي

In this unit you will learn the three letters transliterated **j**, **H** and **kh**. These are distinguished only by dots, the basic form of the letters being identical.

Name	Initial	Medial	Final	Separate	Pronunciation
jiim	جـ	ـجـ	ـج	ج	j
Haa'	حـ	ـحـ	ـح	ح	H
khaa'	خـ	ـخـ	ـخ	خ	kh

Note the nucleus shape (ـحـ) and the flourishes below the line on the final and separate forms. These are medium sized letters, (those in the previous unit having been small, and letters like **laam** (ل) being tall).

The forms given above are the printed ones. In handwriting (including calligraphy on shop and street signs and bank-notes) the joining strokes from the previous letters are often looped over the top like this:

In the following exercise try to match the Arabic on the left with the transliteration on the right. There are a few letters which you have not learned yet, but by this stage you should be able to look them up in the alphabet table at the beginning of the book. Note that double letters, for example, the second 'm' in the name Muhammad, are only written once.

Insight

The second letter in this group (ح) is very common in the numerous personal names which derive from the root **H-m-d** (ح-م-د) meaning praise e. g. Muhammad, Hamid, Mahmoud, Hamdan, etc.

1 محمد	A khaTT (*script*)
2 ثلج	B khaalid (*name*)
3 ثلاجة	C al-baHrain (*place name*)
4 حمام	D thallaajah (*fridge*)
5 خربان	E Hasan (*name*)
6 خط	F muHammad (*name*)
7 البحرين	G thalj (*ice*)
8 حسين	H Husain (*name*)
9 حسن	I kharbaan (*broken*)
10 خالد	J Hammaam (*bathroom*)

Test yourself

This test covers the main vocabulary, phrases and language points given in Unit 8. If you are not sure about your answers, go back to the dialogues and exercises for some revision, before going on to Unit 9. For the answers, see the **Key to the exercises.**

Match these questions with the appropriate answer.

1 tiriid ghurfah li-shakhS waaHid aw shakSain?	(a) min as-saa:ah sab:ah li-ghaayat as-saa:ah iHda:shar wa-nuSS
2 fii ayy taarikh?	(b) tafaDHDHal
3 li-kam lailah?	(c) yoom as-sabt, waaHid w-:ishriin oktoobir
4 fiih takyiif fi-l-ghurfah?	(d) na:am, laakin al-fanaadiq kull-ha fiih takyiif
5 al-ghurfah bi-kam?	(e) ajiib-uh
6 as-saa:ah kam tooSaluun?	(f) al-lailah bi-arba:ah miyyat diinaar
7 al-:asha s-saa:ah kam?	(g) na:am, kull al-ghuraf fii-haa takyiif
8 maa fiih Saabuun fii ghurfat-i	(h) nooSal aDH-DHuhur
9 al-jaww Haarr fii dubai fi S-Saif?	(i) li-shakhSain
10 mumkin ta:Tiini jawaaz as-safar min faDhl-ak?	(j) lailatain

9

الهوايات والإجازات

al-hawaayaat wa l-ijaazaat

Interests and holidays

In this unit you will learn how to

- Talk about your interests and say what you do in your spare time
- Talk about your plans for the future
- Talk about the weather
- Say what you did on holiday

New words and phrases

CD 2, TR 3

Listen to the recording.

Hiwaar 1 (Dialogue 1) حوار ١

CD 2, TR 3, 0:18

Mohammad and some of the people at the university in Al-Ain are being asked what they do in their spare time.

Interviewer	gul-li yaa muHammad, aish hawaayaat-ak?
Mohammad	:ind-i hawaayaat kathiirah Tab:an. aHibb al:ab kurah. in shaa' Al-laah al:ab fii fariig al-Jaami:ah ha s-sanah. wa al:ab lu:ab fi l-kambyuutar maal-i
Interviewer	wa t(i)sawwi shay ghair?
Mohammad	al:ab tanis hina fi l-:ain .... wa fi S-Saif aruuH aSTaad samak ma:a ikhwaan-i wa awlaad :amm-i
Interviewer	miin :allam-ak Said as-samak?
Mohammad	jadd-na :allam-na wa niHna Sughaar

Now the interviewer asks Farida, from Abu Dhabi.

Interviewer	fariidah, aish t(i)sawwiin fii wagt al-faraagh? tiHibbiin til:abiin ar-riyaaDHah?
Farida	laa, maa aHibb ar-riyaaDHah khaaliS. hina fi l-:ain agra w aruuH as-suug ma:a Sadiigaat-i, aw ashuuf t-tilifizyuun aw astami: ila l-musiiga
Interviewer	w aish tisawwiin Hiin tiruuHiin al-bait fii abuu DHabi?
Farida	ya:ni .... nafs ash-shay

Note: verbs are now given in two parts, past tense then present. See the grammar section later in this unit.

QUICK VOCAB

gaal yigúul (B1)	*to say*
hawáayah (-aat)	*interest, hobby*
lá:ab yíl:ab (A)	*to play*
kúrah, or more formally **kúrat al-gádam**	*football*
faríig (furúug))	*team*
tánis	*tennis*
Said as-sámak	*fishing*
iSTáad yiSTáad (B1) (sámak)	*to hunt (fish), fish*
miin	*who? (alternative to* man*)*
:állam yi:állim (A)	*to teach*
Saghíir (Sugháar)	*small, young*
wagt al-faráagh	*leisure, free time*
riyáaDHah (-aat)	*sport*

kháaliS	*at all (after negative)*	QUICK VOCAB
gára yígra (C)	*to read*	
raaH yirúuH (B1)	*to go*	
Sadíig (áSdiga)	*friend (male)*	
Sadíigah (-aat)	*friend (female)*	
shaaf, yishúuf (B1)	*to see, watch, look at*	
istáma: yistámi: íla (A)	*to listen to*	
musíiga	*music*	
Hiin	*when, at the time when*	

(a) What does Mohammad do in the summer?
(b) Who does he go fishing with?
(c) Which of Farida's interests is the most active?

---

mulaaHaDHaat (Notes) ملاحظات

1 **ha s-sánah: haadha/haadhi** can sometimes be shortened in this way.

2 to hope, intend to do something

You will recall that the phrase **in shaa' Al-laah** is used wherever there is some doubt about what will happen. To say you hope to do something, put **in shaa' Allaah** (*God willing*) before the verb for what you intend to do in the present tense:

in shaa' Al-laah naruuH iskutlanda shahar sab:ah
We hope to go to Scotland in July (lit. 'month seven').
in shaa' Al-laah naruuH al-hind fi S-Saif
We intend to go to India in the summer.

3 verbs, past tense

See grammar points at the end of the unit. The present tense has both prefixes and (sometimes) suffixes; the past tense has only suffixes.

4 **wa niHna Sughaar** (*when we were young*).

The Arabic idiom says literally *and we young* (at that time). The plural adjective **Sughaar** agrees with the (plural) human beings.

Insight

Remember that when you are talking about things, the Arabic adjective takes the same form as the feminine singular, usually the ending **-ah**, e.g. **hawaayaat kathiirah** (*many hobbies*).

When talking about people, use the plural form of the adjective. This usually has the suffix **-iin**, but a number of common adjectives take special forms, e.g. **Saghiir/Sughaar** as here. If no plural form is given in the vocabularies, the **-iin** suffix should be used.

Hiwaar 2 (Dialogue 2) حوار ٢

CD 2, TR 3, 1:34

Next he interviews Dr Jones, who is ending a year's exchange as a history lecturer at the university. First he asks him about living in Al-Ain.

Dr Jones	al-:ain :ajabat-ni kathiir, wa T-Tullaab kaanu mujtahidiin jiddan
Interviewer	ya:ni .... aT-Tullaab fii ingiltarra kaslaaniin?
Dr Jones	(*laughs*) na:am .... ba:DH-hum
Interviewer	doktoor joonz, mumkin tiguul l(a)-na maa sawwait fi l-:ain?
Dr Jones	al-Hagiigah sawwaina ashyaa' kathiirah. kamaa ta:raf ana mudarris taariikh, fa zurt gilaa: w mataaHif kathiirah fi l-imaaraat, w niHna .... ya:ni ana w al-:aa'ilah sawwaina riHlaat ila jabal Hafiit w al-baHar. ishtarait kaamira jadiidah fii dubay, w Sawwart kathiir. w aHyaanan shufna sibaag al-jimaal ti sh-shita.
Interviewer	w aish min ar-riyaaDHaat?
Dr Jones	na:am, la:abt goolf ma:a zamiil waaHid, wa ruHna kathiir nisbaH fi l-baHar, wa fi l-ijaazaat, al-awlaad ta:allamu al-ghooS, ya:ni as-skuuba, fii khoor fakkaan
Interviewer	shukran jaziilan yaa doktoor joonz.

:ájab yí:jab (A)	*to impress, cause wonder; used in the idiom to like*
Táalib (Tulláab or **Tálabah)**	*student (male)*
Táalibah (-aat)	*student (female)*
mujtáhid	*hard-working, diligent*
kasláan	*lazy*
ba:DH	*some*
al-Hagíigah	*really, actually. (lit. the truth)*
shay (ashyáa')	*thing*
kámaa tá:raf	*as you know*
taaríikh	*date; history*
fa	*so*
zaar yizúur (B1)	*to visit*
gál(a):ah (giláa:)	*fort*
mátHaf (matáaHif)	*museum*
ríHlah (-aat)	*outing, trip, journey*
jábal (jibáal)	*mountain, desert*
ishtára yishtári (C)	*to buy*
káamira (-aat)	*camera (more formally* **áalat taSwíir***)*
Sáwwar, yiSáwwir (A)	*to photograph, take photographs*
sibáag al-jimáal	*camel racing*
goolf or **lá:bat al-goolf**	*golf*
zamíil (zúmala)	*colleague*
sábaH, yísbaH (A)	*to swim, bathe*
ijáazah (-aat)	*holidays*
ta:állam, yit:állam (A)	*to learn*
ghooS	*diving*

QUICK VOCAB

(a) Which of Dr Jones' interests is in keeping with his job?
(b) Which are his most active pursuits?
(c) Who learned to scuba dive?

---

mulaaHaDHaat (Notes) ملاحظات

1 ba:DH (*some, some of*)
Usually followed by a noun with al- or a suffix pronoun:

ba:DH aT-Tullaab	*some of the students*
ba:DH-hum	*some of them*

2 Jebel Hafit

A mountain near Al-Ain, popular for visitors as it is the only feature nearby. Other words relating to the landscape are:

raas	*headland. point*
al-barr	*inland, the desert*
wáadi (widyáan)	*dried -up river bed, wadi*
bálad (biláad)	*town, village*
bándar	*town on the coast, port*
wáaHa (-aat)	*oasis*

3 **(mumkin) tiguul l(a)-na** *can you tell us . . . ?*

The verb **gaal/yiguul** (*to tell/say*) is frequently followed by the preposition **li/la** (*to*).

Insight

The full form is given here for the sake of clarity, but in practice this would be pronounced **tigul-l-na** condensed into one word **tigullna.**

mumkin tigulli *can you tell me . . . ?*

4 **:allam + t(a):allam** (*teach* and *learn*)

This is a common type of verb pair in Arabic, equivalent to what is called the active and the passive in English. **:allam** (lit. *to make know*) and **t(a):allam** (*to be made to know*).

ma:luumaat thaqaafiyyah (Cultural tips) معلومات ثقافية

The Arabs have many words for varieties of camel. **jámal** (plural **jimáal**) is the only one you really need, and the one from which the English is derived.

Similarly there are many words for the desert, depending on whether it is sandy, rocky, salt-flat and so on. **al-barr** (*the land, country*) is the most useful general term. **aS-SáHraa** (whence we get Sahara) is the literary word, and **rimáal** (lit. *sands*) refers to that type of desert landscape. **ar-ruba: al-khaali** (*the Empty Quarter*) is a term not originally used by inhabitants of the area (who call it **ar-rimaal**), but everybody knows it now from literary sources.

Hiwaar 3 (Dialogue 3) حوار ٣

CD 2, TR 3, 2:59

Mike and Salim are in Abu Dhabi, discussing their holiday plans.

Salim	wain bi-truuH fii ijaazat aS-Saif yaa maayk?
Mike	in shaa' Al-laah bi-nruuH ingilterra haadhi s-sanah :a shaan nazuur al-:aa'ilah. as-sanah l-maaDHiyah ruHna :umaan.
Salim	:umaan bilaad jamiilah jiddan. ruHt hinaak min gabil?
Mike	laa, kaan haadha awwal marrah. inta ta:raf :umaan?
Salim	na:am, ruHna hinaak min sanatain. aish sawwaitu fii :umaan?
Mike	saafarna ila masqaT bi T-Tayyaarah w ga:adna fii fundug jamb al-baHar. ba:dain ista'jarna sayyaarah w tajawwalna shwayyah.
Salim	aish kaan ra'y-ak fii-ha?
Mike	:ajabat-na kathiir. ruHna bi s-sayyaarah ila DHufaar fi l-januub, w shufna ghailam w Tuyuur kathiirah w asmaak w nakhiil maal narjiil. bitna fii khaimah fi l-barr, wa l-awlaad inbasaTu waajid nun haadha.
Salim	kaif kaan al-jaww?
Mike	al-usbuu: al-awwal kaan al-jaww Haarr jiddan, laakin al-usbuu: ath-thaani kaan fiih bard w maTar w hawa shwayyah.
Salim	yaa khaSaarah!
Mike	laa, niHna l-ingliiz mit:awwidiin :ala l-hawa wa l-maTar!

QUICK VOCAB

ijáazat aS-Saif	*summer holiday*
haadhi s-sanah	*this year*
:a shaan	*in order to (short for* **:ala shaan***)*
maaDHi	*past, last (year, week etc.)*
as-sánah l-máaDHiyah	*last year*
jamíil	*beautiful*
biláad (fem.)	*country*
min gábil	*before, beforehand*
kaan yikúun (B1)	*was; will be (see notes)*
áwwal márrah	*the first time*
:áraf yí:raf (A)	*to know*
min san(a)táin	*two years ago*
sáafar yisáafir (A)	*travel*
bi	*by (when talking about means of transport)*
Tayyáarah (-aat)	*plane*
istá'jar yistaá'jir (A)	*to hire, rent*
tajáwwal yitjáwwal (A)	*to tour around*
ra'y (aaráa')	*opinion*
aish kaan rá'y-ak fii-ha	*what was your opinion of it?*
DHufáar	*Dhofar (southern region of Oman)*
al-janúub	*the south*
gháilam	*turtles (in Oman; elsewhere* **Hámas***)*
Tair (Thyúur)	*bird*
sámak (asmáak)	*fish*
nákhlah (nakhíil)	*palm tree*
narjíil	*coconuts*
baat yibáat (B1)	*to spend the night*
khaimah (khiyáam)	*tent*

inbásaT yinbásiT min (A)	*to enjoy*
jaww	*air, atmosphere, weather*
usbúu: (asabíi:)	*week*
Haarr	*hot*
bard	*cold (noun)*
máTar	*rain*
háwa	*wind, air*
khaSáarah	*a pity*
mit:áwwid :ála	*used to, accustomed to*

QUICK VOCAB

(a) Where does Mike intend to go on holiday this year?
(b) When did Salim go to Oman?
(c) What did the children particularly enjoy?
(d) How was the weather in the second week?

---

mulaaHaDHaat (Notes) ملاحظات

1 kaan (*was, were*: verb)

Although no verb is used in Arabic for *is/are*, there is a verb **kaan** (*was, were*). It has a present tense form **yikuun**, but this implies a future or potential event. (See Unit 10 and the verb tables at the end of the book for the formation of the tenses).

kaan fi l-bait	*He was in the house.*
kunt fii ghurfat-i	*I was in my room.*

kaan has many other uses, the main one being to give everything which comes after it a past aspect:

fiih *there is/are*	**kaan fiih** *there was/were*
:ind-i *I have*	**kaan :ind-i** *I had*
mumkin nazuur *we can visit*	**kaan mumkin nazuur** *we could/were able to visit*
laazim yiruuH *he must/has to go*	**kaan laazim yiruuH** *he had to go*

2 *going to . . .*

In English you say 'he goes *to* work'; in Arabic there is no translation of the word *to*:

yi-ruuH ash-shughal	*He goes to work* (lit. *he goes the work).*
naruuH ingilterra	*We are going (to) England.*

Insight

If you use the word **yisaafir** (*he travels* from which our word *safari* comes), then you may use **ila** (*to*): **yisaafir ila taaylaand** *He is going (travelling) to Thailand.*

3 **al-jaww** (*the weather*)

When talking about *good, bad, hot* and *cold* weather you can use an adjective:

al-jaww zain/muu zain	*The weather is good/not good*
al-jaww baarid	*The weather is cold.*
al-jaww Haarr	*The weather is hot.*

Alternatively you can use a noun:

fiih bard	*It is cold (*lit. *there is cold).*
fiih Harr	*It is hot (*lit. *there is heat).*

This noun construction is the only one available for talking about any other weather condition:

fiih shams	*It is sunny (*lit. *there is sun).*
fiih ghaim	*It is cloudy (*lit. *there are clouds).*
fiih hawa	*It is windy (*lit. *there is wind).*
fiih maTar	*It is raining (*lit. *there is rain).*
fiih thalj	*It is snowing (*lit. *there is ice, snow).*
fiih :aaSifah	*It is stormy (*lit. *there is a storm).*
darajat il-Haraarah thalathiin	*It is 30°C (*lit. *degree the-heat [is] 30).*

4 To talk about the weather in the past, put **kaan** before the statement:

kaan al-jaww baarid	*It was cold.*
kaan fiih maTar	*It was raining, it rained*

5

(a) What does the name of the bus mean in English?
(b) Which word is missing from the English transliteration?

6 **bi** (*by, by means of*)
When you want to talk about a means of transport, you use the word **bi** (*by, by means of*). Note that where you say *by car, plane* etc., in Arabic you always say *by the*.

bi T-Tayyaarah	*by plane*
bi s-sayyaarah	*by car*
bi l-baaS	*by bus*
bi t-taksi	*by taxi*
bi s-safiinah	*by ship*
ruHna masqaT bi T-Tayaarah	*We went to Muscat by plane.*

But to say you go on foot, use the verb **yiruuH** (*he goes*) with **yímshi** (*he walks*):

muu ba:iid, naruuH nimshi	*It's not far, we'll walk.*

7 The points of the compass

ash-shamáal	*the North*
al-janúub	*the South*
ash-sharq (or **ash-sharg**)	*the East*
al-gharb	*the West*
shamaal al-khaliij	*the North of the Gulf*
ash-sharg al-awsaT	*the Middle East*
al-gharb	*the West (*i.e. *Europe and the USA*)

The adjectives from these compass directions are formed by adding **-i** (fem. **-iyyah**) to the noun:

urúbba l-gharbíyyah	*Western Europe*

---

ma:luumaat thaqaafiyyah (Cultural tips) معلومات ثقافية

As you might expect, Arabs accept hot weather as a fact of life, and only comment on it if the temperature rises above about 40°C, or if it is excessively humid. They are however very interested in rain, which in most of the region generally comes in the winter. Naturally the success of the harvest depends on the arrival of rain, which is often sudden and can result in flash floods, but usually the sun comes out again and the ground dries up quickly.

The Bedouin have many words for clouds, depending on whether they are rain-bearing or not. The Dhofar area of southern Oman catches the monsoons and has a regular annual rainfall pattern. It is covered with lush green vegetation for considerable periods of the year.

ta:biiraat haammah (Key phrases) تعبيرات هامة

Talking about what you like to do in your spare time

aish tisawwi fii wagt al-faraagh?	*What do you do in your free time?*
al:ab tanis/skwaash	*I play tennis/squash.*
aruuH as-suug	*I go shopping* (lit. *to the souq*).
ashuuf at-tilifizyuun	*I watch television.*
agra	*I read.*
azuur :aa'ilat-i/aSdigaa'-i	*I visit my family/friends.*

Talking about what you like and don't like to do

tiHibb la:bat at-tanis?	*Do you like to play tennis?* (lit. *the game of tennis*).
aHibb la:bat as-skwaash	*I like to play squash.*
maa aHibb as-sibaaHah	*I don't like swimming.*

Talking about what you did in the past

la:abt goolf	*I played golf.*
ruHt ad-dooHa	*I went to Doha.*
shuft sibaag al-Jimaal	*I watched the camel-racing.*
sawwait riHlah	*I went on a trip* (*made a trip*).

núqaT naHwíyyah (Grammar points) نقط نحوية

The Arabic Verb: Past tense

The past tense uses a past stem with suffixes only. These suffixes are more or less the same for all Arabic verbs, with only slight variations to smooth out pronunciation. There are only two verbs in Arabic which could be called irregular, and these are fully explained in the verb tables at the end of the book which you should look at regularly.

All verbs in Arabic can be categorised into four types, depending on the nature of the stems. The following is a summary:

TYPE A The simplest type, with one stem for each tense.

The next three types have more than one stem in either or both of the tenses. Which stem is used depends on the part of the verb you are using (*he*, *we*, *they*, etc.)

TYPE B1 has two past stems and one present stem.

TYPE B2 also has two past and one present stem, but is of a different nature.

TYPE C verbs have two stems for each of the past and present tenses.

Important note

Because Arabic does not have the handy infinitive form (*to go, to read* etc.) found in most European languages, we use its most basic part, the past tense *he*-form, which has neither prefixes nor suffixes. From this lesson onwards, verbs are given as follows:

Past tense *he*-form followed by present tense *he*-form followed by verb type, e.g. (A) given between brackets and then the meaning expressed as *to* . . .

For example:

raaH, yiruuH (B1) *to go* (lit. *he went, he goes*)

Note: Only two parts are given for each verb. For types other than group (A) you must check in the verb tables.

Below are two examples with the suffixes picked out in bold type.

TYPE A has only one past stem. An example is **akhadh** to *take* (actually, of course, *he took*):

Singular		Plural	
I	akhadh - **t**	we	akhadh - **na**
you (masc.)	akhadh - **t**	you (m. and f.)	akhadh - **tu**
you (fem.)	akhadh - **ti**		
he/(it)	akhadh - (no suffix)	they (m. and f.)	akhadh - **u**
she (it)	akhadh - **at**		

TYPE B1 has two past stems. The main stem has been picked out in italics. An example is **raaH** *to go* (he went):

Singular		Plural	
I	ruH - **t**	we	ruH - **na**
you (masc.)	ruH - **t**	you (m. and f.)	ruH - **tu**
you (fem.)	ruH - **ti**		
he/(it)	*raaH* - (no suffix)	they (m. and f.)	*raaH* - **u**
she (it)	*raaH* - **at**		

Insight

Where verbs have more than one past stem the main one (i.e. that given first in the vocabularies and glossary) is used with the *he*, *she* and *they* form, or, put another way, when either there is no suffix or the suffix begins with a vowel.

Note that as with present tense verbs, there is usually no need to put in the pronoun (*I*, *you* etc.), as it is already implied by the verb itself. However, in the following exercises it has often been supplied for the sake of clarity.

tamriinaat (Exercises) تمرينات

◀) **CD 2, TR 3, 4:50**

1 Listen to the recording or read the transcript at the end of the book, and make a note of what these five people say they do in their spare time.

QV

booling	*bowling*
síinima	*cinema*

2 (a) How would you ask Mohammad, in Arabic, if he would like to:

(i) go fishing? (ii) play tennis? (iii) go to the market?

What do you think his reply would be to each question?

(b) How would you ask Faridah, in Arabic, if she would like to:

(i) play tennis?
(ii) watch television?
(iii) go swimming?

What do you expect her answers would be?

3 You are describing a trip you made while staying in the Gulf. Match up the two halves of the sentences so that they make sense.

(a) ga:adt	(i) matHaf
(b) ista'jart	(ii) baarid
(c) akalt	(iii) sayyaarah
(d) zurt	(iv) fi l-fundug
(e) shuft	(v) samak w baTaaTis
(f) kaan al-jaww	(vi) ghailam

gá:ad, yíg:ad (A) *to sit, stay, remain*

QV

4 Look at the map of Saudi Arabia and say whether the statements below are true or false.

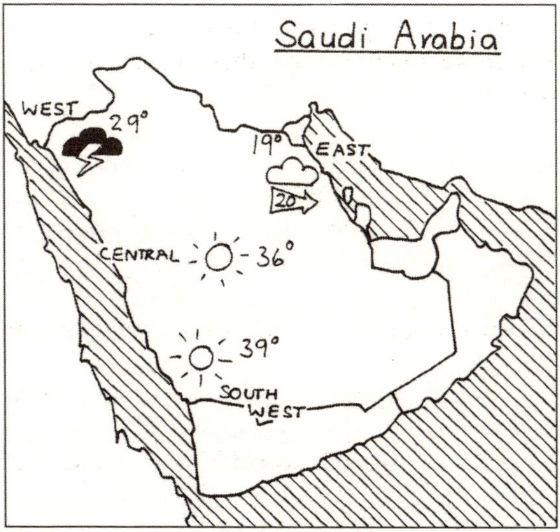

QUICK VOCAB

mánTigah (manáaTig)	*area, region*
ghaim (ghuyúum)	*cloud*
áwsaT, fem. **wúsTaa**	*middle, central*
rá:ad	*thunder*
bárg	*lightning*
:áaSifah (:awáaSif)	*storm*

(a) fi l-manTigah al-gharbiyyah ghuyuum w hawa, sittah w :ishriin darajah

(b) fi l-manTigah l-wusTaa shams, sittah w thalaathiin darajah

(c) fi manTigat al-januub al-gharbi shams, khamsah w thalaathiin darajah

(d) fi l-manTigah ash-shargiyyah :awaaSif, ra:ad w barg, tis:ata:shar darajah

5 Jim and Eleanor are with their friends Khaled and Samirah in Muscat, and are planning to spend Friday with them and their family. Read the conversation and check your comprehension by answering the questions below.

Khaled	aish al-barnaamij baakir?
Jim	ayy shay. aish barnaamij-ak inta?
Khaled	niHna aHyaanan nisawwi riHlah ma:a l-awlaad yoom al-jum:ah. niruuH al-baHar, al-mazra:ah, ayy makaan
Samirah	mumkin banruuH nakhal. al-jaww jamiil hinaak, wa l-awlaad yiHibbuun-uh
Eleanor	aish nsawwii hinaak fii nakhal?
Samirah	fiih gala:ah w :ain saakhinah, w kull-uh akhDHar w Hilw. al-awlaad mumkin yil:abuun w naakul piikniik hinaak
Jim	n-zain. laazim naakhudh akil w mashruubaat baaridah Hagg al-piikniik
Khaled	laa, nashtari kull shay fi T-Tariig. fiih dukkaan gariib min al-:ain.

(a) What does Khaled ask about tomorrow?
(b) What do Khaled and Samirah sometimes do on Fridays?
(c) Why does Samirah suggest going to Nakhal?
(d) What is there to see in Nakhal?
(e) What could they do there?
(f) What does Jim suggest?
(g) What will they buy?
(h) Where can they buy it?

QUICK VOCAB

barnáamij (baráamij)	*programme, plan of activity*
mázra:ah (mazáari:)	*farm, country estate*
makáan (-aat)	*place*
ayy makaan	*anywhere*
:ain (fem.) **(:uyuun)**	*spring; eye*

sáakhin	*warm, hot*	QV
Hilw	*sweet, pleasant, pretty*	
Hagg	*for*	

CD 2, TR 3, 5:12

6 Listen to the weather forecast for the Gulf Region on the recording, or read the transcript, and note down what the weather will be like for tomorrow in (a) the North (b) Bahrain and Qatar (c) the Emirates and Dhofar.

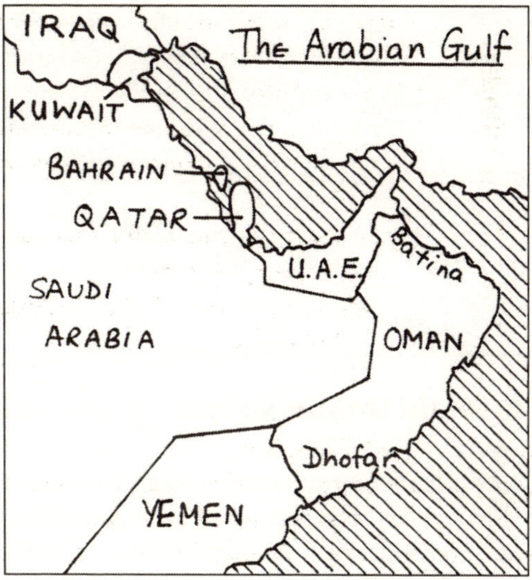

mánTigat al-khalíij (al-:árabi)	*the (Arab) Gulf region*	QUICK VOCAB
Haráarah	*heat*	
dárajat al-Haráarah	*temperature (*lit. *degree of heat)*	
al-báaTinah	*the Batinah, eastern coastal strip of Oman*	

7 You have been on holiday in the Gulf and get chatting to the taxi-driver on the way to the airport. Fill in your part of the conversation.

inta	*Ask him where he is from.*
sawwáag at-taksi	ana min al-hind, min bangaloor fi l-januub. inta zurt al-hind?
inta	*Tell him you went last year, to Delhi.*
sawwáag at-taksi	aish sawwait hinaak?
inta	*Tell him you did a tour, and you took a lot of photographs, and you went shopping.*
sawwáag at-taksi	shuft al-jibaal?
inta	*Say yes, but from far away. Say they were very beautiful.*
sawwáag at-taksi	laakin al-jaww waajid baarid fi sh-shita, w fiih thalj
inta	*Tell him it's not cold here in the Gulf in the winter!*

qv

dálhi *Delhi*
jáwlah (-aat) *tour*

---

al-khaTT al-:árabi (Arabic script) الخط العربي

In this unit you will learn two more sets of Arabic letters, the equivalents of **d** and **dh** and **r** and **z**. The second of each pair is distinguished by having one dot above it. You already know two of them from the currency units **dirham**, **diinaar** and **riyaal** in Unit 5.

Name	Initial	Medial	Final	Separate	Pronunciation
daal	د	ـد	ـد	د	d
dhaal	ذ	ـذ	ـذ	ذ	dh
raa'	ر	ـر	ـر	ر	r
zaay	ز	ـز	ـز	ز	z

These are all non-joiners, so there are really only two forms for each.

At first the two pairs look similar. However the **daal** and the **dhaal** are written above the line, and have an upright stroke leaning towards the left. The **raa'** and the **zaay** start on the line and go below it, and have no upward stroke except the tiny one where they meet the ligature. They have a much less pronounced hook than the first pair.

Insight

There is no difficulty in pronunciation here, but remember that **dh** is the sound of English *th* in words like *that, those, then.* Also remember the **r** must be trilled as in Scots or Spanish.

Since you know all the words below, this time here are some Arabic words and their translations for you to match up.

(a) good, fine	١– برد
(b) journey, flight, trip	٢– درجة
(c) cold (adj.)	٣– حجز
(d) cold (noun)	٤– جزيرة
(e) step, degree	٥– بحر
(f) heat, temperature	٦– حرارة
(g) booking, reservation	٧– ثلج
(h) island	٨– رحلة
(i) sea	٩– بارد
(j) ice, snow	١٠– زين

Test yourself

This test covers the main vocabulary, phrases and language points given in Unit 9. If you are not sure about your answers, go back to the dialogues and exercises for some revision, before going on to Unit 10. For the answers, see the **Key to the exercises.**

Some tourists are on holiday in Ras al-Khaimah, and are telling Mahmoud at the hotel reception what they did during the day and what they hope to do tomorrow. You fill in the correct form of the verb; the stem has been put in brackets for you. You will need the following new vocabulary:

QV

naam, yináam (B1)	*to sleep, go to sleep*
víidiyoo (viidiyooh// áat)	*video*

1 ana (ishtara **C**) banjari fi s-suug adh-dhahab
2 jaan (la:ab **A**) tanis ma:a zoojat-uh
3 niHna (sabaH **A**) fi l-masbaH
4 ana (akal **A**) al-ghada ma:a ukhti fii maT:am :arabi
5 maryam (naam **B1**) w ba:dain (shaaf **B1**) viidiyoohaat fii ghurfat-ha
6 Khaled wa Nasser (ista'jar **A**) sayyaarah wa (raaH **B1**) Hatta
7 niHna (raaH **B1**) ash-shaarjah wa (zaar **B1**) as-suug
8 piitar wa saara (saafar **A**) ila gaTar wa (sawwa **C**) ghooS as-skuuba
9 kaan yuusif maa (:araf **B**) aish (sawwa **C**), fa (ga:ad **A**) fi l-fundug, maa (kharaj **A**).
10 (raaH **B1**) naaSir wa-khaalid dubay wa (shaaf **B1**) sibaag al jimaal

10

تاريخ العرب

taariikh al-:arab

The history of the Arabs

In this unit you will learn

- How to say what you were doing or used to do in the past
- More ways of describing things
- To describe how and when you do things

New words and phrases

CD 2, TR 4

Listen to the recording.

Hiwaar 1 (Dialogue 1) حوار ١

CD 2, TR 4, 0:16

Bill asks his friend Suleiman to give him an outline of the history of the Arabs.

Bill	mumkin tikhabbir-ni shwayyah :an taarikh al-:arab yaa akh-i?
Suleiman	Tab:an. aish tiriid ta:raf?
Bill	awwalan, al-:arab aSal-hum min wain?
Suleiman	al-:arab aSal-hum min jaziirat al-:arab.
Bill	ya:ni maa kaan fiih :arab fii maSir mathalan?
Suleiman	laa, haadha ba:d DHuhuur al-islaam.
Bill	w aish Saar ba:d DHuhuur al-islaam?
Suleiman	fi l-guruun ba:d DHuhuur al-islaam, al-:arab intasharu li-ghaayat aS-Siin fi sh-sharg w al-andalus - ya:ni isbaanya - fi l-gharb.
Bill	idhan al-junuud al-:arab fataHu buldaan kathiirah!
Suleiman	na:am. Hatta al-aan tishuuf inn al-:arab la-hum duwal kathiirah.
Bill	wa fii haadhi d-duwal kull-ha an-naas yitkallamuun :arabi?
Suleiman	bi-DH-DHabT. al-lughah l-:arabiyyah hiyya lughat al-umm li-Hawaali miiyyah w khamsiin milyoon min sukkaan al-:aalam al-mu:aaSir.

QUICK VOCAB

khábbar, yikhábbir (A)	*to tell, inform*
:an	*of, about*
áwwalan	*firstly*
:árabi (:árab)	*Arab, Arabic*
áS (a)l (uSúul)	*origin*
jazíirat al-:árab	*the Arabian peninsula (lit. the island of the Arabs)*
máS(i)r	*Egypt*
máthalan	*for example*
DHuhúur	*emergence, appearance*
al-isláam	*Islam*
Saar, yiSíir (B1)	*to happen, become*
garn (gurúun)	*century*
intáshar, yintáshir (A)	*to spread, spread out*
aS-Siin	*China*
al-ándalus	*the Arab name for their empire in Spain*
isbáanya	*Spain (modern name)*
júndi (junúud)	*soldier*
fátaH, yíftaH (A)	*to open, conquer*

biláad (buldáan) (fem.)	*country*
Hátta	*until*
al-'aan	*now*
inn	*that (conjunction)*
dáwlah (dúwal)	*state, country, nation*
takállam, yitkállam (A)	*to speak*
lúghah (-aat)	*language*
lúghat al-úmm	*mother tongue (*lit. *language of the mother)*
Hawáali	*about, approximately*
sáakin (sukkáan)	*inhabitant, resident*
al-:áalam	*the world*
mu:áaSir	*contemporary*

QUICK VOCAB

(a) Where did the Arabs originally come from?
(b) What happened after the appearance of Islam?
(c) How many people speak Arabic as their mother tongue in the contemporary world?

---

mulaaHaDHaat (Notes) ملاحظات

1 taariikh al-:arab (*the history of the Arabs*)
This is the possessive construction again: noun without **al-** followed by noun with **al-**.

2 :arab
See grammar section on nouns and adjectives of nationality.

3 fataHu (*they conquered*)
This verb usually means simply *to open* but in military contexts it is also used for *to conquer*.

4 al-lughah l-:arabiyyah hiyya lughat al-umm li- . . .
The **hiyya** (*it*) here lends some emphasis to the sentence. **li-** (*to, for*) here expresses possession (an alternative to **:ind** used sometimes).

ma:luumaat thaqaafiyyah (Cultural tips) معلومات ثقافية

This is not a history book, but it is as well to know something about and show an interest in the Arab heritage. As mentioned in the dialogue, the Arab empire was very extensive, and their scholars and writers made many important contributions to science, medicine, engineering and other subjects.

This generally receives scant attention in European education, which tends to jump from the Graeco-Roman era to the Renaissance. In the centuries preceding this Renaissance (i.e. 're-birth') of European culture, the torch of learning was carried by the Arabs, who were far ahead of the West in practically all fields of endeavour.

Arab occupation of Southern Spain (roughly Andalucia which is the same word as the Arabic **al-andalus**), the last outpost of the Arab Empire in Europe, ended with the fall of Granada in 1492, the year in which Columbus discovered America.

Hiwaar 2 (Dialogue 2) حوار ٢

CD 2, TR 4, 1:32

Bill asks Suleiman to tell him something about Islam.

Bill	mumkin tikhabbir-ni :an ad-diin al-islaami shwayyah?
Suleiman	akiid. anzal Al-laah al-qur'aan al-kariim :ala muHammad rasuul Al-laah, Salla Al-laahu :alai-hi wa sallam, fii awáa'il l-garn as-saabi: al-miilaadi.
Bill	kaan an-nabi muHammad min makkah, muu kidha?
Suleiman	na:am. mawluud fii makkah al-mukarramah, w ba:dain haajar ila l-madiinah l-munawwarah fii sanat sitt miyyah ithnain wa :ishriin miilaadiyyah. haadhi nasammii-ha l-hijrah, w naHsab at-taariikh min haadhi s-sanah.

diin (adyáan)	*religion*
isláami	*Islamic*
ánzal, yúnzil (A)	*to reveal, send down (of God, the Koran)*
al-qur'áan	*the Koran*
karíim	*generous, noble (in this context holy)*
rasúul Al-láah	*the Apostle of God*
Sálla Al-láahu :alái-hi wa sállam	*Peace be upon Him*
awáa'il	*the first, early part of (used with months, years, centuries)*
miiláadi	*pertaining to the birth (of Christ)*, i.e. *A.D.*
nábi (anbiyáa')	*prophet*
mákkah	*Mecca*
kídha, also **chídha, chídhi**	*like this, so*
muu kídha	lit. *isn't it so?*
mawlúud	*born*
al-mukárramah	*Holy (honorific adjective used after Mecca)*
háajar, yiháajir (A)	*to emigrate*
al-madíinah	*Medinah*
al-munáwwarah	*resplendent, illuminated (honorific adjective used after Medinah)*
sámma, yisámmi (C)	*to call, name*
al-híjrah	*the Hegirah (see below)*
Hásab, yíHsab (A)	*reckon, count, calculate*

QUICK VOCAB

(a) Where was the Prophet Muhammad born?
(b) In which year did he migrate to Medinah?
(c) Why is this date important in Arab history?

---

mulaaHaDHaat (Notes) ملاحظات

1 Written, especially classical, Arabic differs from the spoken variety. Since all Islamic religious scriptures, especially the Holy Koran,

are couched in a high style of Classical Arabic, people tend to import words and phrases from this register of the language when discussing such subjects.

Apart from words and phraseology, pronunciation is also affected, especially the letter **q** (see pronunciation notes, p. 15), especially in the Arabic word for the Koran, **al-qur'aan**.

2 The verb **anzal** (*to send down, reveal*) (of the Koran) is not used in other contexts.

3 Phrases such as **Salla l-laahu :alai-hi wa sallam** (*peace be upon him*) and **laa iláaha ílla l-láah** (*there is no other god but God*) (see exercises below) also preserve some of the old Classical endings which have long since been dropped in everyday speech.

Insight – **hijri** and **miilaadi**

These are the terms used to distinguish between the Islamic and Christian dating systems, often abbreviated in writing to هـ and م written after the date. The Islamic dating system, now (except in Saudi Arabia) almost restricted to use in religious connections – although still given along with the Christian date on most Arabic newspapers – began on 16th June 622 AD, the date of the Prophet's **hijrah** (often spelled in English *Hegirah* for some reason) from Mecca to Medinah.

THE NEWS الآخبار

الجمعة ٢٢ يناير ٢٠١٠ الموافق ٦ صفر ١٤٣١ هـ

Friday 22 January 2010, 6 Safar 1431 A.H.

4 miilaadi

The adjective (see grammatical points) from **miilaad** birth, i.e. that of Christ.

5 Honorific adjectives and phrases.

These are automatically used after certain nouns referring to religious persons, places and things. Muslims do not expect Westerners to know or use these, but you will hear them frequently. Each place, religious figure or group of figures has a specific one:

al-qur'aan al-kariim	*the Holy Koran*
makkah al-mukarramah	*Holy Mecca*
al-madiinah al-munawwarah	*Medina the Resplendent*
muHammad rasuul Al-laah, Salla Al-laah :alai-hi wa sallam	*Muhammad the Prophet of God, peace be upon Him*

Jesus Christ is counted among the general ranks of the prophets in Islam, and merits the honorific **:alai-hi s-salaam** (*peace be upon him*).

Insight

nasammíl-ha (*we call it*) and **ma:náa-ha**
Remember that any final vowel at the end of a word is lengthened (and stressed) when a pronoun suffix is added.

---

ta:biiraat haammah (Key phrases) تعبيرات هامة

CD 2, TR 4, 2:28

More examples of Arabic past (continuous):
akhi maHmuud kaan yiruuH al-madrasah as-saa:ah sab:ah S-SubaH *My brother Mahmoud used to go to school at seven o'clock in the morning.*
kaanat ukhti faaTimah tidarris al-lughah l-:arabiyyah fii landan *My sister Fatima was teaching/used to teach Arabic in London.*

---

núqaT naHwíyyah (Grammar points) نقط نحوية

1 Adjectives formed from nouns

In English you have several ways of forming adjectives from nouns, for example adding *-ic* (*e.g. historic, photographic*), or *-an* (*e.g. American,*

Belgian). Some of these require a slight alteration to the base noun, e.g. the final *-y* in *history* has to be omitted, and the *-um* from Belgium.

Arabic mainly uses one ending **-i**, which becomes **-iyyah** in the feminine, and usually **-iyyiin** in the plural when applied to human beings. However, changes to the base-word are also required in certain cases.

Probably the largest class of such adjectives in Arabic are those referring to nationality, places of origin or tribal/family affiliations, such as:

Country	Masc.	Fem.	Plural	Translation
gáTar	**gáTari**	**gaTaríyyah**	**gaTariyyíin**	*Qatari*
:umáan	**:umáani**	**:umaaníyyah**	**:umaaniyyíin**	*Omani*
máS(i)r	**máSri**	**maSríyyah**	**maSriyyíin**	*Egyptian*

Note that:

(a) If the place name from which the adjective is derived has the definite article **al-**, this is dropped when forming the adjective:
al-yaman → **yamani**
al-kuwait → **kuwaiti**
al-urdun → **urduni** (*Jordanian*)

(b) If it has the **-ah** feminine ending, this is also dropped, and there are certain anomalies with words ending in **-a**, which can omit this final vowel and add **-i**, or take the ending **-aani**, **-aawi**, or even use a completely different base.

These are best learned as they come, but here are a few common examples. The plurals are sometimes irregular:

Country	Masc.	Fem.	Plural	Translation
ingiltérra	**inglízi**	**ingliizíyyah**	**inglíz**	*English*
amríika	**amríki**	**amriikíyyah**	**amriikáan**	*American*
fauránsa	**faransáawi***	**faransíyyah**	**faransiyyíin**	*French*
dubáy	**díbawi**	**dibawíyyah**	**dibawiyyíin**	*from Dubai*
al-mághrib	**maghribi**	**maghribíyyah**	**magháar(i)bah**	*Moroccan*

* or **faránsi**

(c) **:arabi** (*Arab, Arabic*) has the irregular plural **:arab**

Insight

These adjective formations are not restricted to countries of origin. Almost all personal names in the Gulf end in such an attributive adjective formed from the name of a person's tribe or family, e.g. **khamíis bin Hamad al-baTTaashi** (i.e. *Khamis bin* [*son of*] *Hamad of the Battash tribe*).

You can improve your reading by trying to spot the Arabic letter ي – which is how this ending **-i** is spelled in Arabic – at the end of names on business cards or shop signs. It won't always be there, but there is a very good chance that it will.

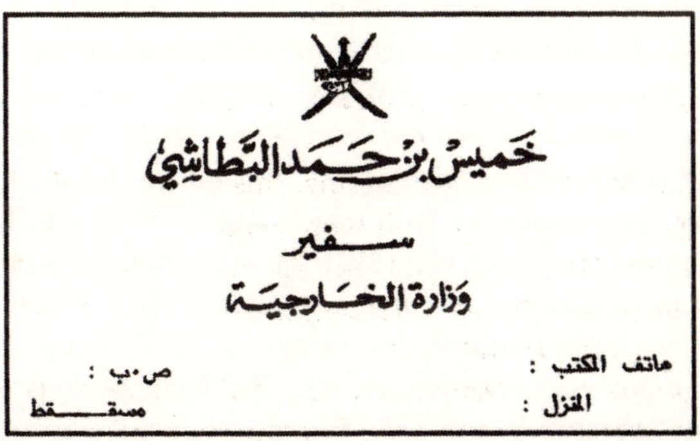

(d) This adjectival ending can be added to ordinary nouns, as for instance in dialogue 3 we have:
islaami (*Islamic*) from **islaam**
miilaadi from **miilaad** (AD, referring to the birth of Christ)

The adjective used for the Islamic year **hijri** illustrates the dropping of the feminine ending of the base noun **hijrah**.

In this category fall also the 'non-primary' colours, which are adjectives formed from natural objects, usually fruits or flowers:

ward (*roses*) → **wardi** (*pink*)
burtugaal (*oranges*) → **burtugaali** (*orange*)
banafsaj (*violets*) → **banafsaji** (*violet*)

There are more examples in the exercises at the end of the unit.
As a final illustration, the Arabic name for the Kingdom of Saudi Arabia is: **al-mámlakah al-:arabíyyah as-sa:uudíyyah** (lit. *the Kingdom the Arab the Saudi*) where both *Arab* and *Saud* become adjectives to agree with *Kingdom*.

2 The past continuous/habitual

You have already learned that there are only two main verb tenses in Arabic, the present and the past. The future is merely the present with the prefix **b(a)-**. These three will get you through most situations, but there are one or two more possibilities, the main one being that used to express continual or habitual action in the past. This shade of meaning is not always immediately apparent in English. For instance, when you say *he was doing, he used to do,* etc., the words show that you intend a continuous/habitual meaning. However, if you consider *he worked in the oil company for three years, she lived most of her life in London,* the bare past tense verb gains its continuous aspect from the context. In Arabic, however, the simple past tense has a sort of 'sudden death' instantaneous action. This can be softened into a continuous or habitual happening simply by using the verb string: **kaan** (past tense) + main verb (present tense). The **kaan** here as usual puts the whole sentence in the past. Examples of this construction are given below.

kaan is a TYPE B1 verb. For convenience, here is its past tense in full:

Singular		Plural	
I was	**kunt**	we were	**kunna**
you (m.) were	**kunt** (same as above)	you were	**kuntu**
you (f.) were	**kunti**		
he was	**kaan**	they were	**kaanu**
she was	**kaanat**		

as-sanah l-maaDHyah kunt adrus at-taarikh al-islaami fi jaami:at al-kuwait *Last year I studied (was studying) Islamic history in (at) Kuwait university.*
as-saa:ah kam kaanu yiruuHuun al-maktab? *What time did they go (used to go) to the office?*
kunt aHibb al-kurah kathiir, laakin al-Hiin afaDHDHil at-tanis *I used to like football a lot, but now I prefer tennis.*
umm-i kaanat tiTbukh akil ladhiidh *My mother used to cook delicious food.*

Tábakh, yíTbukh (A)	*to cook*
ladhíidh	*delicious*

3 Adverbs

Adverbs are words which describe *how*, *when* or *where* the action of verb takes/took place, and in English you usually form them by adding the ending *-ly*, as in *quickly, formerly*.

Arabic has two ways of forming adverbs:

(a) Using the suffix **-an**, as in **Tab(a):an** (lit. *naturally*) **jíddan** (*very*) **aHyáanan** (*at times*). In this unit you have **máthalan** (*for example*) from **máthal** (*an example*).

(b) Using a preposition + noun construction, as the English *with ease* = *easily*. The Arabic preposition used is usually **bi-**. In this unit we have had **bi-DH-DHabT** (*with exactness, exactly*) and another common one is **bi-sur:ah** (*with speed, quickly*).

tamriinaat (Exercises) تمرينات

1 Here are two types of Arabic adverbs:

haadhi T-Tayyaarah tiruuH al-qaahirah mubaasharatan *This plane goes directly to Cairo.*

aHmad yitkallam bi-sur:ah *Ahmed speaks quickly.*

Fit the correct adverbs from the box into the gaps in the sentences below. Only one will make real sense.

bi-suhuulah	**daayman**
fawran	**bi-sur:ah**
jiddan	**mathalan**
abadan	**Tab:an**
bi-DH-DHabT	**aHyaanan**

(a) _______ naruuH nazuur al-:aa'ilah yoom al-jum:ah

(b) inta min Abu Dhabi? na:am. titkallam :arabi? _______ !

(c) tishuuf t-tilifizyuun kathiir? laa _______

(d) as-sayyaarah al-marsaidis al-jadiidah jamiilah _______

(e) :amm-i saalim kaan _______ yishrab finjaan gahwah as-saa:ah khamsah S-SubaH

(f) akh-i S-Saghiir ya:raf ingliizi w faransaawi w almaani. yit:allam al-lughaat al-ajnabiyyah _______

(g) sulaimaan yisuug _______ . haadha khaTar

(h) ithnain w ithnain arba:ah, laa? aywah _______

(i) aHibb ar-riyaaDHaat. al-kurah wa t-tanis _______

(j) aT-Tayyaarah as-saa:ah thamaanyah w nuSS, laazim naruuH al-maTaar _______

QUICK VOCAB

finjáan (fanajíin)	*(small coffee) cup*
almáani	*German*
ájnabi (ajáanib)	*foreign*
saag, yisúug (B1)	*to drive*
kháTar	*danger*
suhúulah	*ease*

ábadan	*never*	QV
dáayman	*always*	

2 These are examples of adjectives formed from nouns.

ad-diin al-islaami *the Islamic religion*
al-lughah l-:arabiyyah *the Arabic language*

In the following sentences, change the nouns in brackets into adjectives, remembering to make them agree with the thing they are describing.

(a) faaTimah (kuwait), laakin tiskun fii dubay
(b) huwwa Taalib (isbaanya) min madriid
(c) al-khaTT al-(:arab) jamiil jiddan
(d) maa a:raf al-lughah al-(faransa)
(e) kaan al-gabaayil al-(:arab) yiskunuun fii jaziirat al-:arab gabil DHuhuur al-islaam
(f) al-:aaSimah al-(:umaan) isim-ha masqaT
(g) maa aHibb al-loon al-(ward)
(h) al-qur'aan al-kariim maktuub bi-l-lughah al-(:arab)
(i) fiih Tullaab (gaTar) kathiiriin fii jaami:at landan
(j) maa ariid gumaash (banafsaj), ariid (burtugaal)
(k) al-bank al-(waTan) gariib min as-suug
(l) akbar markaz (tijaarah) fii dubay huwwa suug al-ghurair

QUICK VOCAB

gabíilah (gabáayil)	*tribe*
:áaSimah (:awáasim)	*capital (city)*
maktúub	*written*
gumáash (agmíshah)	*cloth, material*
wáTan (awTáan)	*nation, homeland*
suug al-ghuráir	*Al Ghorair Centre in Dubai*

3 Change the bold verbs in the following sentences to past continuous/ habitual.

Example:
aHmad **raaH** isbaanya fi S-Saif (*Ahmed went to Spain in the summer.*) → **kaan** aHmad **yiruuH** isbaanya fi S-Saif (*Ahmed used to go to Spain in the summer.*)

(a) **la:abt** goolf
(b) ukhti fariidah **darasat** al-lughah l-ingliiziyyah
(c) **ishtaghalna** fii sharikah fi l-baHrain
(d) **waSal** al-baaS as-saa:ah tis:ah
(e) biil **yitkallam** :arabi zain
(f) aT-Tullaab **darasu** taarikh al-:arab
(g) **raaHat** as-suug as-saa:ah kam?
(h) **agra** l-qur' aan al-kariim
(i) wain **sakantu** fii abu Dhabi?
(j) **ruHna** l-baHar fi S-Saif

QV

dárras, yidárris (A)	*to teach*
dáras, yídrus (A)	*to study*

4 Bill asks Suleiman about the fundamental beliefs of Islam and the main festivals. Listen to the conversation on the recording, or read the transcript, and answer the questions below.

CD 2, TR 4, 2:52

QUICK VOCAB

ahámm	*more/most important*
khaSíiSah (khaSáa'iS)	*characteristic, feature*
asáas (úsus)	*basis, fundamental belief*
áHad	*formal Arabic for* **waaHid** *one*
laa iláaha ílla l-lláah wa muHámmadun rasúul Al-láah	*'There is no God but Allah, and Muhammad is the Apostle of God'. The Muslim creed.*

kálimah (-aat)	*word*
:álam (a:láam)	*flag*
sa:úudi	*Saudi*
aish ghair?	*what else?*
Sálla, yiSálli (C)	*to pray, say one's prayers*
fájir	*dawn*
mághrib	*Sunset*
:ísha	*evening prayer (about an hour after sunset)*
ittijáah	*direction; facing, in the direction of*
al-gíblah	*the direction of prayer, facing Mecca*
:iid (a:yáad)	*eid, religious festival*
al-fíT(i)r	*the breaking of fast*
al-áDHHa	*the sacrifice (of an animal)*
sámi:, yísma: (A)	*to hear*
Saam, yiSúum (B1)	*to fast*
Tuul	*throughout (before an expression of time)*
má:na	*meaning*
al-wáaHid	*one, a person*
fáTar, YífTur (A)	*to break a fast; have breakfast*
Soom	*fast, fasting*
al-Hajj	*the pilgrimage*
móosam (mawáasim)	*season*
al-ká:bah	*the Kaaba, holy shrine in Mecca*
mubáasharatan	*directly*

(a) What is the basic fundamental belief of Islam?
(b) Where do you commonly see it written?
(c) How many times per day do Muslims pray, and at what approximate times?
(d) What is the *giblah* or *qiblah*?
(e) How many main Islamic festivals are there?
(f) What is marked by Eid al-Adha?
(g) What is observed during the month of Ramadan?
(h) What is marked by Eid al-Fitr?
(i) What sacred shrine do Muslims visit during the pilgrimage?

---

al-khaTT al-:árabi (Arabic script) الخط العربي

In this unit we shall look at another 'pair' of consonants, s and **sh**, the latter having three dots above it. The pronunciation is the English *s* as in *bits* (not as in *bins*), and *sh* as in *shin*.

Both these letters are joiners, so there are four forms of each:

Name	Initial	Medial	Final	Separate	Pronunciation
siin	ســ	ـسـ	ـس	س	s
shiin	شــ	ـشـ	ـش	ش	sh

The meaningful part of these letters is the three little spikes, looking like a rounded English *w*, with the ligatures and final flourishes. They are written on the line (except for the final flourishes), and are classed as small letters.

Insight

In fact, these letters have such a low profile that, in many styles of handwriting and calligraphy (for instance, on shop signs), the three little spikes are ironed out, and the letters are reduced to a long line, which the eye has to pick up as a letter from the context. For example, the proper name Hassan–which has, of course, only one *s* in Arabic is written:

حسن

but will often look more like this:

حـــن

with only the length of the stroke between the ح and the ن telling us that there is an *s* in there.

As with the only other letter which has three dots above it (ث) these are often written on the **shiin** in the form of an upside-down *v* or a French circumflex accent ^ (see alphabet section).

Below are some words you already know which include these letters. Try to transcribe them according to the system used in this book. (Remember, no short vowels or doubled letters are shown!)

١–	سيارة	٦–	سنة
٢–	مدرس	٧–	ستة
٣–	سالم	٨–	مباشر
٤–	خمسة	٩–	ساخن
٥–	شمس	١٠–	سليمات

Test yourself

This test covers the main vocabulary, phrases and language points given in Unit 10. If you are not sure about your answers, go back to the dialogues and exercises for some revision, before going on to Unit 11. For the answers, see the **Key to the exercises.**

Change the verb from the past tense to the past continuous in the following sentences:

1 akh-i akal bargharaat kull yoom
2 ishtaghalt fii sharikah kabiirah fii dubay
3 sabaH-naa fi l-baHr fi l-fujairah
4 saafarat ila miSr kull sanah
5 zurt waalidai-k fii nyuu york?
6 la:abuu tanis fi-l-misa
7 akal-naa samak ladhiidh fi l-maT:am al-lubnaani
8 muHammad waSSal awlaad-uh fii sayyarat-uh
9 al-awlaad darasu al-lughah l-ingliiziyyah fii jaami:at qaTar
10 ishtarait fawaakih fi-s-suug

11

الصحة

aS-SiHHah

Health

In this unit you will learn how to

- Say you don't feel well
- Ask for a chemist or doctor
- Buy remedies

New words and phrases

CD 2, TR 5

Listen to the recording.

Hiwaar 1 (Dialogue 1) حوار ١

CD 2, TR 5, 0:14

Bill Stewart is not feeling well, and he goes to a chemist in Dubai.

Chemist	kaif mumkin asaa:id-ak?
Bill	:ind-i waja: fii baTn-i. :ind-ak dawa Hagg haadha?
Chemist	Saar l-ak aishgadd :ind-ak haadha l-waja:?

Bill	min awwal ams
Chemist	:ind-ak ishaal?
Bill	na:am, shwayyah.
Chemist	:ind-i haadhi l-Hubuub hina. hiyya mufiidah jiddan.
Bill	kam marrah fi l-yoom laazim aakhudh-ha?
Chemist	khudh Habbah waaHidah arba: marraat fi l-yoom li muddat khamsat ayyaam. ishrab maay kathiir w laa taakul fawaakih wala akil magli
Bill	shukran

QUICK VOCAB

wája:(awjáa:)	*ache, pain*
báT(i)n	*stomach*
dáwa (adwíyah)	*medicine (incl. weedkiller, chemicals)*
min	*from, since*
isháal (pronounced **is-háal)**	*diarrhœa*
Hábbah (Hubúub)	*pill*
mufíid	*effective, beneficial*
kam márrah	*how often, how many times*
ákhadh, yáakhudh (A irreg.)	*to take*
laa táakul	*do not eat*
fáakihah (fawáakih)	*fruit*
wála	*or, nor (*lit. *and not)*
mágli	*fried*

(a) How long has Bill felt ill?
(b) How often does Bill need to take the pills?
(c) For how many days should he take them?
(d) What advice does the chemist give him?

---

mulaaHaDHaat (Notes) ملاحظات

1 min (*from*) + period of time = *since*

2 ishaal (*diarrhœa*)
The s and the h here are two separate letters, not the single letter shiin.

Hiwaar 2 (Dialogue 2) حوار ٢

🔊 **CD 2, TR 5, 1:04**

Kamil in Doha is going to work but he doesn't look well. His wife Rayyah is worried about him.

Rayyah	aish Haal-ak?
Kamil	al-Hagiigah, ana ta:baan shwayyah.
Rayyah	aish fii-k?
Kamil	:ind-i waja: al-asnaan
Rayyah	min mata?
Kamil	ibtada min yoomain, laakin ams bi l-lail Saar al-waja: shadiid, wa l-Hiin yooja:-ni kathiir
Rayyah	laish maa khabbart-ni? laazim tiruuH :ind Tabiib al-asnaan
Kamil	SaHiiH, laakin al-Hiin niHna waajid mashghuuliin fi l-maktab, w maa :ind-i wagt. akhadht asbriin, w in shaa' Al-laah yikuun aHsan ba:d shwayyah
Rayyah	al-mafruuDH tiruuH fawran gabil maa yiSiir awHash w yikuun laazim yigla: la-k sinn-ak!
Kamil	laa tit:abiin nafs-ich. huwwa laa shay.
Rayyah	idha kaan laa shay, kaif shakl-ak mariiDH kidha? ana battaSil fii Tabiib as-asnaan al-Hiin aakhudh maw:id

QUICK VOCAB

al-Hagíigah	*the truth, actually*
ta:báan	*tired, ill*
aish fii-k?	*what is wrong with you?* (lit. *what is in you?*)
sinn (asnáan)	*tooth*
wája: al-asnáan	*toothache*
máta	*when? (in questions only)*
ibtáda, yibtádi (C)	*to begin, start*
ams bi-l-lail	*last night*
shadíid	*violent, acute*
wája:, yóoja: (A)	*to hurt, give pain*

QUICK VOCAB

laish	*why*
Tabíib al-asnáan	*dentist (*lit. *doctor [of] the teeth)*
SaHíiH	*right, correct*
mashghúul	*busy*
wag(i)t	*time*
asbríin	*aspirin*
al-mafrúuDH	lit. *that which is required, should be done*
áwHash	*worse*
gála:, yígla: (A)	*pull out*
tá:ab, yít:ab (A)	*to tire*
laa tit:abíin nafs- ich	*don't worry (*lit. *don't tire yourself* (fem.)
laa shay	*nothing*
idha, idha kaan	*if*
shák(i)l (ashkáal)	*appearance; shape, type, kind*
maríiDH (márDHa)	*ill; sick person, patient*
máw:id (mawa:íid)	*appointment; plural. schedule, operating hours*

(a) When did Kamil begin to feel worse?
(b) Why doesn't he want to go to the dentist?

---

mulaaHaDHaat (Notes) ملاحظات

1 ta:baan (lit. *tired*)
This word is commonly used as a euphemism for *ill*, when the complaint is not severe. The real word for *ill* is **mariiDH**.

2 wája:, yóoja: (*to give pain*)
Remember that a type A verb whose past begins with a **w** smooths this out in the present which becomes **yooja:**.

3 tiruuH :ind Tabiib al-asnaan
The **:ind** here implies *at the house/place of* (French *chez*). In everyday English you talk about 'the dentist's', 'the doctor's' meaning the same thing.

4 yikuun

Here are two examples of **yikuun** putting the rest of the sentence into the future: **yikuun aHsan** (*it will be better, you'd better*), **yikuun laazim** (*it will be necessary, you will have to*). See Unit 8.

5 **(al-)mafruuDH** (used with or without the article) literally means some thing that *is required of you, imposed upon you.*

Insight

In Gulf Arabic **mafruuDH** is a stronger form of **laazim.** If one person says **laazim,** someone who agrees with him will often reply **aywa mafruuDH.**

6 gabil maa (*before*)

For this **maa** before verbs, see grammar points. It is not the negative **maa.**

7 yigla: la-k sinn-ak

The preposition **li** or **la** means *to* or *for*, and is often used in Gulf Arabic after a verb, as here, to imply a sense of immediate personal involvement. English *will pull your tooth out for you* gives much the same flavour. See also grammar points.

8 laa tit:abíin nafs-ich (masc. **laa tit:ab nafs-ak**)

This means either literally *don't trouble yourself* or, jocularly, *don't get into a state*. It is another example of the negative imperative.

9 idha

Very often followed by **kaan, :idha** is probably the most common word for *if* in Gulf Arabic. You have also come across **law** in the phrase **law samaHt** (*please, if you permit*).

10 aakhudh maw:id (*I'll make an appointment*)

English says *make*, Arabic says *take.*

11 **ana ta:baan** (fem. **ta:baanah**) **shwayyah** (*I don't feel very well*) This is the easiest way to say you are unwell, although there is a word in Arabic for *feeling*, **Háasis** (fem. **Háassah**):

ana Haasis nafs-i ta:baan	lit. *I am feeling myself ill.*

12 **aish fii-k** or **aish bii-k** (fem. **fii-ch/bii-ch**) (What is wrong with you?) There are three ways to say what is wrong with you:

(a) **:ind-i waja: fii . . . -i** *(I have a pain in my . . .)*
(b) You can use the verb **yooja:** *(to hurt, give pain)*:
. . . -i yooja:-ni *(my . . . hurts (is hurting) me)*.
(c) With some common ailments - especially toothache - use the posessive construction:

ind-i waja: al-asnaan	*I have pain [of] the teeth.*

Insight

There is a special word for a *headache*, **Sudáa:**, the verb from which is often used figuratively when referring to problems or difficulties:

haadha yiSadda:-ni	*That gives me a headache.*

Hiwaar 3 (Dialogue 3) حوار ٣

CD 2, TR 5, 2:16

Rayyah telephones the dentist's surgery.

Receptionist	SabaaH al-khair, haadhi :iyaadat ad-doktoor maHmuud al-badawi
Rayyah	ariid aakhudh maw:id Hagg zooj-i
Receptionist	khallii-ni ashuuf . . . . mumkin yiiji yoom al-arba:ah al-gaadim as-saa:ah :asharah w ruba:? ad-doktoor faaDHi . . . .

Rayyah	laa, haadha maa yinfa:. yiguul inn-uh bi waja: kathiir wa l-mafruuDH inn-uh yiiji fii asra: wagt mumkin. maa fii maw:id faaDHi :ind ad-doktoor al-yoom?
Receptionist	haadha Sa:b . . . . ad-doktoor mashghuul jiddan al-yoom, :ind-uh marDHa kathiiriin. nashuuf . . . mumkin yiiji as-saa:ah sittah al-misa? fiih iHtimaal yikuun laazim yintaDHir shwayyah
Rayyah	n-zain, bakhabbir-uh. shukran jaziilan.
Receptionist	:afwan, ma:a s-salaamah.

QUICK VOCAB

khálla, yikhálli (C)	*to let leave*
khallíi-ni ashúuf	*let me see*
fáaDHi	*free, empty*
náfa:, yínfa: (A)	*to be suitable, useful*
fii ásra: wagt múmkin	*as soon as possible*
Sá:(a)b	*difficult*
nashúuf . . .	*let's see*
jaa, yíiji (C irreg.**)**	*to come*
iHtimáal	*possible,* lit. *possibility*
intáDHar, yintáDHir (A)	*to wait*

(a) When does the receptionist first suggest Kamil comes?
(b) What has been the problem today?
(c) What might he have to do?

mulaaHaDHaat (Notes) ملاحظات

1 ad-doktoor (*doctor*, borrowed from English)
The 'official' word for *doctor* is **Tabiib**, from the Arabic root **Tibb** (*the science of*) *medicine*. **Hakiim** (lit. *wise man*) and **dakhtar** (a corruption of doctor) are also heard. **doktoor** only can also be used as a title, when it always takes the definite article: **ad-doktoor :aziiz as-saalimi** (*Dr Aziz al-Salimi*). A dentist is referred to simply as **doktoor** although the formal word is **Tabiib al-asnaan** (*doctor [of the] teeth*).

2 **jaa, yiiji** (*to come*)
This irregular verb is given in full in the verb tables. Its imperative **ta:áal** (fem. **ta:áali**, plural **ta:áalu**) (*come!*) derives from a completely different root.

3 (**fiih**) **iHtimaal** (lit. *there is a possibility*)
Whereas **mumkin**, or its verbal equivalent **yimkin**, can be used both for ability and possibility, **iHtimaal**, which originally means *it is conceivable that*, can only be used for the latter, i.e. something that might happen.

muu mumkin yiiji as-saa:ah khamsah	*He can't come at five o'clock.*
mumkin or **iHtimaal yikuun fiih maTar baakir**	*It could/might rain tomorrow.*

---

ta:biiraat haammah (Key phrases) تعبيرات هامة

CD 2, TR 5, 3:50

Asking what's wrong with someone

kaif Haal-ak, shloon-ak	*How are you?*
ana muu bi-khair, ana ta:baan	*I'm not very well.*
aish fii-k, aish bii-k	*What's wrong with you?*

Describing your ailments

:ind-i Sudaa:	*I have a headache.*
:ind-i zukaam	*a cold.*
:ind-i Humma	*a fever*
:ind-i waja: al-asnaan	*toothache.*
:ind-i fluu	*flu.*
:ind-i ishaal	*diarrhœa.*
(**ana**) **akuHH**	*I have a cough (*lit. *I cough)*
:ind-i waja: fii bal:uum-i/bal:uum-i yooja:-ni	*I have a sore throat.*

:ind-i waja: fii baTn-i/baTn-i yooja:ni	*I have a stomach-ache.*
:ind-i waja: fii DHahr-i/DHahr-i yooja:-ni	*I have back-ache.*
:ind-i waja: fii :ain-i/:ain-i tooja:ni	*My eye is sore.*
:ind-i waja: fii rjuul-i/rjuul-i tooja:-ni	*My legs are aching.*

QV

iid or **yad (iidain)** — *hand, arm*
rijl (rujúul) — *foot, leg*

Insight

iid (*hand*) and **rijl** (*foot*) can refer to the whole upper and lower limbs respectively. These words are feminine as are most parts of the body which come in pairs, such as **:ain** (*eye*) above.

Saying how you feel

ána bardáan (f. **bardáanah**)	*I feel cold.*
niHna bardaaníin	*We feel cold.*
ána maríiDH	*I'm ill.*
ána ta:báan	*I'm tired, unwell.*
ána Háasis inn-i múmkin azúu:	*I feel sick (*lit. *I am feeling that I shall vomit).*
ráas-i yidúukh	*I feel dizzy, faint (*lit. *my head is spinning).*

QV

zaa:, yizúu: (B1) — *to vomit*

Wounds, cuts and stings

ta:awwárt fii uSbu:-i	*I have cut my finger.*
ta:awwárt fii iid-i	*I have cut my hand/arm.*
kasárt iid-i	*I have broken my arm.*
rijl-i maksúurah	*My leg is broken.*
ladaghat-ni naHlah	*I have been stung by a bee (*lit. *a bee stung me).*
ladagh-ni :agrab	*I have been stung by a scorpion*

QUICK VOCAB

ta:áwwar, yit:áwwar (A)	*to be wounded*
kásar, yíksir (A)	*to break*
maksúur	*broken*
náHla (náHal)	*bee*
:ágrab (:agáarib)	*scorpion*

Saying how long you have felt ill

min ams	*since yesterday*
min aS-SubaH	*since this morning*
min yoomain	*for two days*
min usbuu:	*for a week*

Asking for help

laazim aruuH :ind aT-Tabiib	*I need to go to the doctor's.*
ariid aruuH :ind Tabiib al-asnaan	*I want to go to the dentist.*
laazim aruuH aS-Ṣaydaliyyah	*I need to go to the chemist.*
laazim nawaddii-h l-mustashfa	*We have to take him to the hospital.*
aHsan awaddii-ch al-:iyaadah	*I'd better take you (fem.) to the clinic.*

QV

wádda, yiwáddi (C)	*to take to, deliver*

Medicines and remedies

:ind-ak dawa Hagg waja: al-bal:uum?	*Do you have anything for a sore throat?*
:ind-i Hubuub Hagg Sudaa:	*I have pills for a headache.*
khudh (fem. **khudhi**, pl. **khudhu**) **Habbah waaHidah/Habbatain/ thalaath Habbaat**	*Take one/two/three pills.*
gafshah waaHidah	*One spoon(ful).*
marrah waaHidah/marratain/ thalaath marraat	*Once/twice/three times.*
gabil maa tiruuH tinaam	*Before going to bed (*lit. *sleep).*

kull saa:ah/saa:atain/thalaath saa:aat	*Every hour/two hours/ three hours.*
aS-SubaH/aDH-DHuhur/al-misa	*In the morning/at noon/in the evening.*
gafshah waaHidah gabil al-akil	*One spoonful before meals.*
khamsah mililitir ba:d al-akil	*5 mls after meals.*

---

núqaT naHwíyyah (Grammar points) نقط نحوية

1 Imperatives

These, you remember, are special parts of the verb used for giving orders, or telling people to do something. In this unit you have met a negative imperative, telling someone *not* to do something. In this case, use the negative **laa** (*not*), which is also the word for *no*, followed by a simple present tense verb.

laa tit:abiin nafs-ich	*Don't trouble yourself (to a woman).*
laa titkallam bi-sur:ah kidha	*Don't speak quickly like that (to a man).*
laa tiruuHuun yoom as-sabt	*Don't go on Saturday (plural).*

2 gabil *and* ba:d

When these words are used before a verb, they must be followed by the word **maa**. This is meaningless in English, and has nothing to do with the negative **maa** (*not*).
Examples:

Before a noun: **ba:d al-ghada**	*after [the] lunch*
but, before a verb: **gabil maa tinaam**	*before you [go to] sleep*

3 khallíi-ni ashuuf *let me see* (lit. *leave-me I-see*)

This verb string or phrase has an imperative (+ pronoun suffix) followed by the main verb in the present tense. Remember that all words ending in a vowel lengthen and stress this when a prefix is added.

Insight

In many parts of the Gulf, verbs of the **khalli** type lose their final vowel in the (masculine) imperative, in which case this phrase would be **kháll-ni**. You need only be aware of this for listening purposes, as you will be understood whichever variety you use.

4 The preposition li-/la- (*to, for*)

This little word is frequently used with pronoun suffixes and sometimes changes or omits its vowel:

l-i	*to/for me* (*the vowel is pronounced long:* **l-ii**; *sometimes also* **lí-yya**)
l-ak	*to you (masc.)*
l-ich	*to you (fem.)*
l-uh	*to him*
la-ha	*to her*
la-na	*to us*
la-kum	*to you (plural)*
la-hum	*to them*

---

tamriinaat (Exercises) تمرينات

CD 2, TR 5, 4:27

1 The street map below has four places marked on it. Four people are trying to get to the doctor, the dentist, the clinic and the hospital, so listen to the instructions they are given, or read the transcript, and make a note of which number is which place.

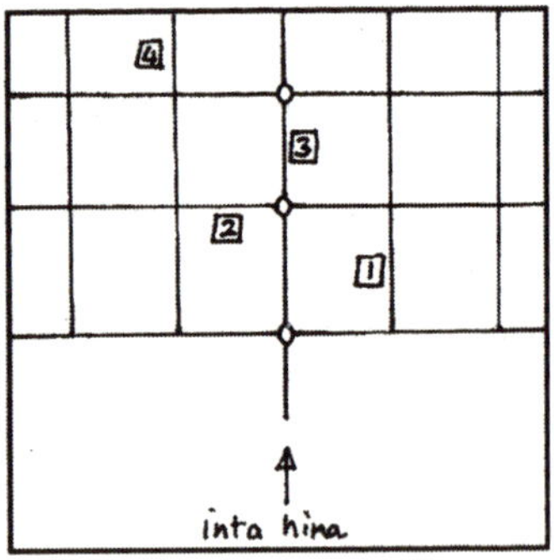

🔊 **CD 2, TR 5, 5:14**

2 You overhear four Kuwaitis asking the chemist for the following items. Listen to the recording or read the transcript, and match the people up with the appropriate remedies below.

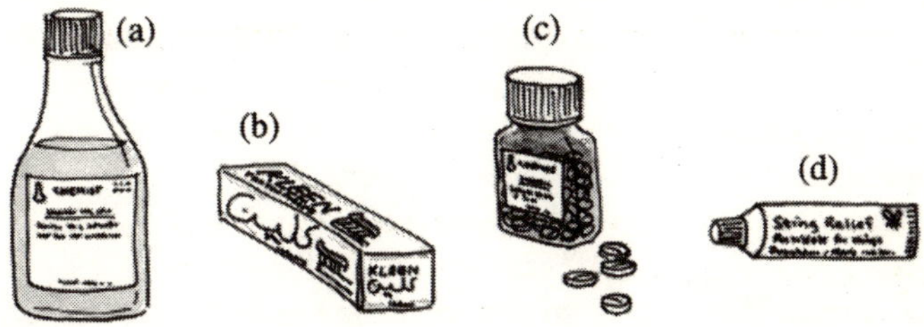

márham	*cream (medical)*
ládghat náHlah	*bee-sting*
ma:júun al-asnáan	*toothpaste*

3 You are not well and go into a pharmacy. How do you tell the chemist that you:

(a) have a headache
(b) have hurt your leg
(c) feel dizzy
(d) have cut your hand
(e) have a sore throat

4 There must be something wrong at this office – nearly half the employees are getting their relatives to call in to say that they are sick on Saturday morning!

– What is wrong with them?
– How long have they had the symptoms?
– What have they done about it?

(a) faaTimah raagidah l-yoom. :ind-ha zukaam min thalaathat ayyaam. akhadhat asbriin
(b) as:ad mariiDH. :ind-uh waja: fi l-baTn min ams, fa raaH :ind ad-doktoor fi S-SabaaH. ad-doktoor a:Taa-h dawa, fa in shaa' Al-laah yikuun ahwan baakir

(c) Hasan ta:baan. :ind-uh Sudaa: w Humma min yoomain, wa gult l-uh aHsan yirgad li ghaayat maa tiruuH :ann-uh l-Humma
(d) khawla maa tigdar tiiji sh-shughul al-yoom. gaalat inn-uh :ind-ha waja: fi DH-DHahar min awwal ams, w laazim tistariiH Tuul al-usbuu: w taakhudh Hubuub Hagg al-waja:
(e) laazim nawaddi walad-na Haamid al-mustashfa. :ind-ma kaan yil:ab wiyya akhuu-h aS-SabaaH DHarab :ain-uh. hiyya waarimah jiddan, w laazim aT-Tabiib yishuuf-ha

QUICK VOCAB

ráagid (adj.)	*in bed (* lit. *lying down)*
a:Táa-h	*(he) gave him*
áhwan	*better (from an illness)*
rágad, yírgad (A)	*to lie down, stay in bed*
li gháayat maa	*until (with a verb)*
tirúuH :ánn-uh	*goes from him, leaves him*
gádar, yígdar (A)	*to be able*
ínn-uh	*that*
istaráaH, yistaríiH (B1)	*to rest, relax, take one's ease*
Tuul al-usbúu:	*all week, the whole week, throughout the week*
:índ-ma	*when, while*
wíyya	*with, together with*
akhúu-h	*his brother*
DHárab, yíDHrab (A)	*to hit, strike, knock*
wáarim	*swollen*

5 You are staying with a friend, Aisha, but she thinks you don't look very well today. Fill in your half of the conversation.

Aisha	kaif Haal-ich?
inti	*Say actually you don't feel very well*
Aisha	aish fii-ch?
inti	*Say you have a headache*
Aisha	salamt-ich!
inti	*Ask if she has anything for it*
Aisha	na:am, khudhi haadhi l-Hubuub ma:a shwayyat maay

Insight

salámt-ak/-ich (lit. *your welfare*). Said to someone who says they are ill. The reply is **Al-laah yisal(l)m-ak/-ich.**

CD 2, TR 5, 5:43

6 Listen to the recording, or read the transcript, of the conversation between two Saudis, and answer the questions below.

QUICK VOCAB

Sákhrah (Sukhúur)	*rock*
aT-Tawáari'	*casualty, emergency*
:aks eksrai	*x-ray photograph*
iftákar, yiftákir (A)	*to think, consider*
áwwal	*(at) first*
HaTT, yiHúTT (B2)	*to put, place*
ribáaT (rúbaT)	*bandage*
gádar, yígdar (A)	*to be able*
másha, yímshi (C)	*to walk*

(a) What is the matter with him?
(b) How did he get to hospital?
(c) Has he broken any bones?
(d) How does it feel now?

al-khaTT al-:árabi (Arabic script) الخط العربي

In this lesson, you will learn two more pairs of letters, distinguished only by one dot placed above the second member of each. These letters are of medium size. All are joiners and show the usual ligatures and final flourishes.

Name	Initial	Medial	Final	Separate	Pronunciation
Saad	صـ	ـصـ	ـص	ص	S
Daad	ضـ	ـضـ	ـض	ض	D

Taa’	ـط	ـطـ	طـ	ط	T
DHaa’	ـظ	ـظـ	ظـ	ظ	DH

Insight

In writing the second pair, **Taa’** and **DHaa’**, the bottom ‘egg shape’ is produced first, and the upright ‘stick’ added later at the next lift of the pen in the same way as we dot our i’s and cross our t’s.

These four letters are often called the ‘emphatic’ letters, as they have a powerful sound produced by greater tongue tension and more violent release of breath.

Note: In the Gulf, **D** and **DH** are both pronounced the same, (i.e. like an emphatic **dh**). (See alphabet section.)

The following exercise is of the crossword clue type (not very subtle). Remember, there are no short vowels or double letters, and ـة at the end of a word is always the (feminine) ending **-ah**. Also, the **al-** in many Arabic place names is frequently omitted in English.

Write down the consonants you recognize, check them for potential long vowels and you should get the right answer.

Clues:	**Arabic words**
1 City in southern Iraq	١- البصرة
2 Internal part of the body	٢- بطن
3 Common Arab male first name	٣- صالح
4 One of the United Arab Emirates	٤- ابو ظبي

Clues:	Arabic words
5 Someone attending an institute of higher learning	٥– طالب
6 Fast means of international transport	٦– طيارة
7 Capital of the largest country in Arabia	٧– الرياض
8 Healer	٨– طبيب
9 Former leader of a Northern Arab state	٩– صدام
10 Method or style of writing	١٠– خط
11 Where you would go to catch a 6	١١– مطار
12 A more down-to-earth means of transport	١٢– باص

Test yourself

This test covers the main vocabulary, phrases and language points given in Unit 11. If you are not sure about your answers, go back to the dialogues and exercises for some revision, before going on to Unit 12. For the answers, see the **Key to the exercises.**

Match the questions below with the appropriate replies. Example:

kaif Haal-ak?	ana ta:baan shwayyah
1 aish fii-k?	(a) mumkin kaan al-akl fi l-maT:am maa zain
2 Saar la-k gaddaish w-inta ta:baan?	(b) aakhudh l-ak maw:id bukrah S-SubH
3 :ind-ak dawa Hagg zukaam?	(c) khudh Habbatain arba:ah marraat fi l-yoom ma:a maa'

4	aakhudh al-Hubuub kam marrah fi l-yoom?	(d)	umm-ii Saar la-haa usbuu:ain fi l-mustashfa
5	ana mariiDH, mumkin :ind-ii fluu	(e)	laazim tiwaddii-h l-mustashfa bi-sur:ah
6	:ind-ii waja: al-asnaan, wa laazim aruuH :ind Tabiib al-asnaan	(f)	a:Tii-haa haadha l-marham
7	ibn-ii rijl-uh maksuurah	(g)	yoomain
8	kaan yizuu: bi-l-lail wa :ind-uh ishaal	(h)	:indii waja: fii baTn-i
9	kaif Haal waaldai-k?	(i)	:ind-ii haadhii l-Hubuub Hagg az-zukaam
10	zoojat-ii ladaghat-haa naHlah fii yad-haa	(j)	laazim taakhudh asbriin wa-tirgad

12

الإجراءات الرسمية
al-ijraa'áat ar-rasmíyyah
Official procedures

In this unit you will learn how to

- Find a bank cashpoint
- Cash travellers' cheques and change money
- Buy stamps, send letters and parcels
- Deal with government departments and embassies

New words and phrases

CD 2, TR 6

Listen to the recording.

Hiwaar 1 (Dialogue 1) حوار ١

CD 2, TR 6, 0:19

Mark, a visitor to Saudi Arabia, wants to get some cash. He stops a passer-by.

Mark	:afwan, mumkin tisaa:id-ni min faDHl-ak?
rajjáal	Tab:an. b-aish asaa:id-ak?
Mark	laazim aruuH bank
rajjáal	fiih bank hinaak, gariib
Mark	laazim yikuun bank fii-h makíinat Sarf. ayy bank aruuH?
rajjáal	aaa. idhan . . . laazim tiruuH al-bank al-:arabi fii shaari: al-malik khaalid. fii-h makíinat Sarf yaakhudh kuruut maal bank min kull shakil.
Mark	shukran jaziilan

QUICK VOCAB

bank (bunúuk)	*bank*
makíinat Sarf	*cash machine*
malik	*king*
kart (kurúut)	*card*
kurúut maal bank	*bank cards*

(a) What does Mark ask for?
(b) What exactly does he want?
(c) What is the name of the bank he is directed to?

---

mulaaHaDHaat (Notes) ملاحظات

1 **ayy,** (fem. **ayyah**) (*which*)
This comes before the noun and agrees with it in gender:

ayy bank	*Which bank?*
ayyah sayyaarah	*Which car?*

2 **al-malik khaalid** (*King Khaled*)
With Dr. and other titles you must use the definite article.

3 **kull** is used before the noun for *each, every, all*. See **Grammar points**.

Hiwaar 2 (Dialogue 2) حوار ٢

🔊 **CD 2, TR 6, 1:09**

Tony has been in Jeddah on business, and he has come to Taif for a couple of days. He needs to change money, and finds his way to the First Saudi Bank.

Tony	as-salaamu :alai-kum.
Káatib	w :alai-kum as-salaam. asaa:id-ak bi shay?
Tony	ariid aSraf chaik siyaaHi
Káatib	Tab:an, ayyah :umlah?
Tony	doolaaraat
Káatib	kam doolaar?
Tony	khams miyyah. aish si:r ad-doolaar al-amriiki al-yoom?
Káatib	laHDHah min faDHl-ak . . . (*consulting his computer screen*) si:r ad-doolaar al-amriiki thalaathah riyaalaat w khamsah w sab:iin halalah. jawaaz as-safar law samaHt.
Tony	tafaDHDHal
káatib	shukran . . . waggi: hina min faDHl-ak
Tony	(*signs*) tfaDHDHal
káatib	min faDHl-ak khudh haadhi l-waragah li S-Sarraaf hinaak, w huwwa ya:Tii-k al-mablagh.
Tony	shukran
káatib	:afwan

QUICK VOCAB

Sáraf, yíSraf (A)	*to cash, change money*
chaik (-aat)	*cheque*
chaik siyáaHi	*travellers' cheque*
:úmlah (-aat)	*currency*
dooláar (-aat)	*dollar*
si:r (as:áar)	*price, exchange rate*

wáragah (awráag) — *(sheet of) paper*
Sarráaf (-iin) — *cashier; money changer*
máblagh (mabáaligh) — *sum, amount of money*

(a) How much does he want to change?
(b) What does the clerk ask for?
(c) What does Tony have to do after showing his passport?

---

mulaaHaDHaat (Notes) ملاحظات

1 Money
The general term is **filúus** (the plural of **fils**, the smallest division of many Arab currencies), or **baizáat** which dates back to the days of the rupee in the Gulf and is still used as a thousandth part of a riyal in Oman (sing. **baizah**).

The two best known foreign currencies in the Gulf are the US dollar, and the **jináih** (**-aat**) **starliini** (*the pound sterling*).

2 Changing money
The verb **Saraf, yiSraf** can be used for either to cash or to change. It is usually assumed that you want to change into the local currency, so this need not be specified. If you want some other currency, simply add **ariid** (*I want*) plus the currency name, or better **:umlah** plus the nationality adjective of the currency.

ariid riyaalaat — *I want riyaals.*
ariid :umlah sa:uudiyyah — *I want Saudi currency.*

---

ma:luumaat thaqaafiyyah (Cultural tips) معلومات ثقافية

There are plenty of banks in the Gulf, but their opening hours are rather brief, generally about 8 am until noon (11 am on Thursdays and closed all day Friday). A clerk will effect your transaction on paper, but if you are withdrawing money, you will have to collect this from the cashier.

Exchange rates are not sacred, so unless you have an established relationship with a certain bank and are sure you are getting the best deal (ask!) it is often worth shopping around, especially if you intend to exchange a significant amount.

An alternative to the banks are the money-changers (**Sarraafiin**, same as cashiers) who have offices in the souks of most large Gulf towns. These are perfectly legal operations, and you can sometimes get a better rate. They also have the advantage of being open for much longer hours, including evenings.

Hiwaar 3 (Dialogue 3) حوار ٣

CD 2, TR 6, 2:14

Eleanor has gone to the post office in Muscat to buy stamps for the letters and postcards she and Mike have written.

Eleanor	al-buTaagah li ingilterra bi-kam min faDHl-ak?
káatib	miyyah w khamsiin baizah
Eleanor	wa r-risaalah?
káatib	idha kaan al-wazn agall min :asharah ghraam, miitain baizah, w min :asharah li-ghaayat :ishriin ghraam thalaath miyyah w khamsiin baizah.
Eleanor	zain, a:Tii-ni arba:ah Tawaabi: bi-miitain baizah, w ithna:shar bi-miyyah w khamsiin min faDHl-ak.
káatib	arba:ah bi-miitain, w ithna:shar bi-miyyah w khamsiin. haadha kull-uh riyaalain w sitt miyyat baizah.
Eleanor	tfaDHDHal (*she gives him three riyaals*)
káatib	arba: miyyat baizah. tfaDHDHali.

QV

buTáagah (-aat) *postcard*
risáalah (rasáayil) *letter*
wazn (awzáan) *weight*
agáll min *less than*

QUICK VOCAB

ghraam (-aat)	*gramme*
li gháayat . . .	*up to . . .*
Táabi: (Tawáabi:)	*stamp*
bi	*(here) to the value of, at*
kúll-uh	*all of it, all together*
báagi	*change, remainder of something*
ághla	*more expensive*

True or false?

(a) al-buTaagah aghla min ar-risaalah bi-khamsiin baizah.

(b) kaanat :ind-ha arba: rasaayil wazn-ha agall min :asharah ghraam

(c) kaan al-baagi sitt miyyat baizah

mulaaHaDHaat (Notes) ملاحظات

1 If (see **Grammar points.**)

2 **ghraam** (*gram*) + plural **ghraamaat**
This is often left in the singular, just like **kíilo** (*kilo(metre), kilo (gram)*).

Hiwaar 4 (Dialogue 4) حوار ٤

CD 2, TR 6, 3 : 11

Mike needs a local driving licence, so he goes to the Ministry of Transport in Abu Dhabi.

Mike	law samaHt, ariid laisan maal siwaagah
muwaDHDHaf	haadha maa min hina. hina wizaarat al-muwaaSalaat. laazim tiruuH :ind ash-shurTah, daa'irat al-muruur.
Mike	wain-ha daa'irat al-muruur?
muwaDHDHaf	hina gariib, fii nafs ash-shaari:
Mike	shukran.

At the Traffic Department, he looks for the right desk.

Mike	SabaaH al-khair. aakhudh laisan maal siwaagah min hina?
muwaDHDHaf	na:am
Mike	aish tiriid min awraag?
muwaDHDHaf	jiib al-laisan al-dawli maal-ak, w Suuratain maal jawaaz, w mablagh khamsiin dirham
Mike	:ind-i hina. (*gives him the papers*) tfaDHDHal
muwaDHDHaf	(*examines the papers and fills out a form*) min faDHl-ak waggi: hina (*Mike signs*). law tiiji ba:d bukrah, yikuun al-laisan jaahiz in shaa' Al-laah w mumkin taakhudh-uh
Mike	shukran jaziilan. fii amaan Al-laah
muwaDHDHaf	fii amaan al-kariim

QUICK VOCAB

láisan (layáasin)	*licence*
laisan maal siwáagah	*driving licence*
muwaaSaláat	*communications, transport*
shúrTah	*police*
dáa'irah or **dáayirah (dawáayir)**	*(government) department*
murúur	*traffic*
jaab, yijíib (B1)	*to bring, get, hand over*
dáwli	*international*
law tiiji	*if you come*

(a) Where does Mike have to go to get his licence?
(b) Where is it?
(c) What papers does he need?
(d) When will his licence be ready?

mulaaHaDHaat (Notes) ملاحظات

1 laisan

The proper word for *licence* is **rúkhSat siyáagah** (*driving permit*), but this adaptation of the English word is very current (along with its real Arabic plural formation).

2 **wain-ha daa'irat al-muruur** (*where is the traffic department?*)
The suffix pronouns are sometimes added to **wain** (*where*) giving the sentence more emphasis. The **wain** can come either before or after the noun:

muHammad wain-uh	*Where's Mohammad?*
wain-ha s-sayyaarah maal-ak	*Where is your car?*

3 **aish tiriid min awraag**
Note the way this is phrased: lit. *what do you want of papers* (i.e. what papers do you want?).

Insight maal (*for*)

Here are more examples of this useful word which expresses belonging, pertaining to something.

laisan maal siwaagah	*driving licence* (lit. *licence for driving*)
Suuratain maal jawaaz	*two passport photographs* (lit. *two pictures for passport*)

ma:luumaat thaqaafiyyah (Cultural tips) معلومات ثقافية

wizáarah (*ministry*) is derived from **waziir** (*minister*) (the Vizier of the Arabian Nights). Ministries are usually expressed by the possessive construction, with the hidden **-t** appearing.

Here are a few:

wizaarat at-ta:líim	(*Ministry of Education*)
wizaarat aS-SíHHah	(*Ministry of Health*)
wizaarat ad-daakhilíyyah	(*Ministry of the Interior*)
wizaarat al-khaarijíyyah	(*Ministry of Foreign Affairs*)
wizaarat ath-thaqáafah	(*Ministry of Culture*)

sifaarah *embassy* is derived in exactly the same way from **safiir** *ambassador* (itself in turn derived from **safar** *travel*).

Embassies are usually referred to by the adjectives of nationality:

as-sifaarah l-kuwaitiyyah	(*Kuwaiti Embassy*)
as-sifaarah l-amriikiyyah	(*American Embassy*)
as-sifaarah l-briiTaaniyyah	(*British Embassy*)
as-sifaarah al-hindiyyah	(*Indian Embassy*)

Note however that their official titles are often in the possessive construction: e.g.

sifaarat mamlakat al-baHrain *Embassy of the Kingdom of Bahrain*

Ministries and embassies are run by armies of **muwáDHDHaf (-iin)** (*officials*) (lit. *one appointed to an official position*). They tend to open from about 8 am until 2 pm and close on Thursdays and Fridays.

Whatever you go for, you will inevitably be asked for several passport photographs, so keep a good supply with you as automatic machines are not plentiful in the Gulf.

---

ta:biiraat haammah (Key phrases) تعبيرات هامة

CD 2, TR 6, 4:22

Changing money

ariid aSraf filuus *I want to change (some) money.*
ariid aSraf miitain jinaih starliini *I want to change £200.*
mumkin tiSraf l-i miitain w khamsiin doolaar amriiki? *Can you change $250 for me?*
ariid :umlah sa:uudiyyah *I want Saudi (Arabian) currency.*

Cashing travellers' cheques

ariid aSraf chaik siyaaHi bi-mablagh miyyat jinaih (starliini) *I want to cash a traveller's cheque for the sum of £100.*

a:Tii-ni jawaaz as-safar min faDHI-ak *Give me your passport please.*
waggi: hina *Sign here.*
taakhudh al-mablagh min :ind aS-Sarraaf *You will get (take) your money (the sum) from the cashier.*

Asking about posting an item

al-buTaagah li amriikah bi-kam? *How much is a postcard to the USA?*
ar-risaalah li l-mámlakah l-muttáHidah bi-kam? *How much is a letter to the United Kingdom?*
aT-Tard li urubba bi-kam? *How much is a parcel to Europe?*

QV

al-mámlakah l-muttáHidah	*the United Kingdom*
Tard (Turúud)	*parcel, package*

Asking for stamps

Taabi:ain bi-miitain fils min faDHl-ak *two stamps at 200 fils please*
thalaathah Tawaabi: bi-riyaal (waaHid) *three stamps at one riyal*

Note that **waaHid** *one* here is optional, and, if used, must come after the noun as usual.
ariid Taabi: (waaHid) bi miyyah w khamsiin fils *I'd like one stamp at 150 fils.*

---

núqaT naHwíyyah (Grammar points) نقط نحوية

1 *Each, every* and *all*

These are all expressed by the single word **kull** (also pronounced **kill**), which never changes.

For *each* and *every* use it before an indefinite singular noun:

kull yoom	*every day*
kull sanah	*every year*

kull bank fii-h makíinat Sarf *every bank has a cash machine.*
kull waaHid laazim yiSraf miyyat doolaar *each one must change $100.*

Insight

kull sanah (or **:aam**, another word for *year*) **w inta bi-khair** is the Arabic felicitation for any annual event (birthdays, Eids, etc.), usually *Happy* . . . (birthday, Christmas etc.) in English. The literal meaning is *every year and (may) you (be) well.*

There are two ways to use **kull** for *all*:

(a) Follow it by a plural noun with either the definite article or a suffix pronoun:
kull al-bunuuk maftuuHah yoom al-ithnain *All the banks are open on Monday(s).*
kull-hum kaanu mashghuuliin ams *They were all busy yesterday.*

(b) Put the plural noun first, and then follow it with **kull** + the agreeing suffix pronoun referring back to the noun:
al-bunuuk kull-ha maftuuHah *The banks are all open (*lit. *the banks all [of] them [are] open).*
al-ghuraf kull-ha maHjuuzah *The rooms are all booked (*lit. *the rooms all [of] them [are] booked).*

maHjúuz *booked, reserved* V

Insight

Remember that the plurals of non-humans are considered feminine singular in Arabic, hence the **-ha** (*her*) suffix used in the above examples to refer to *banks* and *rooms* respectively. For humans you use **-hum** (*them*):

al-muwaDHDHafiin kull-hum mawjuudiin *The officials are all here.*

2 *If*

The three words for *if* (**idha, in** and **law/loo**) are used virtually interchangeably in colloquial Gulf Arabic. The last suggests a lesser (or even zero) chance of the condition being fulfilled, but is also used in the common polite phrase **law samaHt** (*please, if you please, if you would permit*).

A strange thing about *if* sentences in Arabic is that the verb is often, though not always, put in the past tense (even though the action hasn't happened yet, or might never happen).

All three words are often followed by **kaan** with no particular change in meaning. Here are a few examples:

idha jaa rashiid khabbirii-h :an barnaamij bukrah *If Rashid comes, tell him about tomorrow's programme.*
in kaan :ind-ak chaikaat siyaaHiyyah laazim tiSraf-ha *If you have travellers' cheques, you'll have to cash them.*
law kaan sawwa kidha, kaan aHsan *If he had done this, it would have been better.*
loo kunt :araft haadha, maa ruHt *If I had known this, I wouldn't have gone.*
idha tiruuH ash-shaarjah, laazim tizuur al-matHaf al-jadiid *If you go to Sharjah, you should visit the new museum.*

And the classic:

in shaa' Al-laah lit. *if God wished,* (i.e. *wishes)*

---

tamriinaat (Exercises) تمرينات

1 You want to post some mail home. How would you ask the cost of the following:
(a) a letter to the USA?
(b) a postcard to Australia?
(c) a parcel to the Emirates?
(d) a letter to Saudi Arabia?

2 Now how would you ask for the following stamps:

(a) three at 150 fils
(b) one at two dinars
(c) five at one dirham
(d) 20 at half a riyaal
(e) six at 200 baizas

3 Each line of the puzzle represents one of the words below in Arabic. They must be entered in the correct order to reveal in column A another word a tourist might need at the bank.

cheque
stamp
letter
postcard
exchange rate
bank
dollar
credit card
moneychanger

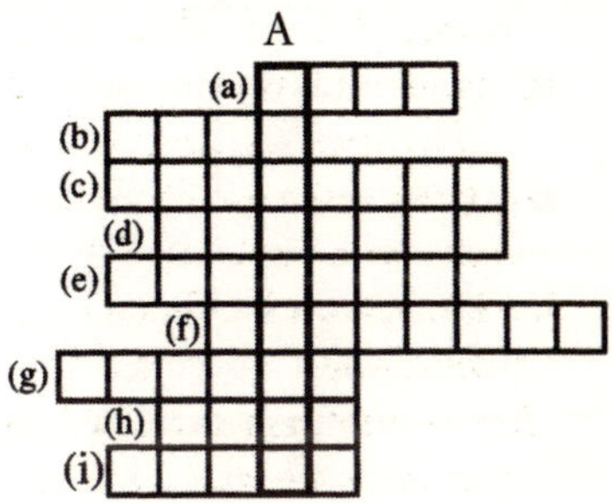

🔊 **CD 2, TR 6, 5:02**

4 You are on holiday in Dubai, and you ask a friend where to go to change some money. You complete your side of the conversation.

Sadiig-ak	ayyah :umlah :ind-ak?
inta	*Say sterling pounds.*
Sadiig-ak	tiriid tiSraf kam?
inta	*Say £250.*
Sadiig-ak	aHsan tiruuH :ind aS-Sarraafiin fi s-suug
inta	*Ask why.*

Sadiig-ak mumkin taakhudh si:r aHsan.
inta *Ask which one of them you should go to.*
Sadiig-ak illi :ala l-yisaar jamb al-baab. huwwa :ind-uh aHsan si:r

illi *who, the one who, which*

---

al-khaTT al-:árabi (Arabic script) الخط العربي

This time you have **:ain** and **ghain**, again distinguished by one dot above the second letter:

Name	Initial	Medial	Final	Separate	Pronunciation
:ain	عـ	ـعـ	ـع	ع	:
ghain	غـ	ـغـ	ـغ	غ	gh

To distinguish a nucleus form here requires some imagination, so it's better just to remember that the medial and final forms have a different shape from the initial and separate ones.

For the sounds, refer to the section on the alphabet at the beginning of the book and, more importantly, listen to native speakers and emulate them. Here are some examples in words you already know:

عندي	**:ind-i**	*I have*
يعني	**ya:ni**	*that is, um . . .*
صغير	**Saghiir**	*small*
غالي	**ghaali**	*expensive*

This is a good opportunity to look at one of the most common forms for first names in Arabic. The names of God (Allah) are said to number 99, and an age-old naming formula is to precede one of these divine epithets with the word **:abd** (Arabic عبد), *worshipper* (*of*).

The popular English abbreviation 'Abdul' does not exist in Arabic.

The name Abdallah or Abdullah meaning *worshipper* of *Allah* has an irregular spelling, with the **alif** of the long **a**-vowel in Arabic being missed out: عبد الله (**:abd al-laah**).

The same thing occurs in another common name **:abd ar-raHmáan** (عبد الرحمن) Abd ul-Rahman which features the same omission of the **alif** to mark the long **-aa**.

Match up the following pairs. The Arabic names all begin with عبد الـ, and the divine attributes of Allah are given in transcription, along with their approximate meanings.

A ar-raHiim (*the Merciful*)	١– عبد العزيز
B an-naaSir (*the Victorious*)	٢– عبد الغانم
C aS-Sabuur (*the Patient One*)	٣– عبد الجليل
D al-waaHid (*the One*)	٤– عبد المنعم
E al-majiid (*the Magnificent*)	٥– عبد الناصر
F al-ghaanim (*the Bestower of the spoils of war*)	٦– عبد الواحد
G al-jaliil (*the Majestic*)	٧– عبد الصبور
H al-:aziiz (*the Noble*)	٨– عبد المجيد
I ar-raHmaan (*the Compassionate*)	٩– عبد الرحيم
J al-mun:im (*the Giver of blessings*)	١٠– عبد الرحمن

Test yourself

This test covers the main vocabulary, phrases and language points given in Unit 12. If you are not sure about your answers, go back to the dialogues and exercises for some revision, before going on to Unit 13. For the answers, see the **Key to the exercises.**

Put **kull** *each, every, all* and an appropriate suffix pronoun if necessary in the following sentences:

1. ______ waaHid mumkin yit:allam lughah jadiidah
2. aT-Turuq fi l-imaaraat ______ jayyidah
3. an-nisaa' ______ Tabakhuu akl Hagg al-:iid
4. a:Ta Taariq ______ al-awlaad filuus
5. niHna ______ ta:baaniin

Can you do the following?

6. Ask where you can change $200.
7. Say you want to cash a traveller's cheque.
8. Ask how much it costs to post a letter to America.
9. Ask for 5 stamps at 3 dirhams and 2 stamps at 50 fils.
10. Ask if this bank has a cash machine.

13

الى أين؟

li-wain?

Where to?

(Note: the written word for *where* is different from the spoken.)

In this unit you will learn how to

- Tell people to do things
- Take a taxi
- Book and buy bus tickets
- Hire a vehicle
- Buy petrol
- Deal with car problems

New words and phrases

CD 2, TR 7

Listen to the recording.

Hiwaar 1 (Dialogue 1) حوار ١

CD 2, TR 7, 0:16

Janet, a solicitor, is taking a taxi across Kuwait to the office of a client. The driver is not sure exactly where to go and Janet is not too happy about his driving, as he is chatting to her and not watching the traffic.

Janet	khudh baal-ak! min faDHl-ak, khalli baal-ak :ala T-Tariig
sawwaag at-taksi	maa fiih mushkilah
Janet	khaffif as-sur:ah. laa tisuug bi-sur:ah kidha. haadha huwwa sh-shaari: . . . laa, liff yisaar fi sh-shaari: ath-thaani
sawwaag at-taksi	haadha hina? inti mit'akkidah?
Janet	aywa. (*he drives past the street*) fawwatt-uh! irja: shwayyah. (*he reverses*) haadha huwwa, fi l-:imaarah al-kabiirah al-baiDHa hinaak. zain. waggiff hina :ind al-baab.
sawwaag at-taksi	(*stopping the car*) hina maDHbuuT?
Janet	na:am zain. (*getting out*) ana aruuH awaddi risaalah hina w arja: ba:d khamas dagaayig. khallii-k fi s-sayyaarah, laa tisiir makaan.
sawwaag at-taksi	zain. bantaDHir hina.

QUICK VOCAB

baal	*attention*
khudh báal-ak	*take care, be careful*
khálli báal-ak :ála	*pay attention to, watch*
kháffaf, yikháffif (A)	*to lighten, reduce*
súr:ah	*speed*
mit'ákkid	*sure*
rája:, yírja: (A)	*to return, come back, go back*
:ímaarah (-aat)	*apartment building, block*
wággaf, yiwággif (A)	*to stop*
baab (biibáan)	*door*
maDHbúuT	*exact, correct*
sáar, yisíir (B1)	*to go (common alternative to* raaH, yiruuH*)*

(a) Why does Janet complain about the taxi driver's speed?
(b) Where does she tell him to stop?
(c) Where does she tell him to wait?

mulaaHaDHaat (Notes) ملاحظات

1 **fawwatt-uh** (*you've passed it*)
When verbs ending in **-t** take a suffix beginning with **t-**, the letter must be clearly doubled in pronunciation.

2 **haadha huwwa** (*that's it*)

3 **laa tisíir makáan** (*don't go [any] place*)
This dialogue contains some imperatives or commands, telling someone to do or not to do something. These are dealt with in full in the grammar section later in this Unit.

Hiwaar 2 (Dialogue 2) حوار ٢

CD 2, TR 7, 1:20

Nasir, a Saudi student in Riyadh, is going to visit his brother who works in Doha. He can't afford to fly, so he goes to the bus station to enquire about the bus service to Doha.

Nasir	fiih baaS yiruuH ad-dooHa min faDHl-ak?
kaatib	laa, maa fiih baaS yiruuH mubaasharatan. laazim tiHawwil fi l-hufuuf
Nasir	maa yikhaalif. at-tadhkarah bi-kam?
kaatib	dhihaab bass aw dhihaab w iyaab?
Nasir	dhihaab w iyaab
kaatib	miyyah w khamsah w :ishriin riyaal
Nasir	al-baaS yiTla: as-saa:ah kam?
kaatib	as-saa:ah thamaanyah bi DH-DHabl.
Nasir	zain, w mata yooSal ad-dooHa?
kaatib	yooSal al-hufuuf as-saa:ah ithna:shar aDh-Dhuhur, w al-baaS li d-dooHa yooSal as-saa:ah sab:ah w khams dagaayig al-misa.
Nasir	a:Tii-ni tadhkarat dhihaab w iyaab Hagg baakir min faDHl-ak.

QUICK VOCAB

Háwwal, yiHáwwil (A)	*to change*
maa yikháalif	*that's OK, it doesn't matter*
tádhkarah (tadháakir)	*ticket*
dhiháab	*single (ticket,* lit. *going)*
dhiháab w iyáab	*return (ticket,* lit. *going and coming back)*
Tála:, yíTla: (A)	*to leave, depart, go out*
wáSal, yóoSal (A)	*to arrive*

(a) Can you go direct from Riyadh to Doha?
(b) How much is a return ticket?
(c) When does the bus arrive in Doha?

---

mulaaHaDHaat (Notes) ملاحظات

1 fiih baaS yiruuH (*is there a bus that goes*)
No word for *that* or *which* is required in Arabic. This type of sentence is dealt with in Unit 14.

2 maa yikhaalif (*it doesn't matter*)
You also frequently hear the Egyptian Arabic import **maa :aláish** with the same meaning, or the modified form **maa :alái-h.**

Hiwaar 3 (Dialogue 3) حوار ٣

CD 2, TR 7, 2:24

Charlie and Stella are on holiday in Dubai, and they want to rent a car for a few days with some friends they have made in the hotel, so that they can see a little more of the Emirates. First they talk to Muhammad at Reception in their hotel.

Charlie	:ind-na fikrah nasta'jir sayyaarah :ala shaan naruuH khaarij dubay Hatta nashuuf al-balad shwayyah. ta:raf sharikah zainah mumkin nasta'jir min :ind-hum?
Muhammad	khalii-ni afakkir. . . . fiih naas kathiiriin min hina raaHu :ind sharikat al-:aaSimah, laakin ba:DH-hum gaalu inn as:aar-hum ghaalyah shwayyah. laish maa tiruuH sharikat sayyaaraat al-khaliij fii shaari: al-waHdah. haadhi sharikah mashhuurah, w as:aar-hum ma:guulah.
Charlie	nzain, shukran. baruuH as'al-hum.

Charlie and Stella go to Gulf Cars.

al-baayi:	SabaaH al-khair
Charlie	SabaaH an-nuur, nariid nasta'jir sayyaarah. aish min sayyaaraat-kum munaasibah Hagg l-jabal?
al-baayi:	intu kam nafar?
Charlie	arba:at anfaar
al-baayi:	al-aHsan yikuun sayyaarah fii-ha dabal. :indi toyoota landkraizir, sayyaarah naDHiifah mumtaazah, tisiir ayy makaan.
Charlie	fii-ha kandaishan?
al-baayi:	Tab:an, as-sayyaaraat maal-na kull-ha fii-ha kandaishan
Charlie	w al-iijáar kam fi l-yoom?
al-baayi:	thalaath miyyah w khamsiin dirham. tiriiduun-ha li muddat aish?
Charlie	nariid-ha min yoom al-khamiis aS-SabaaH li ghaayat yoom as-sabt aS-SabaaH idha kaan mumkin.

al-baayi:	zain. a:Tii-kum si:r makhSuuS. sitt miyyat dirham li l-muddah kull-ha
Charlie	haadha ma:a t-ta'miin?
al-baayi:	na:am, w thalaath miyyat kiilomitr majjaanan
Charlie	zain. mumkin tiwaddii s-sayyaarah :ind-na fi l-fundug aw laazim najii najiib-ha min hina?
al-baayi:	nawaddii-ha l-fundug. maa fii mushkilah.

QUICK VOCAB

fíkrah (afkáar)	*thought, idea*
kháarij	*outside*
Hátta	*in order to, so that*
bálad (biláad)	*country (see notes)*
naas	*people*
al-khalíij (al-:árabi)	*the (Arabian) Gulf*
mashhúur	*famous, well known*
ma:gúul	*reasonable*
sá'al, yís'al (A)	*to ask*
báayi:	*salesman*
munáasib	*suitable, convenient*
náfar (anfáar)	*individual, person*
dábal	*4-wheel drive*
naDHíif	*clean, in good condition*
mumtáaz	*excellent, super (petrol)*
makhSúuS	*special*
ta'míin	*insurance*
majjáanan	*free, gratis*

(a) Why do Charlie and Stella want to hire a vehicle?
(b) What suggestion does the car hire man make?
(c) Is insurance included in the rate?

---

mulaaHaDHaat (Notes) ملاحظات

1 ba:DH (*some*)
This is used before a plural noun with the definite article.

2 **sharikat al-:aaSimah** (*Capital Company*, lit. *Company [of the] Capital*)

The names of trading companies in the Gulf are often composed of phrases like this (possessives) followed by **li** (*for*), then the name of their commercial activity:

sharikat aHmad ash-shanfari li bai: as-saa:aat	*Ahmed al-Shanfari Watch Company* (lit. *company [of] Ahmed al-Shanfari for [the] sale [of] watches*).

3 **inn** (*that*)

The use of **inn** is very common after verbs such as **gaal** (*to say*), **khabbar** (*to tell, inform*) and **iftákar** (*to think, consider, be of the opinion that*). This differs from the verb in the text **yifakkir**, which means *to think* in the sense of *to devote thought to*.

iftakart inn-ha waSalat ams	*I thought she arrived yesterday.*
khallíi-ni afakkir	*Let me think.*

4 **balad**

The meaning of this word has to be interpreted from the context. It can mean *town, village or country*. Its plural **bilaad** can mean *towns, villages* or (singular) *country, nation state* and this again has a further plural form **buldáan** which can only mean *countries, nations, states*.

5 **al-aHsan yikuun** (*the best thing would be to*)

This is the present tense of **kaan** in its usual meaning *will be, would be*.

6 **dabal** (*4-wheel drive*).

This apparently comes from *double*, although the term is not used in this context in English. Gulf Arabic has many words (mainly technical) borrowed from English (and other languages) like **kandaishin** (*air conditioning*), also **ai sii** (*AC*) and the proper Arabic word **takyiif**, and **fáinri** (*refinery*).

7 **kam nafar . . . arba:at anfaar** (*How many persons? . . . Four people*)

This word is only used when counting individuals.

8 **al-iijáar** (*the hire, rent*)
On a taxi you might see a slightly different word, **li-l-ujrah** (*for hire*).

---

ma:luumaat thaqaafiyyah (Cultural tips) معلومات ثقافية

In some Gulf countries bus services are very sporadic, mainly transporting foreign workers to and from the cities, but in others there is a well-established bus network with a frequent service.

Taxis are either service, or standard. Service means that the taxi runs along a (roughly) prescribed route and will pick up people if there are spare seats and charge a (roughly) standard fare. If you want the taxi solely for yourself or your party, you must specify this by saying **ariid ingáij** – another quaint borrowing presumably from English *engage*. This is, of course, more expensive and you should agree the fare with the driver before getting into the car:

tiruuH . . . (name of destination) **bi-kam?** (*How much to . . . ?*)

---

ta:biiraat haammah (Key phrases) تعبيرات هامة

CD 2, TR 7, 4:13

Telling someone to do something

tfaDHDHal	*Come in! Sit down! Take (what I am offering you)!*
tfaDHDHal istariiH	*Sit down, relax.*
ta:aal hina	*Come here!*
ijlis or **ig:ad**	*Sit down!*
khaffif as-sur:ah	*Go slower.*
ruuH bi-sur:ah	*Go fast, quickly.*
waggif as-sayyaarah hina	*Stop the car here.*
khallii-k fi s-sayyaarah	*Wait/stay (*lit. *leave yourself) in the car.*

Asking about going somewhere

inta faaDHi/mashghuul? *Is this taxi (*lit. *'you' meaning the driver) free/busy?*
tiruuH fundug aS-SaHra bi-kam min faDHl-ak? *How much to the Sahara Hotel please?*
waddii-ni l-maTaar min faDHl-ak *Take me to the airport, please.*

Asking about bus or train tickets

kaif aruuH ash-shaarjah min faDHl-ak? *How do I get to Sharjah please?*
thalaath tadhaakir dhihaab w iyaab ila madiinat al-kuwait *Three return tickets to Kuwait City.*
tadhkarah waaHidah li r-riyaaDH, daraja uula *One first-class ticket to Riyadh.*
tadhkaratain li l-hufuuf darajah thaanyah *Two second-class tickets to Hofuf.*

úula fem. of **áwwal** (*first*) V

Asking about bus and train times

awwal baaS li abu DHabi s-saa:ah kam? *When is the next (*lit. *first) bus to Abu Dhabi?*
awwal giTaar li l-hufuuf yiTla: as-saa:ah kam? *When does the next train to Hofuf leave?*
yooSal as-saa:ah kam min faDHl-ak? *When does it arrive, please?*
al-baaS yiTla: min wain? *Where does the bus leave from?*

giTáar *train* V

Hiring a vehicle

ariid asta'jir sayyaarah fii-ha dabal *I would like to hire a 4WD vehicle.*
kam al-iijáar li yoom waaHid/yoomain/usbuu:? *How much is the rental for a day/two days/a week?*
mumkin adfa: bi l-kart? *Can I pay by credit card?*
tfaDHDHal al-laisan maal-i *Here is my driving licence*

haadha s-si:r ma:a t-ta'miin? *Does this price include insurance?*
at-tanki matruus? *Does it have a full tank?* (lit. *is the tank full?*)
mumkin aakhudh as-sayyaarah min al-maTaar? *Can I collect the car from the airport?*
mumkin tiwaddii-ha l-fundug maal-i? *Can you deliver it to my hotel?*
as-saa:ah kam laazim arajji:-ha? *What time must I return it?*

QV

dáfa:, yídfa: (A)	*to pay*
tánki	*tank (car)*
matrúus	*full*
rájja:, yirájji: (A)	*to return something, give it back*

Buying petrol

:abbii-ha :aadi *Fill it up with regular.*
ariid :ishriin laitir mumtaaz *I want 20 litres of premium.*
ariid khamsah galoonaat bi-duun raSaaS *5 gallons of lead-free.*
ariid daizil bi khamasta:shar diinaar *15 dinars' worth of diesel.*

(Petrol is sold by the gallon in the UAE but by the litre elsewhere.)

QUICK VOCAB

banzíin	*petrol*
:ábba, yi:ábbi (C)	*to fill*
:áadi	*regular (petrol)*
láitir, lítir (-aat)	*litre*
galóon (-aat)	*gallon*
raSáaS	*lead (metal)*
dáizil	*diesel*

Problems with the car

fiih shíishah gariibah min hina? *Is there a petrol station near here?*
wain agrab garaaj/warshah maal sayyaaraat? *Where is the nearest garage/car workshop?*
as-sayyaarah maal-i kharbaanah *My car is broken down.*
:ind-i banchar *I have a puncture.*
mumkin tichayyik at-taayraat? *Can you check the tyres please?*
aftakir inn al-laitaat kharbaanah *I think the lights are broken.*
mumkin tiSalliH l-i s-sayyaarah l-yoom min faDHl-ak? *Can you repair the car for me today please?*

QUICK VOCAB

shíishah/maHaTTat banzíin	*filling station*
ágrab	*nearer, nearest*
wárshah (-aat)	*workshop*
bánchar	*puncture*
chayyák, yicháyyik (A)	*to check*
biráik	*brakes*
taayr (-aat)	*tyre*
áayil	*(engine) oil*
lait (-aat)	*light (of a car)*
SállaH, yiSálliH (A)	*to repair*

núqaT naHwíyyah (Grammar points) نقط نحوية

1 Imperative verbs: how to form them

The imperative form of the verb is used when you want to tell someone to do something, and it is easy to form in Arabic. Verbs in this book are given in the *he*-form, with the past tense followed by the present: **raaH, yiruuH** (*to go*). (The verb type given in brackets after the verb doesn't matter in this connection.)

First isolate the present stem of the verb by removing the **yi-** prefix from the present tense: **yiruuH** gives **ruuH**.

If the word resulting from this process does not begin with two consonants, you have the masculine singular imperative form, as here: **ruuH** (*go!*).

However, if it does begin with two consonants, you have to add a helping vowel prefix, usually **i-** as in: **intaDHar, yintaDHir** (*to wait*).

Removing the **yi-** gives **ntaDHir**, which begins with two consonants (**n** and **t**), so you have to supply an initial **i-**: **intaDHir** (*wait!*).

Insight

The term 'beginning with two consonants' must be interpreted as two Arabic consonants. Combinations of English letters used to represent one Arabic consonant must be regarded as one and not two. The combination letters used in this book are: **th, kh, dh, sh, DH, gh** and occasionally **ch**.

For example the verb **khabbar, yikhabbir** yields **khabbir**. This begins with one Arabic consonant, and therefore is the correct imperative form and does not require any helping initial vowel.

A few common verbs vary slightly from these rules in forming the imperative. These are:

(a) verbs whose past tense begins with **w**.
The present tense of these begins with **yoo-** and the imperative is formed by dropping the **y-**. The two most common verbs of this type are:
waSal, yooSal (*to arrive*); imperative **ooSal**
wagaf, yoogaf (*to stop*); imperative **oogaf**

(b) two common verbs which have a shortened imperative:
akal, yaakul (*to eat*); imperative **kul** (the **yaa-** is dropped)
akhadh, yaakhudh (*to take*); imperative **khudh**

(c) the verb **jaa, yiiji** (*to come*) which has an imperative totally unrelated to the verbal form: **ta:aal**.

2 Gender

The form obtained by the above method is the masculine singular imperative, i.e. used when you are telling one male to do something. If you are talking to a woman, add **-i** to the masculine form (if it doesn't have one already, in which case one absorbs the other):

ruuH to a man	**ruuHi** to a woman	(*go!*)
intaDHir	**intaDHiri**	(*wait!*)
khudh	**khudhi**	(*take!*)

khalli from **khalla, yikhalli** (*to leave*) is the same for both because it already has a final **-i.**

For the plural, men or women, add a final **-u,** again omitting any final vowel present: **ruuHu, intaDHiru, khudhu, khallu** (from sing. **khalli,** final -i dropped).

Insight

The above are the base forms and will always be understood, but you will hear slightly different versions in different areas of the region. The golden rule is to imitate the native speakers around you.

3 Negative imperatives

The above forms are not used when you are telling someone not to do something. In this case use **laa** + the ordinary present form of the verb.

kul	*Eat!*
laa taakul/taak(u)li/taak(u)lu	*Don't eat!*

tamriinaat (Exercises) تمرينات

CD 2, TR 7, 5:07

1 You are on business in Dubai and decide to hire a car. In the car hire office you overhear an Emirati asking the car rental assistant

some questions about renting a car. What three questions does he ask? Listen to the recording, or read the transcript.

2 You need to buy fuel and have stopped at a service station. How would you ask the attendant for the following in Arabic?
(a) fill up with diesel
(b) 15 litres of premium
(c) RO5 of regular?

3 Your car needs attention. How would you ask the attendant:
(a) to check the oil and water
(b) if he can mend a puncture for you?
(c) if he can repair it today?

4 Look at the bus timetable opposite and say if the following statements are true or false.
(a) al-baaS yiTla: min masgaT as saa:ah thamaanyah wa nuSS iS-SubaH
(b) yooSal dubay gabil as-saa:ah waaHidah w nuSS ba:d aDH-DHuhur
(c) muu mumkin naHaSSil akil fii SuHaar
(d) fii shahar ramaDHaan al-kariim al-baaS min masgaT yooSal burj aS-SaHwa as-saa:ah :asharah S-SubaH
(e) si:r tadhkarat dhihaab w iyaab miyyah w khamsiin dirham

HáSSal, yiHáSSil (A) — *get, find, obtain*
shahar ramaDHaan al-kariim — *the holy month of Ramadan*
burj aS-SaHwa — *Sahwa Tower*

5 Saif, an Omani, wants to take a taxi from Muttrah to Muscat. He has to go to the main post office. Fill in the missing words of his side of the conversation with the taxi driver, choosing an appropriate word from the box.

Oman - Dubai Express

Daily Timetable

Muscat, Ruwi Bus Station	dep	0730	1630
Seeb International Airport		0755	1655
Sahwa Tower		0800	1700
Mabailah BP Station		0810	1710
Barka Roundabout		0830	1730
Musannah Roundabout		f 0845	f 1745
Khaburah Roundabout		f 0930	f 1830
Saham Roundabout		f 0945	f 1845
Sohar - Shell Station R	arr	1005	1905
Sohar - Shell Station R	dep	1020	1920
Shinas turnoff		f 1100	f 2000
Wajajah - Border Post	arr	1125	2025
Dubai, Dnata Car park	arr	1325	2225
			★
Dubai, Dnata Car park	dep	0730	1730
Wajajah - Border Post	arr	0900	1900
Shinas turnoff		f 1010	f 2010
Sohar - Shell Station R	arr	1050	2050
Sohar - Shell Station R	dep	1105	2105
Saham Roundabout		f 1125	f 2125
Khaburah Roundabout		f 1140	f 2140
Musannah Roundabout		f 1225	f 2225
Barka Roundabout		1240	2240
Mabailah Shell Station		1300	2300
Sahwa tower		1310	2310
Seeb International Airport		1315	2315
Muscat, Ruwi Bus Station	arr	1340	2340

R - *refreshment stop*

f - *flag stop, bus stops on request only, timings approximate*

HR - *in the holy month of Ramadan departs at 1930 and runs 2 hours later throught*

Fares :	***Adult RO***	***Single Dhs***
Muscat - Dubai	***9***	***85***
Muscat - Sohar	***5***	***-***
Sohar - Dubai	***4***	***35***
Return Fare Muscat - Dubai	***16***	***150***
FAMILY FARE (upto 2 adults and 2 children)	***36***	***350***

Saif	inta ______?
sawwaag at-taksi	laa, ana faaDHi
Saif	mumkin tiwaddii-ni ______, min faDHl-ak?
sawwaag at-taksi	haadha bi riyaalain

The taxi is rather slow, and Saif is impatient

Saif	ruuH ______ min-faDHl-ak
sawwaag at-taksi	muu mumkin aruuH bi-sur:ah, fiih sayyaaraat kathiirah fi T-Tariig

They arrive and Saif is only going to be a few minutes.

Saif	______ fi s-sayyaarah, ana barja: ba:d shwayyah
sawwaag at-taksi	zain, ana bantaDHir hina

Saif has more business in Muscat.

Saif	ruuH ______ wa ______ yisaar hina
sawwaag at-taksi	yisaar, zain
Saif	______ as-sayyaarah hina. kam tiriid?
sawwaag at-taksi	riyaalain min-faDHl-ak

siidah	**waggif**
khallii-k	**maktab al-bariid**
liff	**bi-sur:ah**
mashghuul	

6 The sign inside the circle, in the photograph opposite, says:

للأجرة

١٨٨٨/مسقط

مسقط

(a) Does the sign in the top half of the circle say: Taxi/Al-Bourj Taxis/For Hire?
(b) Is the number of the taxi: 1888/7771/1777?
(c) Is the taxi registered in: Muscat/Muttrah/Oman?

al-khaTT al-:árabi (Arabic script) الخط العربي

The pair of letters to learn in this unit are **faa'** and **qaaf**. These are both joiners and fairly simple to write. This time they both have dots, one and two respectively. They are identical in all forms except the final and the separate, in which the **faa'** has its final flourish or tail on the line, but the **qaaf** has a more curved tail extending below the line.

Name	Initial	Medial	Final	Separate	Pronunciation
faa'	فـ	ـفـ	ـف	ف	f
qaaf	قـ	ـقـ	ـق	ق	g

Here are another ten words to try:

١- نفر

٢- فندق

٣- قبل

٤- فرنسا

٥- فلوس

٦- غرفة

٧- مسقط

٨- رقم

٩- دقيقة

١٠- قريب

Test yourself

This test covers the main vocabulary, phrases and language points given in Unit 13. If you are not sure about your answers, go back to the dialogues and exercises for some revision, before going on to Unit 14. For the answers, see the **Key to the exercises.**

Can you provide the correct form of the imperative verbs in the following sentences? The verbs are given for you in the past tense *he* form. You will need the following new vocabulary:

iksbráis	*express*
wájabah (-aat)	*meal*
khafíif	*light*

1 yaa Sadiiq-l (akhadh) haadha l-filuus
2 yaa faaTimah, (jaa) hin bi-sur:ah
3 (jalas) hinaak min faDHl-kum
4 laa (takallam) ingliizi, yaa maryam
5 laa (:abba) haadhi s-sayaarah daizal

You and a friend want to travel by bus from Doha to Abu Dhabi tomorrow. Complete your half of the conversation with the bus clerk.

6 *Say good morning. Ask if there is a bus to Abu Dhabi tomorrow afternoon.*
kaatib na:am, al-iksbrais as-saa:ah khamsah w-nuSS

7 *Ask what time it gets to Abu Dhabi.*
kaatib yooSal as-saa:ah tisa:a illa thilth bi l-lail

8 *Ask if it stops anywhere so that you can buy food.*
kaatib na:am, yoogaf fii ruwais w mumkin tiHaSSil wajabaat khafiifah hinaak fii maHaTTat al-banziin

9 *Ask how much a single ticket costs.*
kaatib Hida:ashar riyaal

10 *Say you'd like two single tickets.*
kaatib ithnain wa-:ishriin riyaal, min faDHl-ak

14

في البيت

fi l-bait

In this house

In this unit you will learn how to

- Talk about where you live
- Talk about renting a flat or house
- Get things made for you

New words and phrases

CD 2, TR 8

Listen to the recording.

Hiwaar 1 (Dialogue 1) حوار ١

CD 2, TR 8, 0:14

Salim and his wife Amal are considering renting a larger flat in Dubai than the one they live in at present. They have been to see one, and they are discussing it with Salim's parents Abdel Aziz and Suad.

Abdel Aziz	guuli aish ra'y-ich fi sh-shaggah
Amal	:ajabat-na kathiir. hiyya akbar min ash-shaggah illi nasta'jir-ha l-Hiin bi kathiir.
Abdel Aziz	wain-ha?
Salim	al-:imaarah jamb :imaarat-na. ash-shaggah fi d-door ar-raabi:, w fiih shaggatain kamaan fii nafs ad-door
Saud	fii-ha kam ghurfah?
Salim	fiih majlis w ghurfat akil, w thalaath ghuraf noom, w maTbakh w Hammaamain, w Saalah kabiirah
Abdel Aziz	wa l-iijaar kam fi sh-shahar?
Salim	al-iijaar thalaathat aalaaf dirham, ya:ni akthar mimma nadfa:-uh l-Hiin bi-khams miyyah, w idha akhadhnáa-ha, laazim nadfa: iijaar shahrain muggadam
Abdel Aziz	wa aish bitsawwuun?
Salim	banfakkir shwayyah. muu laazim nakhabbar SaaHib al-milk al-Hiin

QUICK VOCAB

májlis (majáalis)	*sitting, reception room*
ghúrfat (ghúraf) akil	*dining room*
ghúrfat (ghúraf) noom	*bedroom*
máTbakh (maTáabikh)	*kitchen*
Sáalah	*hall*
mugaddam	*in advance*
SáaHib al-milk	*landlord*

(a) Which floor is the flat on?
(b) How many rooms are there apart from the hall?
(c) How much will they have to pay in advance?

mulaaHaDHaat (Notes) ملاحظات

1 **akbar … bi kathiir** (lit. *bigger by much,*) i.e. much bigger. Note the same construction relating to the higher rent, *more than .... by.*

2 **ghurfat noom** (lit. *room of sleep, bedroom*) and **ghurfat akil.** (lit. *room of food*).
These are two more examples of the possessive construction showing the hidden **t**.

3 **mimma**
Short for **min maa** (*than what*).

---

ma:luumaat thaqaafiyyah (Cultural tips) معلومات ثقافية

Although traditional Arab houses are still to be seen in villages, homes in the Gulf cities are mainly in apartment blocks either built on new ground or on the sites of traditional buildings which have sadly been demolished.

The apartments in these buildings are basically western style, with furniture in the taste of the area, and plenty of mirrors and ornaments. More affluent families live in detached houses or villas.

Hiwaar 2 (Dialogue 2) حوار ٢

CD 2, TR 8, 1:40

Abdel Aziz and Suad are wondering now about the furnishing of the flat.

Abdel Aziz	ash-shaggah mafruushah?
Salim	laa. yikuun laazim najiib al-athaath maal-na. w iHtimaal yikuun laazim nashtari karaasi jadiidah Hagg al-majlis. huwwa majlis kabiir waasi: w al-karaasi illi :ind-na al-Hiin Saghiirah
Suad	aish fiih min ajhizah kahrabaa'iyyah?
Amal	fiih ghassaalah, thallaajah w Tabbáakhah jadiidah. SaaHib al-milk jaab waaHidah jadiidah li-ann as-sukkaan illi min gabil kassarúu-ha

Salim	fiih takyiif markazi, w fiih marwaHah fi l-majlis Hagg ash-shita
Abdel Aziz	wa s-sayyaarah maal-ak, wain tiHuTT-ha?
Salim	taHit. fiih garaaj kabiir taHt al-:imaarah, w fiih miS:ad yiwaSSil-ak foog li sh-shaggah.

QUICK VOCAB

mafrúush	*furnished*
aatháath	*furniture*
jiháaz (ájhizah)	*appliance, piece of equipment*
káhrab(a)	*electricity*
kahrabáa'i	*electrical*
ghassáalah (-aat)	*washing machine*
thalláajah (-aat)	*refrigerator*
Tabbáakhah (-aat)	*cooker*
wáasi:	*spacious*
li'ánn	*because*
kássar, yikássir (A)	*to break, smash*
márkazi	*central*
marwáHah (maráawiH)	*fan*
HaTT, yiHúTT' (B2)	*to put*
táH(i)t	*underneath, below, downstairs*
garáaj	*garage*
foog	*above, upstairs*
wáSSal, yiwáSSil (A)	*to transport, take*

True or false?

(a) They don't need to buy new chairs
(b) There is a new fridge
(c) There is a fan in the living room only
(d) There is a lift in the building

mulaaHaDHaat (Notes) ملاحظات

1 The general word for *furniture* is **aatháath**.
Other items you might have in a house are:

QUICK VOCAB

maiz (amyáaz)	*table*
saríir (saráayir)	*bed*
raff (rufúuf)	*shelf*
kábat (-aat)	*cupboard, wardrobe*
miráayah (-aat)	*mirror*
lámbah (-aat)	*lamp*
lóoHah (-aat)	*(framed) picture*
mighsalah	*washbasin/sink*
shárshaf (sharáashif)	*sheet*
barnúuS (baraníiS)	*blanket*
sitáarah (satáayir)	*curtain*
zoolíyyah (zawáali)	*carpet*
SáH(a)n (SuHúun)	*plate*
giláas (glaasáat)	*glass*
Sufríyyah (Safáari)	*pan*
gáfshah (gfáash)	*spoon*
sikkíin (sakaakíin)	*knife*
chingáal (chanagíil)	*fork*

2 yikuun laazim (*it will be necessary, will have to*). Remember that **yikuun** always has a future or potential meaning.

Insight

marwaHah is the Arabic word for *fan* but one frequently hears the Indian word **pánkah** for a *ceiling fan.*

Hiwaar 3 (Dialogue 3) حوار ٣

CD 2, TR 8, 2:45

Amal and her mother are in a furnishing store ordering curtains for the new flat. They have been looking at materials, and Amal has decided what she would like. She has taken in another pair for the shop to copy.

Amal	haadha l-akhDHar hina gumaash mumtaaz. yi:jab-ni. al-mitir bi-kam?
SaaHib al-maHall	haadha waajid zain. al-mitir bi thalaathiin dirham, wa t-tafSiil khamsah w :ishriin.
Amal	haadha kathiir. mumkin tisawwíi-li takhfiiDH?
SaaHib al-maHall	zain, a:Tíi-ch takhfiiDH :ishriin fi l-miyyah. arba:ah w :ishriin dirham, w :ishriin Hagg at- tafSiil
Amal	zain, nariid-ha haadha sh-shakil. (*She shows him the old pair*) mumkin tisawwíi-ha mithil haadhi?
SaaHib al-maHall	mumkin tikhalli waaHidah :ind-na Hatta na:raf shakl-ha bi DH-DHabT?
Amal	haadha l-magaas illi ariid-uh Hagg al-majlis, w ariid haadha l-gumaash al-azrag Hagg ghurfat an-noom. haadha guTun, laa?
SaaHib al-maHall	ai na:am, guTun
Amal	mata yikuun jaahiz?
SaaHib al-maHall	mumkin . . . yoom al-arba:a al-gaadim
Amal	mumkin tisawwi as-sataayir al-khaDHrah awwal? yimkin yoom as-sabt?
SaaHib al-maHall	mmmm . . . haadha Sa:b shwayyah. zain, nakhallaS al-khaDHra yoom as-sabt, wa th-thaanyah yoom al-arba:a
Amal	shukran

QUICK VOCAB

tafSíil	*making, fashioning (esp. with material)*
takhfíiDH	*discount*
haadha sh-shák(i) l	*this form, shape; like this*
magáas	*size*
gúTun	*cotton*
khállaS, yikhálliS (A)	*to finish, complete something*

(a) How much discount does Amal get for the material?
(b) What colour has she chosen for the bedroom?
(c) When will the living-room curtains be ready?

mulaaHaDHaat (Notes) ملاحظات

1 **SaaHib al-maHall**
Larger shops are called **maHáll** (**-aat**). The word **dukkáan** (**dakaakíin**) is applied to smaller enterprises, stalls in the market, etc.

2 **:ishriin fi l-miyyah** *20 in the hundred, i.e. 20%*

3 **khaDHra** (*green*)
Remember the adjectives for the basic colours change their form slightly in the feminine; **ázrag** behaves in the same way, fem. **zárga**.

ma:luumaat thaqaafiyyah (Cultural tips) معلومات ثقافية

Whereas we, in the UK or the States, buy most of our clothes and furnishings ready made, people in the Middle East are accustomed to having things made for them, often at extremely low prices, by an army of craftsmen.

Tailors will measure you and make you a suit in a couple of days, dressmakers can make a dress overnight, and curtains similarly can be made up in a day or two.

There is a huge choice of materials from all over the world, and because the cost of making-up is so low, while imported clothes and furnishings are relatively expensive, many people are happy to have some garments made for them. However, the quality of workmanship varies tremendously, and the best tailors are found by personal recommendation.

ta:biiraat haammah (Key phrases) تعبيرات هامة

Asking about renting a villa or flat

nariid nasta'jir shaggah/bait *We would like to rent a flat/a house.*
al-bait/ash-shaggah mafruush/-ah? *Is the house/flat furnished?*

fiih kam ghurfah? *How many rooms are there?*
al-iijaar ma:a l-kahraba? *Is the electricity included in the rent?*
al-iijaar kam? *How much is the rent?*
idha akhadhna l-filla, laazim nadfa: iijaar shahar migaddam? *If we take the villa, will we have to pay one month's rent in advance?*

fíllah (fílal)	*villa*	V

Talking about where you live

naskun fii shaggah/filla	*We live in a flat/villa.*
namlik-ha/nasta' jir-ha	*We own/rent it.*
fii-ha sab: ghuraf	*It has seven rooms*
:ind-na . . .	*We have a . . .*
majlis	*living-room*
ghurfat akil	*dining-room*
maTbakh	*kitchen*
Hammaam	*bathroom*
ghurfat noom	*bedroom*
Saalah	*hall*
garaaj	*garage*
Hadiigah	*garden*

málak, yímlik (A)	*to own*	V
Hadíigah (Hadáayig)	*garden*	

Asking someone to make something for you

mumkin tifaSSil l-i badlah/lubsah/sataayir? *Can you make a suit/dress/pair of curtains for me?*
mumkin tisawwi waaHid mithil haadha? *Can you copy this for me? (lit. make one like this).*
ariid-uh agSar/aTwal/akbar/aSghar shwayyah *I want it a bit shorter/longer/bigger/smaller.*
mumkin tikhalliS-uh yoom al-khamiis? *Can you finish it by Thursday?*
mata yikuun jaahiz? *When will it be ready?*

fáSSal, yifáSSil (A)	*to make, fashion, tailor*	V
badlah (-aat)	*(man's) suit*	

lúbsah (-aat) or **fustáan (fasatíin)**	*(lady's) dress*
ágSar	*(shorter)*

---

núqaT naHwíyyah (Grammar points) نقط نحوية

Which, what, whose, etc.

We are not referring to the question words here, but the *which* featuring in sentences such as. 'The book which I ordered came in the post today'. These words are called relative pronouns.

To express such sentences in Arabic, you must distinguish between definite and indefinite concepts. A definite concept in English is one either preceded by *the*, *this*, *that*, etc., (the book) or the name of a person or place (Jack, Muhammad, Abu Dhabi).

(a) If the concept is *definite*, the word for *which, that, who* etc. is **illi**
(b) If it is *indefinite*, no word at all is used.

Insight

illi does not change for gender, etc., and there are no different words for *whom*, *whose* or *which*.

In both cases, the part of the sentence after English *which*, etc. must be able to stand on its own, like a complete utterance.

Definite concept

ash-shaggah illi nasta'jir-ha l-Hiin	*The apartment which we are renting now (the apartment which we-rent it now).*
ad-doktoor illi yishtaghal fii dubay	*The doctor who works in Dubai (the doctor who he-works in Dubai).*

ar-rajjaal illi nasta'jir shaggat-uh	*The man whose apartment we rent (the man who we-rent his apartment).*
al-muhandis illi :ind-uh bait jamb bait-na	*The engineer who has a house next to ours (the engineer who with-him a house next to our house).*

Indefinite concept

shaggah nasta'jir-ha l-Hiin	*An apartment which we are renting now (apartment we-rent it now).*
doktoor yishtaghal fii dubay	*A doctor who works in Dubai (a doctor he-works in Dubai).*
rajjaal nasta'jir shaggat-uh	*A man whose apartment we rent (a man we-rent his apartment).*
Hurmah :ind-ha thalaath banaat	*A woman who has three daughters (a woman with-her three daughters).*

Húrmah (**Haríim**) *woman*
The plural is the source of English 'harem'; also **mára** (**niswáan**) is used (note irregular plural).

---

tamriinaat (Exercises) تمرينات

CD 2, TR 8, 4:28

1 Listen to these four 'people talking about where they live in Bahrain. Make notes about their homes and the rooms they have, and check your answers in the **Key to the exercises.**

shájarah (ashjáar)	*tree*
looz	*almonds*
zuhúur	*flowers*
was(a)T	*middle, centre*

2 Now it's your turn. How would you say that you lived in the following:

(a) A small flat with living-room, one bedroom, kitchen and bathroom?
(b) A villa with lounge, dining-room, four bedrooms, two bathrooms, kitchen and garage?
(c) A house with a large living-room, two bedrooms, bathroom and kitchen?

3 You are moving house. Look at the following words and decide which items will go into which rooms of the house. We have given you suggestions in the **Key to the exercises**.

thallaajah sariir	**sittah karaasi**
tilifizyoon	**baraniiS**
fuwaT	**kabat**
maiz	**Tabbaakhah**

(a) fi l-majlis
(b) fi l-maTbakh
(c) fii ghurfat an-noom
(d) fi l-Hammaam
(e) fi ghurfat al-akil

4 You intend to rent a flat while you are working in Doha. The agent takes you to see one. Ask him the relevant questions below, trying at first not to look at the dialogue or **Key phrases** for help.

(a) Ask how many rooms it has.
(b) Ask if it is furnished.
(c) Ask how much the rent is.
(d) Ask what electrical appliances are included.
(e) Ask how much money you will have to pay in advance if you take the flat.

5 This wordsearch puzzle contains 14 articles which you will find around the house. Clues are written for you in English.

furniture
bed
table
chair
carpet
telephone
lamp
cupboard
fridge
washing machine
spoon
knife
shelf
plate

g	t	s	i	k	k	i	i	n	a
h	h	S	n	r	u	s	H	m	i
a	a	a	n	a	r	r	n	b	r
y	l	H	s	u	m	i	o	h	a
y	l	n	k	s	l	i	o	a	t
i	a	j	a	i	a	r	f	h	h
l	a	m	b	a	h	a	i	s	a
o	j	r	a	f	f	s	l	f	a
o	a	H	t	i	S	t	i	a	t
z	h	s	l	n	z	a	t	g	h

6 You have a favourite shirt but it is wearing out, so you go to the souk and choose some material for a new one. You take it to the tailor and ask him to copy your old shirt. Fill in your side of the conversation, using **Dialogue 3** as a guide.

inta	*Say you like this red material here. Ask how much it costs per metre.*
SaaHib ad-dukkaan	haadha gúTun khaaliS. al-mitir bi khamsah w :ishriin dirham
inta	*Tell him that's a lot. Ask if he can give you a discount.*
SaaHib ad-dukkaan	n-zain. a:Tíi-k takhfiiDH – :ishriin dirham al-mitir
inta	*Say yes, you'll take it.*

Now you go to the tailor, and tell him you want a shirt like this one

inta	*(Show him your old shirt) Ask him if he can copy this shirt for you.*
khayyaaT	maa fiih mushkilah. agiis-ak.

The tailor measures you.

inta	*Tell him you want it a bit longer than the old one.*
khayyaaT	zain

inta	*Ask if he can make it for you quickly.*
khayyaaT	yikuun jaahiz yoom al-aHad al-misa in shaa' Al-laah
inta	*Tell him that's fine.*

kháaliS *pure*
khayyáaT (-iin or **khayaayiiT)** *tailor*
gaas, yigíis (B1) *to measure*
gamíiS (gumSáan) *shirt*

---

al-khaTT al-:árabi (Arabic script) الخط العربي

Our final two letters are the Arabic equivalents of *k* and *h*. These two are not related in shape in any way, and neither has any dots. Both join to the letter on either side, so have the usual four forms. There are no pronunciation difficulties.

Name	Initial	Medial	Final	Separate	Pronunciation
kaaf	كـ	ـكـ	ـك	ك	k
haa'	هـ	ـهـ	ـه	ه	h

kaaf is quite a tall letter. It is best to write the main part of the letter first, then come back to do the 'tail' at the top, or the little squiggle inside at the first lift of the pen, like dotting i's and crossing t's in English. Note also that, while the first two forms lean to the left, the final and separate forms are vertical.

The **haa'** is more difficult. as the forms seem to bear little or no relation to each other. It is quite small – and you have already met its final form in Unit 2 in the guise of the 'hidden **t**' of the feminine ending where it acquires two dots above it. You have also met its initial form in the currency word درهم **dirham** and its plural دراهم **diraahim**. Have another look at some bank notes!

There is one final character, the so-called **hamzah**. Not technically regarded as a letter of he alphabet, it is counted among the 'signs' used for the short vowels and so on. However, unlike them, it is usually represented in written Arabic. Its sound is a glottal stop (like the *t* in the Cockney version of such words as *bottle*). The rules for writing it are complex and it is a common spelling mistake in Arabic. However, so that you can recognise it, the general rules for writing it are given in the alphabet section at the beginning of the book.

Here are some words with **k** and **h** in them for you to transliterate:

١– هللة

٢– كرسي

٣– مملكة

٤– مشهور

٥– شهر

٦– دكان

٧– كهرباء

٨– هواء

٩– فكرة

١٠– تذكرة

Insight

In 7 and 8 the endings are pronounced simply as **-a** (instead of written **-aa'**) in spoken Arabic.

Test yourself

This test covers the main vocabulary, phrases and language points given in Unit 14. If you are not sure about your answers, go back to the dialogues and exercises for some revision. For the answers, see the **Key to the exercises**.

Are these sentences definite or indefinite? Join them, using an appropriate relative pronoun if necessary. Example:

This is house. I live in it. haadha huwa l-bait illi askun fiih

1. Bring the book. I bought it yesterday.
2. This is the apartment. I rented it.
3. I don't like the dress. You bought it.
4. A film. I saw it on Friday.
5. The town is beautiful. I live in it.
6. A large apartment. It has four bedrooms.
7. The plates are on the table. It is in the kitchen.
8. Give me a key. It opens this door.
9. The tailor in the market. His prices are reasonable.
10. A student can speak Arabic. He reads this book!

Key to the exercises

Unit 1

Translations of dialogues

Dialogue 1

Jim	Hello.
Khaled	Hello.
Jim	How are you?
Khaled	Praise be to God well. And you, how are you?
Jim	Well, praise be to God. What's your news?
Khaled	Praise be to God.
Eleanor	Hello.
Khaled	Hello.
Eleanor	How are you?
Khaled	Praise be to God. And you, how are you?
Eleanor	Praise be to God.

Dialogue 2

Muhammad	Good morning.
Khaled	Good morning.
Muhammad	Welcome.
Khaled	Welcome to you.
Muhammad	How are you?
Khaled and Jim	Praise be to God
Muhammad	Goodbye.
Khaled	Goodbye.

Dialogue 3

Jack	Hello.
Muhammad	Hello.
Jack	What's your name?

Muhammad	My name is Muhammad. And you?
Jack	My name is Jack.
Muhammad	Where are you from?
Jack	I'm from England. And you?
Muhammad	I'm from Dubai.
Jack	Welcome.
Muhammad	Welcome to you.
Jack	Good evening.
Faridah	Good evening.
Jack	What's your name?
Faridah	My name is Faridah. And you?
Jack	My name is Jack. Where are you from?
Faridah	I'm from Abu Dhabi. Are you from America?
Jack	No, I'm from England.
Faridah	Welcome.
Jack	Welcome to you.

Dialogue 4

Jack	Hello.
Yasin	Hello. Do you know Arabic?
Jack	Yes I know Arabic. Where are you from?
Yasin	We are from Bahrain. Are you from America?
Jack	No, I am from England. He is from America.
Yasin	Welcome.
Ken	Welcome.

Questions

3 (a) Dubai. (b) Abu Dhabi. (c) America.

4 (a) Do you know Arabic? (b) Bahrain. (c) America.

Exercises

2 (a) :alái-kum (b) al-Hámdu (c) aish (d) ísm-i (e) masáa' (f) Háal-ak (g) sáhlan (h) min

3 as-salaamu: alai-kum/kaif Haal-ich?/bi-khair, al-Hamdu li-l-laah. aish akhbaar-ich?

4 masaa' an-nuur/ahlan bii-ch/al-Hamdu li-llaah/fii amaan Al-laah

5 (a) masaa' al-khair/masaa' an-nuur/kaif Haal-ak?/al-Hamdu li-l-laahbi-khair, wa inta kaif Haal-ak?/al-Hamdu li-l-laah

(b) masaa' al-khair/masaa' an-nuur. kaif Haal-ak?/al-Hamdu li-l-laah. wa intu kaif Haal-kum?/al-Hamdu li-l-laah bi-khair (c) SabaaH al-khair/SabaaH an-nuur. kaif Haal-ich?/al-Hamdu li-l-laah. aish akhbaar-kum?/al-Hamdu li-l-laah. wa inti aish akhbaar-ich?/al-Hamdu li-l-llaah

6 wa :alai-kum as-salaam/ana ism-i . . ., wa inta aish ism-ak?/ana min . . ., wa inta min wain?/ahlan wa sahlan

7 (a) intu min as-sa:uudiyyah? (b) niHna min ash-shaarjah (c) humma min landan? (d) laa, huwwa min ingilterra wa hiyya min al-kuwait (e) inti min al-imaaraat? (f) na:am, ana min abu DHabi

8 (a) How are you? (b) Abu Dhabi (c) Oman (d) aish ism-ich? (e) inti min wain? (f) Do you speak English?

Test yourself

1f, 2h, 3i, 4j, 5a, 6g, 7c, 8e, 9d, 10b

Unit 2

Translations of dialogues

Dialogue 1

Bill	Good morning.
taxi driver	Good morning.
Bill	The Sheraton hotel please.
taxi driver	O.K., God willing.
Bill	Is the hotel far from the airport?
taxi driver	No, it's near. Only ten minutes, no more.
Bill	Thanks.
taxi driver	You're welcome.

Dialogue 2

Bill	Good morning.
Mahmoud	Good morning. How are you?
Bill	Well, praise God. And you?
Mahmoud	Praise God.
Bill	(If you) please, is there a bank near here?

Mahmoud	Yes there is, the National Bank. Do you know Rashid Street?
Bill	No, I don't (know).
Mahmoud	OK. Go out of the door and turn left, then go straight ahead and take the first street on the right. The bank is on the left.
Bill	Thanks very much.
Mahmoud	Don't mention it.

Dialogue 3

Bill	Please, which way is the market?
man	The market is that way, on the left
Bill	And which way is the museum?
man	The museum is in Dubai, not here. This is Deira. Go straight ahead, turn right, and the museum is after the bridge.
Bill	Thanks.
man	Don't mention it.

Dialogue 4

Bill	Good evening.
Shopkeeper	Good evening.
Bill	Is this the road to Ras al-Khaimah?
shopkeeper	Yes. Go straight on from here, pass the hospital, then turn right at the second round-about – no, the third round-about, before the school. Then turn left, after that go straight ahead.
Bill	Is it far from Dubai?
shopkeeper	By God . . . 90 kilometres from here.
Bill	OK. Many thanks. Good bye.
shopkeeper	Goodbye.

Questions

1 (a) no, it's near (b) ten minutes **2** (a) if there is one nearby (b) left (c) first on the right **3** (a) left (b) museum (c) in Dubai, past the bridge **4** (a) afternoon/evening (b) straight ahead (c) third

Exercises

1 (a) iii (b) ii (c) v (d) i (e) iv **2** (a) háadhi (b) haadhóol (c) háadha (d) háadha (e) háadhi

3 (a) Post office. On the right (b) Sea View Hotel. Go straight, then turn left. (c) The port. At the end of the road. (d) The university. After the third round-about (e) The bus station. Take the 2nd street on the right, and the bus station is on the left.

4 (a) khudh; (b) íTla; (c) fáwwit: (d) liff (e) ruuH.

5 (a) duwwáar al-burj min wain min fáDHl-ak? (b) kaif arúuH al-míina min fáDHl-ak? (c) kaif arúuH ábu DHábi min fáDHl-ak? (d) máT:am al-khalíij min wain min fáDHl-ak?

6 (a) al-mustashfa :ala l-yamiin (b) maHaTTat al-baaS siidah (c) khudh thaalith shaari: :ala l-yisaar (d) :ajmaan khamsah kiilo(mitr) min ash-shaarjah (e) liff yamiin, w maktab al-bariid :ala l-yisaar (f) liff yisaar :ind ad-duwwaar

7 (a) at-tilifoon (b) al-matHaf (c) markaz ash-shurTah (d) abu DHabi

8 **Across** 1 jaami: 6 miina 8 maHaTTat al-baaS 10 maTaar 13 markaz tijaari 15 duwwaar 16 fundug 17 saa:ah
Down 2 madrasah 3 mustashfa 4 jaami:ah 5 matHaf 7 maT:am 9 Saydaliyyah 11 jisir 12 gala:ah 14 suug

Test yourself

1e, 2i, 3h, 4g, 5b, 6a, 7j, 8d, 9c, 10f

Unit 3

Translations of dialogues

Dialogue 1

exchange	Which number do you want?
Bill	What is the phone number of the Gulf Trading. Company please?
exchange	The number is 264501.
Bill	Thank you.
exchange	You're welcome.

Dialogue 2

Secretary	Good morning. this is the Gulf Trading Company.
Bill	Good morning. Is Abdel Aziz there please?
Secretary	What is your name please?
Bill	My name is Bill Stewart.
Secretary	One moment, please.
Abdel Aziz	Good morning Bill. Welcome to Dubai. How are you?
Bill	Praise God. What's your news?
Abdel Aziz	Praise God. How is the family?
Bill	Well, praise God. And you, how is your family?
Abdel Aziz	Well thanks. How can I help you?
Bill	Can I come (to you) at the office?
Abdel Aziz	Of course. Give me the phone number of the hotel and I'll ring you in five minutes.
Bill	The number of the hotel is 281573.
Abdel Aziz	And the room number?
Bill	726.
Abdel Aziz	OK. I'll ring you in a little while. Goodbye.
Bill	Goodbye.

Questions

1 a) ayy rágam tiríid? b) 264501 **2** a) 281573 b) 726 c) in 5 minutes

Exercises

1 (a) Dubai 3 – Bahrain 0 (b) Sharjah 7 – Fujairah 2 (c) Kuwait 4 – Abu Dhabi 4 (d) Jeddah 6 – Taif 2 (e) Doha 1 – Hofuf 0

2 (c) wrong, 207; (e) wrong, 231–450; (h) wrong, 872–660.

3

(a)

visitor	aish rágam ghúrfat Husáin :íisa min fáDHl-ak?
clerk	Husáin :íisa fii ghúrfah rágam khamastá:shar fi d-door al-áwwal.
visitor	shúkran

b)	
visitor	aish rágam ghúrfat múuna ábu Háidar min fáDHl-ak?
clerk	múuna ábu Háidar fii ghúrfah rágam miitáin khamsah wa thalaathíin fi d-door ath-thaani.
visitor	shúkran
c)	
visitor	aish rágam ghúrfat ad-doktóor muHámmad al-wardáani min fáDHl-ak?
clerk	ad-doktóor muHámmad al-wardáani fii ghúrfah rágam árba: míyyah wa thamaaníin fi d-door ar-ráabi:.
visitor	shúkran

4 (a) sáb:ah (b) arba:tá:shar (c) sáb:ah wa :ishríin (d) míyyah tís:ah wa :ishríin (e) khámsah wa arba:íin (f) thaláath míyyah síttah wa sittíin (g) :ishríin (h) thamáanyah

Test yourself

1 kam rágam tilifóon al-fúndug?
2 rágam ithnáin síttah árba:ah Sífr khámsah tís:ah
3 ibrahíim al-hussáin mawjúud min fáDHl-ak?
4 rágam al-ghúrfah thaláath míyyah w-:ásharah
5 15
6 97
7 234
8 ithná:shar
9 árba:ah w-khamsíin
10 sitt míyyah wáaHid w-thamaaníin

Unit 4

Translations of dialogues

Dialogue 1	
Bill	What time is it please?
Mahmoud	It's eight o' clock now.

Bill	Exactly eight o'clock?
Mahmoud	Yes, exactly.
Bill	Thanks.
Mahmoud	Don't mention it.
guest	Where is the swimming pool please?
Mahmoud	There on the left. but it's closed now.
guest	What time does it open?
Mahmoud	It opens at nine. In half an hour.
guest	Thank you.
Mahmoud	You're welcome.
guest	What time does the restaurant close?
Mahmoud	Half past 11.
guest	Thanks.
Mahmoud	Don't mention it.

Dialogue 2

Abdel Aziz	Bill?
Bill	Yes, it's me. Abdel Aziz?
Abdel Aziz	Yes, how are you?
Bill	Well, praise God. And how are you?
Abdel Aziz	Praise God. What time are you coming to the office?
Bill	Is 11 o'clock OK.?
Abdel Aziz	Fine, but 11.30 would be better.
Bill	OK. So I'll see you at 11.30, God willing.
Abdel Aziz	God willing.

Questions

1 (a) 4 hours (b) 9am (c) as-sáa:ah kam yíftaH? (d) 11.30pm

2 (a) Come to the office (b) 11.00am (c) 11.30am

Exercises

1 (a) 1.20 (b) 6.35 (c) 10.15 (d) 5.05 (e) 9.00pm

2 (a) as-sáa:ah khámsah (b) as-sáa:ah :ásharah wa nuSS (c) as-sáa:ah thaláathah ílla rúba: (d) as-sáa:ah wáaHidah wa nuSS wa kháms (e) as-sáa:ah sáb:ah wa thilth (f) as-sáa:ah ithná:shar ílla :áshar

3 (a) yoom al-khamíis (b) búkrah (c) yoom al-áHad (d) áwwal :ams

4 (a) True (b) False (c) False (d) True (e) True

5 (a) quarter to eight (b) at the shopping centre on the left (c) at 8am (d) in quarter of an hour

6

DHaif	as-sáa:ah kam min fáDHl-ak?
káatib	as-sáa:ah thaláathah w nuSS
DHaif	fiih Sarráaf garíib min hína?
káatib	ná:am, fi s-suug :a l-yamíin
DHaif	yíftaH as-sáa:ah kam?
káatib	as-sáa:ah árba:ah, ba:d nuSS sáa:ah
DHaif	shúkran jazíilan
káatib	:áfwan

Arabic script

1 *1* 3/12/1952 *2* 19/11/2013 *3* 1/1/2000 *4* 28/2/1990 *5* 17/4/1880

2 (a) sittá:shar wa khámsah wa thalaathíin dagíigah (b) thamantá:shar w khamastá:shar dagíigah (c) tís:ah wa khámsah wa :ishríin dagíigah (d) :ishríin wa khámsah wa khamsiin dagíigah (e) síttah wa khámsah wa arba:iin dagíigah (f) thalathtá:shar wa :ishríin dagíigah (g) :ásharah wa tis:atá:shar dagíigah (h) arba:atá:shar wa síttah wa :ishríin dagíigah (i) wáaHidah wa iHdá:shar dagíigah (j) thaláathah wa :ishríin wa khám:sah wa khamsíin dagíigah

Test yourself

1 as-sáa:ah kam?

2 as-sáa:ah árba:ah wa-nuSS

3 al-bank maftúuH? Laa, húwwa magfúul

4 yoom al-áHad, yoom al-ithnáin, yoom ath-thaláathah, yoom al-árba:ah, yoom al-khamíis, yoom al-júm:ah, yoom as-sábt

5 b

6 c

7 a

8 yíbánnid/yígfil

9 áji

10 tíftaH

Unit 5

Translations of dialogues

Dialogue 1

Matthew	Do you have batteries please?
shopkeeper	Yes, I have (there are).
Matthew	How much is this one?
shopkeeper	This one is two riyals.
Matthew	And this one?
shopkeeper	This one is one and a half riyals.
Matthew	Give me four of this kind.
shopkeeper	Right. Do you want anything else?
Matthew	No thanks.

Dialogue 2

Peter & Sally	Hello.
shopkeeper	Hello. How are you?
Peter	Well, praise God.
shopkeeper	What would you like?
Peter	We just want to look.
Sally	What is this called in Arabic please?
shopkeeper	This is called a **khanjar**.
Peter	Is this (of) silver?
shopkeeper	Yes, silver. Old silver.
Sally	And what is this called?
shopkeeper	This is called a **mijmar**.
Sally	How much is this small one?
shopkeeper	Seven dirhams.
Sally	And the big (one)?
shopkeeper	Eleven dirhams. Do you want the big one?
Sally	Yes … but (it's) expensive.
shopkeeper	No (it's) not expensive! (It's) cheap! OK., nine dirhams.
Sally	OK., I'll take this (one) for nine dirhams.

Dialogue 3

Sally	How much is this chain?
shopkeeper	This one here?

Sally	No, that one there.
Sally	This one is short. Do you have a longer one?
shopkeeper	Yes, this one is a bit longer.
Sally	This one's better. How much?
shopkeeper	Just a moment please ... This one is 230 dirhams.
Sally	(That's) a lot!
shopkeeper	This is 22 ct gold. Is 200 OK.?
Sally	No, (that's a lot). Let it (go) for 180
shopkeeper	No, I'm sorry, (that's) not possible. Give me 190.
Sally	OK. 190 dirhams. Here you are.

Questions

1 (a) 2 riyals (b) 6 riyals

2 (a) to look around (b) the dagger (c) 7 dirhams

3 (a) 230 dirhams (b) it is 22ct gold (c) 190 dirhams

Exercises

1 (a) 2 riyals (b) 3 riyals 200 baiza (c) 90 riyals (d) 500 baiza (e) 7 dinars

2 (a) sittíin dirham (b) sab: míyyah w khamsíin baizah (c) :ásharah riyaaláat (d) diinaaráin (e) diináar w khamsíin fils (t) nuSS riyáal (g) thamantá:shar diináar (h) khamsah daráahim

3 (a) háadhi aish ism-ha bi l-:arabi? bi-kam hiyya? (b) háadhi aish ism-ha bi l-:arabi? bi-kam hiyya?
(c) háadha aish ism-uh bi l-:arabi? bi-kam huwwa? (d) háadha aish ism-uh bi l-:arabi? bi-kam huwwa?
(e) háadhi aish ism-ha bi l-:arabi? bi-kam hiyya?

4 fiih :índ-kum agláam?
a:Tíi-ni waaHid aswad w waaHid aHmar
aríid :ilbat asbriin
maal sittah w thalaathíin
an-naDHDHáarah hináak bi-kam?
laa, haadha kathiir. kam tiriid?

5 (a) faríidah joo:áanah (b) ána :aTsháan (c) ínti ta:báanah? (d) al-lúghah al-:arabíyyah muu Sa:bah (e) al-marsaidis sayyáarah jáyyidah (f) :áayishah bint jamíilah

Test yourself

1 aríid ashúuf bass
2 :indak khanáajir, min fáDHl-ak?
3 laa, haadháak hína
4 haadha muub zain. :ind-ak waaHid aHsan?
5 húwwa gadíim?
6 húwwa bi-kam?
7 háadha wáajid gháali
8 khudh miitáin riyaaláin
9 má:a l-asaf, :índ-i miitáin w khamsíin bass.
10 zain, ákhudh háadha

Unit 6

Translations of dialogues

Dialogue 1

Khaled	What would you like to drink?
Jim	What do they have?
Khaled	What drinks do you have?
shopkeeper	We have tea, coffee, and orange and lime juice.
Jim	I'll take coffee without milk, if possible.
Khaled	And you, what do you want to drink?
Eleanor	I prefer lime juice.
shopkeeper	Lime with sugar?
Eleanor	Yes.
Khaled	And I'll take tea.
shopkeeper	OK. One tea, one coffee and one lime juice.

Dialogue 2

Salim	By God I'm hungry!
Mike	Me too. Let's stop at this petrol station and buy some food. Maybe they have sandwiches.
Salim	What kind of food do you have please?
shopkeeper	We have sandwiches, eggs, cake and crisps.
Salim	What kind of sandwiches do you have?

shopkeeper	We have chicken, meat and egg with salad.
Salim	What do you want to eat Mike?
Mike	I'll take a chicken sandwich. Can you make me an egg sandwich without salad please?
shopkeeper	Of course. And you (sir)?
Salim	I'll take two meat sandwiches.
shopkeeper	Anything else?
Salim	Yes, give me a bit of cake as well.
shopkeeper	Right. One chicken sandwich, two meat, one egg without salad and one cake. We'll make them now.

Dialogue 3

shopkeeper	The sandwiches are ready. Do you want anything to drink?
Salim	What have you got (that's) cold?
shopkeeper	There is milk, (fruit) juice, soda, cola, Seven Up and Masafi water.
Salim	What do you want to drink Mike?
Mike	Anything, but I don't like milk. What (kind of fruit) juice do you have?
shopkeeper	We have orange, lime, mango, pineapple, banana.
Salim	Can you give us an assortment for ten dirhams?
shopkeeper	Yes, all right.
Salim	How much is this all (together)?
shopkeeper	That makes ten plus six plus nine and a half. That is 25 and a half.
Saalim	Here you are.

Questions

1 (a) True (b) False (c) False

2 (a) nashtári shwayyat akil (b) eggs, cake, crisps (c) cake

3 (a) milk (b) a selection for 10 dirhams (c) 25 and a half dirhams.

Exercises

1 (a) 4 teas; (b) 2 orange juices, 1 lemon juice; (c) 1 chocolate milk, 1 laban; (d) 3 Coca Colas*, 1 orange juice; (e) coffee with milk and sugar

*"*COCA COLA*" *is a registered trademark of The Coca Cola Company*

2 (a) láHam (b) shíkar (c) aríid (d) akh
3 (a) 5; (b) 4; (c) 3; (d) 1; (e) 2.
4 (a) huwwa l-aghla (b) miitáin baizah (c) burtugaal, shamaam wa ananaas (d) sitt miyyat baizah (e) viimtoo, tang aw laimóon
5 (a) 1 egg sandwich, 1 coffee (with milk) (b) 3 ice-creams, 1 orange juice, 1 laban (c) 1 chicken and chips, 1 chocolate milk (d) 4 fishburgers and chips, 1 apple juice, 2 orange juices, 1 coffee without milk e) 1 burger, 3 cheeseburgers and chips, 1 orange juice, 3 colas
6 aish :ind–kum min ákil?
aish tiriidíin yaa júuli?
fiih aish min sandwiichaat :ind-kum?
ána maa aHíbb al-láHam. áakhudh sandwíich maal faláafil
ána afáDHDHal al-láHam. a:Tíi–na wáaHid sandwíich faláafil w wáaHid láHam min faDhl-ak
tiHibbíin Sálsat fílfil áHmar? laa shukran, maa naríid-ha min fáDHl-ak, a:Tíi-na kaik w shibs kamáan
haadha kull-uh kam?
tfáDHDHal (al-filúus)
(a) eggs, cake, falafel and crisps (b) red pepper sauce (c) 8 riyals
7 (a) aHíbb-ha (b) afáDHDHal-ha bi-Halíib (c) maa aHíbb gáhwah bi-shíkar (d) ashkúr-kum, maa aríid gáhwah ai-Híin
8 (a) tiríid táakul shay? (b) tiríid dajáaj aw láHam? (c) asawwíi-lak sandwíich (maal) dajáaj (d) tiríid Sálsat fílfil áHmar?

Arabic script

1 (a) **sáalim** (b) **salíim**
2 (a) **muHámmad** (b) **maHmúud**
3 (a) **sa:íid** (b) **sá:ad** (c) **su:áad** (d) **sa:úud**
4 (a) **Hámad** (b) **Háamid** (c) **Hamíid**
5 (a) **rashíid** (b) **ráashid**
6 (a) **zaid** (b) **záayid**
7 (a) **abu DHabi** (b) **:umáan** (c) **ash-sháarigah**
8 (aj **:azíiz** (b) **:azzah**
9 (a) **gaTar** (b) **al-baHráin** (c) **al-:iráaq**
10 (a) **jaddah** (b) **ar-riyáaDH** (c) **al-fujáirah**

Test yourself

1 haa
2 naa
3 nii
4 uh
5 tiriiduun
6 tiriidii
7 tifaDHDHal
8 asawwi
9 tiriid
10 naHibb

Unit 7

Translations of dialogues

Dialogue 1

Samira	How are the children?
Eleanor	Well, thank God.
Samira	How many children do you have now?
Eleanor	Three, a boy and two girls.
Samira	Only three?
Eleanor	Yes, and you?
Samira	We have seven, three boys and four girls.
Eleanor	Good heavens!
Samira	How old are the children?
Eleanor	The boy is 12 and the elder girl is ten and the young girl is seven years (old).
Samira	Where are they?
Eleanor	They are staying with my (the) mother, because they have to go to school.
Samira	The next time you must bring them to Oman
Eleanor	I hope so.

Dialogue 2

Interviewer	Where are you from?
Mohammad	I am from Shuaib, but my family are living in Dubai.
Interviewer	How long have you been in Al-Ain?
Mohammad	I've been here thirteen months now.
Interviewer	Do you like Al-Ain?

Mohammad	Yes, I like it a lot.
Interviewer	And what does your father work at?
Mohammad	My father is a company director in Dubai. My mother doesn't work.
Interviewer	Tell us a little about your family.
Mohammad	I have three brothers and two sisters. My eldest brother is married and works with my father. My brother Karim is an officer in the army, and my youngest brother is still studying. They are not married.
Interviewer	And your sisters?
Mohammad	Both of them are teachers. Nadia lives with us in the house in Dubai. Jamilah is married and lives in Abu Dhabi. Her husband is an official in he Ministry of Information. They have three children (boys).
Interviewer	Thank you Muhammad.

Dialogue 3

Bill	How long have you been working here in the office with your father Salim?
Salim	A year now.
Bill	Do you live with your father?
Salim	No, we live in a flat near here. Father's house is a long way from the office. Because I am at work from early in the morning, and I some times have to work at night.
Bill	Do you see the family a lot?
Salim	Yes, I go to them every day.
Bill	Do you see them on Fridays?
Salim	Yes, we, I mean the whole family, usually go to visit my grandfather and grandmother on Friday.
Bill	Where do they live?
Salim	In Shuaib. My uncle and aunt live with them in the same house.

Questions

1 (a) true (b) false (c) true

2 (a) 13 months (b) 5 - 3 brothers, 2 sisters
(c) Nadia and Jamila (d) official in the Ministry of Information

3 (a) it is too far from work. (b) on Fridays (c) in Shuaib with the grandparents

Exercises

1 (a) student (f.) (b) shopkeeper in Dubai (c) work for a company (d) official in the Ministry of Education (e) teacher (f.) (f) doctor (m.)
2 (a) B (b) A (c) A (d) A (e) B (f) A (g) B (h) B
3 (a) bait (b) imaaraat (c) jaziirah (d) ikhwaan, akhawaat (e) shakhS, karáasi (f) mudarris, mudarrisaat (g) ghurfah (h) duwwaarain
4 (a) waalidat-uh (b) waalidat-uh (c) ibn akhuu-h (d) ukht-uh (e) zoojat-uh (nuur) (f) ibn :amm-uh (g) ibn-uh (h) jaddat-uh
5 min wain intu?
ana min... intu saakiniin fi l-baHrain?
Saar l-i thalaathat ayyaam bass. aish shughul-kum? (e.g.) ana mudarris, ashtaghal fii madrasah
na:am ta:jib-ni kathiir
6 (a) 5 am (b) school (c) 1.30 (d) sleep for two hours (e) 12 midnight

Arabic script

(**1**) bint (**2**) thaani (**3**) ta:baan (**4**) inta or inti (**5**) min (**6**) bait (**7**) laimoon (**8**) bi-duun (**9**) ya:ni (**10**) laban.

Test yourself

1 a-ii (m.), b-iii (m.), c-i (f.), d-iv (f.)
2 **a** akh, **b** waalidah *or* umm, **c** ammah, **d** walad *or* ibn, **e** zoojah
3 **a** awlaad, **b** bunuuk, **c** sayyaaraat kabiirah, **d** muhandisiin kuwaytiyyiin
4 c, b, d, a
5 Saar l-ii khams sanawaat
6 as-saa:ah sab:ah
7 as-saa:ah thamaaniyyah
8 as-saa:ah thintain
9 laa, maa aHibb
10 as-saa:ah asharah wa-nuSS

Unit 8

Translations of dialogues

Dialogue 1

Clerk	Hello. Welcome.
Tony	Hello. Do you have a room please?
Clerk	For one person or two?
Tony	For one, with a bath.
Clerk	For how long?
Tony	Two nights.
Clerk	One minute please . . . Yes, there is a room.
Tony	How much is it please?
Clerk	120 riyals with the service (charge).
Tony	Fine. I'll take it.
Clerk	Fill in this card please. Could you please give me your passport?
Tony	Here you are. What time is breakfast please?
Clerk	Breakfast is from 6.30 am in the restaurant, or you can order it in the room.
Tony	Right.
Clerk	Room number 514. This is the key. Come
Tony	(here) Abdullah. He will help you with the cases.

Dialogue 2

Youssef	Good morning. I am coming to Kuwait next month and I want to book a room please.
Clerk	Right. On what date?
Youssef	I want a single room, from Saturday the 8th of February until the 11th of February.
Clerk	One moment . . . for four days then?
Youssef	Yes, (that's) right.
Clerk	Yes, OK. What time will you be arriving, God willing?
Youssef	God willing, I will arrive on the 8th in the afternoon Maybe it will be cold in Kuwait in the winter. Is there heating in the room?
Clerk	No problem. All the rooms have heating and air-conditioning and colour TV.

Dialogue 3	
Tony	Hello. This is room 514. There's a problem.
Clerk	What's the problem? I hope we'll be able to help you.
Tony	I need more towels in the bathroom, and the air-conditioning is out of order; it doesn't work.
Clerk	We're very sorry. I'll get in touch with hotel services and they will send someone right away to repair it, and he'll bring towels.
Tony	OK. Thanks.

Questions

1 (a) single with bath (b) two nights (c) passport

2 (3) single (b) on the 8th in the afternoon (c) cold

3 (a) not enough towels, air-conditioning not working (b) send someone to bring towels and repair the air-conditioning

Exercises

1 (a) have reserved, double room, two nights, with bath (b) have reserved, single room, one night, without bath (c) have not reserved, one double and two singles, one night, with bath (d) have not reserved, two double rooms, three nights, with bath

2 (a) iii (b) iii (c) ii

3 (a) 22-24 October (b) 13-19 May (c) 10-17 December

4 (a) ithnain li khamsah maars (b) tis:ah li sitta:shar yuulyo (c) waaHid li thamaaniyah sabtambar/shahar tisa:ah

5 (a) al-:asha s-saa:ah kam? (b) al-maT:am yiftaH as-saa:ah kam? (c) mumkin aTlub al-ghada fi l-ghurfah? (d) wain al-miS:ad?

6 SabaaH an-nuur. :ind-ak ghurfah min faDHl-ak?
li shakhS waaHid
bi dushsh
thalaath layaali
al-ghurfah bi kam min faDHl-ak?
al-ghurfah wain min faDHl-ak?
shukran jaziilan. fii amaan Al-laah

7 (a) 64 (b) mini bar, colour TV, direct dialling abroad (c) Arab, Italian and Indian (d) 24 hours (e) at the poolside (f) parties and conferences

Arabic script
1F 2G 3D 4J 5I 6A 7C 8H 9E 10B

Test yourself

1i, 2c, 3j, 4g, 5f , 6h, 7a, 8e, 9d, 10b

Unit 9

Translations of dialogues

Dialogue 1

Interviewer	Tell me Muhammad, what are your hobbies?
Mohammad	I have many hobbies, of course. I like to play football. I hope to play in the university team this year. And I play games on my computer.
Interviewer	And do you do anything else?
Mohammad	I play tennis here in Al-Ain . . . and in the summer I go fishing with my brothers and my cousins.
Interviewer	Who taught you fishing?
Mohammad	Our grandfather taught us when we were young.
Interviewer	Farida, what do you do in your spare time? Do you like playing sports?
Farida	No, I don't like sports at all. Here in Al-Ain I read and go to the market with my friends. or I watch television or listen to music.
Interviewer	And what do you do when you go home to Abu Dhabi?
Farida	Er . . . the same thing.

Dialogue 2

Dr Jones	I liked Al-Ain a lot, and the students were very hard-working.
Interviewer	Do you mean that the students in England are lazy?
Dr Jones	Yes . . . . some of them.
Interviewer	Dr Jones, can you tell us what you did in Al-Ain?

Dr Jones	The fact is, we did a lot of things. As you know, I am a history teacher, so I visited many forts and museums in the Emirates, and we – that is the family and I – made trips to Jebel Hafit and the sea. I bought a new camera in Dubai, and took a lot of pictures. Sometimes we watched the camel racing in the winter.
Interviewer	And what about sports?
Dr Jones	Yes, I played golf with a colleague, and we went swimming in the sea a lot, and in the holidays the children learnt diving, that is scuba, at Khor Fakkan.
Interviewer	Thank you very much, Dr Jones.

Dialogue 3

Salim	Where are you going in the summer holidays Mike?
Mike	We hope to go to England this year, so that we can visit the family. Last year we went to Oman.
Salim	Oman is a very beautiful country. Had you been there before?
Mike	No, that was the first time. Do you know Oman?
Salim	Yes, we went there two years ago. What did you do in Oman?
Mike	We travelled to Muscat by plane and stayed in a hotel by the sea. Afterwards we rented a car and toured a bit.
Salim	What did you think of it?
Mike	We liked it a lot. We went in the car to Dhofar in the south, and saw turtles and many birds and fishes and coconut palms. We spent the night in a tent in the desert, and the children enjoyed that very much.
Salim	How was the weather?
Mike	The first week the weather was very hot, but the second week it was cold and there was rain and some wind.
Salim	What a pity!
Mike	No, we English are used to wind and rain!

Questions

1 (a) goes fishing (b) his brothers and cousins (c) going shopping

2 (a) visiting forts and museums (b) golf and swimming (c) the children

3 (a) England (b) two years ago (c) sleeping in a tent (d) wet and windy

Notes

5 (a) Mountain of the Sun; (b) *the* (**al-**)

Exercises

1 (a) I play squash. (b) I swim. (c) I go (play) bowling. (d) I go to the cinema. (e) I read.

2 (a) (i) tiriid tiruuH tiSTaad samak? (ii) tiriid til:ab tanis? (iii) tiriid tiruuH as-suug? (i) na:am ariid aruuH aSTaad samak (ii) na:am ariid aruuH al:ab tanis (iii) laa, maa ariid aruuH as-suug (b) (i) tiriidiin til:abiin tanis? (ii) tiriidiin tishuufiin at-tilifizyoon? (iii) tiriidiin tiruuHiin tisbaHiin? (i) laa, maa ariid al:ab tanis (ii) na:am ariid ashuuf at-tilifizyoon (iii) laa, maa ariid aruuH asbaH

3 (a) iv (b) iii (c) v (d) i (e) vi (f) ii

4 (a) *False*, cloudy and windy 29° (b) *True* (c) *False*, sun 35° (d) *False*, thunder and lightning 19°

5 (a) the programme (b) go on a trip with the children (c) because the weather is nice there (d) a fort and a hot spring (e) have a picnic, and the children could play (f) to take food and cold drinks (g) food and drinks (h) at a shop near the spring

6 (a) In the North of the Gulf region there will be rain. Temperature in Kuwait 18°. (b) In Bahrain and Qatar there will be wind, and cloud, temperature 23°. (c) In the Emirates, sunny, 25° and in the Dhofar, sunny, 28°.

7 al-akh min wain?
na:am, ruHt as-sanah l-maaDHiyah, ila dalhi
sawwait jawlah w Sawwart kathiir w ruHt as-suug na:am,
laakin min ba:iid. jamiilah jiddan!
hina fi l-khaliij, maa fiih bard fi sh-shita

Arabic script
(a) 10 (b) 8 (c) 9 (d) 1 (e) 2 (f) 6 (g) 3 (h) 4 (i) 5 (j) 7

Test yourself

1 ishtarait
2 la:ab
3 sabaHna
4 akalt
5 naamat, shaafat
6 ista'jaru, raaHu
7 ruHna, zurna
8 saafaru, sawwu
9 ya:raf, yissawwii, ga:ad, kharaj
10 raaH, shaafuu

Unit 10

Translations of dialogues

Dialogue 1

Bill	Could you tell me something about the history of the Arabs, my friend?
Suleiman	Of course, what do you want to know?
Bill	First of all, where are the Arabs originally from?
Suleiman	The Arabs are originally from the Arabian Peninsula.
Bill	You mean there were no Arabs in Egypt for instance?
Suleiman	No, that was after the appearance of Islam.
Bill	And what happened after the appearance of Islam?
Suleiman	In the centuries after the appearance of Islam, the Arabs spread as far as China in the East and al-Andalus, that is Spain, in the West.
Bill	So the Arab soldiers conquered many countries!
Suleiman	Even now you see that the Arabs have many states.
Bill	And in these states, all the people speak Arabic?
Suleiman	Exactly. The Arabic language is the mother tongue of around 150 million of the population of the contemporary world.

Dialogue 2

Bill	Can you tell me a little about the Islamic religion?
Suleiman	Certainly. God revealed the Holy Koran to Muhammad the Apostle of God, prayers and peace be upon Him, in the first part of the 7th Century AD.
Bill	The Prophet Muhammad was from Mecca wasn't he?
Suleiman	Yes. (He was) born in Mecca, then emigrated to Medinah in the year 622 AD. We call this the Hijrah, and we calculate the date from that year.

Questions

1 (a) the Arabian peninsula (b) they spread to other areas (c) 150 million

2 (a) Mecca (b) 622 (c) it is the start of the lslamic calendar

Exercises

1 (a) aHyaanan (b) Tab:an (c) abadan (d) jiddan (e) daayman (f) bi-suhuulah (g) bi-sur:ah (h) bi-DH-DHabT (i) mathalan (j) fawran

2 (a) kuwaitiyyah (b) isbaani (c) :arabi (d) faransiyyah (e) :arab (f) :umaaniyyah (g) wardi (h) :arabiyyah (i) gaTariyyiin (j) banafsaji, burtugaali (k) waTani (1) tijaari

3 (a) kunt al:ab goolf (b) kaanat ukhti fariidah tidrus al-lughah l-ingliiziyyah (c) kunna nashtaghal fii sharikah fi l-baHrain (d) kaan al-baaS yooSal as-saa:ah tis:ah (e) kaan biil yitkallam :arabi zain (f) aT-Tullaab kaanu yidrusuun taarikh al-:arab (g) kaanat tiruuH as-suug as-saa:ah kam? (h) kunt agra l-qur'aan al-kariim (i) wain kuntu tiskunuun fii abu Dhabi? (j) kunna naruuH l-baHar fi S-Saif

4 (a) There is one God. (b) On the Saudi flag. (c) Five: dawn, noon, afternoon, sunset and evening. (d) Direction of Mecca. (e) Two. (f) End of the pilgrimage. (g) Fasting. (h) End of fasting. (i) The Kaabah.

Arabic script

1 sayyaarah **2** mudarris **3** saalim **4** khamsah **5** shams **6** sanah **7** sittah **8** mubaashir **9** saakhin **10** sulaimaan

Test yourself

1 kaan yaakul
2 kunt ashtaghal
3 kunna nasbaH
4 kaanat tisaafir
5 kunt tazuur
6 kaanuu yil:abuun
7 kunna naakul
8 kaan yiwaSSil
9 kaanu yadrusuun
10 kunt ashtarii

Unit 11

Translations of dialogues

Dialogue 1

chemist	How can I help you?
Bill	I have a pain in my stomach. Do you have any medicine for this?
chemist	How long have you had this pain?
Bill	Since the day before yesterday.
chemist	Do you have diarrhoea?
Bill	Yes, a bit.
chemist	I have these pills here. They're very effective.
Bill	How many times a day do I have to take them?
chemist	Take one pill four times a day for five days. Drink a lot of water and don't eat fruit or fried food.
Bill	Thank you.

Dialogue 2

Rayyah	How are you?
Kamil	Actually I'm not very well.
Rayyah	What's wrong with you?
Kamil	I've got toothache.
Rayyah	Since when?
Kamil	It began two days ago, but last night the pain became severe, and now it hurts (me) a lot.
Rayyah	Why didn't you tell me? You'll have to go to the dentist's.
Kamil	(You're) right, but we're very busy in the office at the moment, and I don't have time. I've taken aspirin and I hope it'll be better soon.

Rayyah	You should really go right away before it gets worse and he'll have to take your tooth out!
Kamil	Don't worry yourself. It's nothing.
Rayyah	If it's nothing, why are you looking ill like this? I'll phone the dentist now and make an appointment.

Dialogue 3

receptionist	Good morning, this is Dr Mahmoud al-Badawi's clinic.
Rayyah	I want to make an appointment for my husband.
receptionist	Let me see . . . can he come next Wednesday at 10.15? The doctor is free . . .
Rayyah	No, that's no good. He says he is in a lot of pain, and he should really come as soon as possible. Does the doctor not have an appointment free today?
receptionist	That's difficult. The doctor is very busy today. He has a lot of patients. Let's see . . . could he come at 6 pm? He might have to wait a little.
Rayyah	OK. I'll tell him. Thanks very much.
receptionist	Not at all. Goodbye.

Questions

1 (a) since the day before yesterday (b) four times a day (c) five days (d) drink lots of water and avoid fruit and fried food

2 (a) last night (b) they are busy at work/he has no time

3 (a) next Wednesday (b) busy/too many patients (c) wait a little

Exercises

1 (a) 3 hospital (b) 2 dentist (c) 1 doctor (d) 4 clinic

2 (i) c (ii) d (iii) a (iv) b

3 (a) :ind-i Sudaa: (b) ta:awwart fii rijl-i (c) raas-i yiduukh (d) ta:awwart fii iid-i (e) :indi waja: fi l-bal:uum

4 (a) cold/3 days/aspirins,bed (b) stomach-ache/yesterday/doctor/medicine (c) headache/fever/2 days/bed (d) sore back/day before yesterday/bed/painkillers (e) swollen eye/this morning/hospital/doctor

5 al-Hagiigah ana ta:baanah shwayyah :ind-i Sudaa: :ind-ich dawa Hagg-uh?

6 (a) he hurt his leg (b) brother took him (c) no (d) still painful

Arabic script

1. Basrah (al-baSrah) **2.** stomach, belly (baTn) **3.** Salih (SaaliH) **4.** Abu Dhabi (abu DHabi) **5.** student (Taalib) **6.** aeroplane (Tayyaarah) **7.** Riyadh (ar-riyaaDH) **8.** doctor (Tabiib) **9.** Saddam (Saddaam) **10.** script (khaTT) **11.** airport (maTaar) **12.** bus (baaS)

Test yourself

1h, 2g, 3i, 4c, 5j, 6b, 7e, 8a, 9d, 10f

Unit 12

Translations of dialogues

Dialogue 1

Mark	Excuse me, can you help me please?
passer-by	Of course. (With what) How(can) I help you?
Mark	I have to go to a bank.
passer-by	There's a bank there, near.
Mark	It must be a bank with a cash dispenser. What bank should I go to?
passer-by	Ah. Then . . . you'll have to go to the Arab Bank in King Khalid Street. It has a cash dispenser which takes bank cards of all kinds.
Mark	Thank you very much.

Dialogue 2

Tony	Hello.
bank clerk	Hello. (Can) I help you with something?
Tony	I want to cash a traveller's cheque.
bank clerk	Certainly, what currency?
Tony	Dollars.

bank clerk	How many dollars?
Tony	500. What's the rate for the American dollar today?
bank clerk	One moment please. The rate for the American dollar is 3 riyals 75 halala. Your passport please.
Tony	Here you are.
bank clerk	Thank you . . . sign here please.
Tony	There you are.
bank clerk	Take this paper to the cashier there please and he will give you the (sum of) money.
Tony	Thank you.
Bank clerk	You're welcome.

Dialogue 3

Eleanor	How much is a postcard to England please?
clerk	150 baisa.
Eleanor	And a letter?
clerk	If the weight is less than 10 grammes, 200 baisa, from 10 to 20 grammes 350 baisa.
Eleanor	Right. Give me four stamps at 200 baisa, and 12 at 150 please.
clerk	Four at 200 and 12 at 150. That's 2 riyals 600 baisa altogether.
Eleanor	Here you are.
clerk	400 baisa change. Here you are.

Dialogue 4

Mike	If you please, I would like a driving licence.
official	That's not from here. This is the Ministry of Transport. You have to go to the police, the Traffic Department.
Mike	Where is the Traffic Department?
official	Near here, in the same street.
Mike	Thank you.
Mike	Good morning. Do I get a driving licence from here?
official	Yes.
Mike	What papers do I need?
official	Give (me) your international driving licence, two passport photos and (the sum of) 50 dirhams.

Mike	I have (them) here. There you are
official	Sign here please. If you come the day after tomorrow, hopefully the licence will be ready and you can collect it.
Mike	Thank you very much. Goodbye.
official	Goodbye.

Questions

1 (a) for a bank (b) a cash machine (c) the Arab Bank.

2 (a) $500 (b) his passport (c) sign

3 (a) F; (b) T; (c) F

4 (a) the police traffic department (b) in the same street as the Ministry of Transport (c) his international licence, two passport photos and the fee (d) in two days

Exercises

1 (a) bi-kam ar-risaalah li amriika (b) bi-kam al-buTaagah li-oSTraalya (c) bi-kam aT-Tard li-l-imaaraat (d) bi-kam ar-risaalah li s-sa:uudiyyah

2 (a) thalaathah bi-miyyah w khamsiin fils (b) waaHid bi-diinaarain (c) khamsah bi-dirham waaHid (d) :ishriin bi-nuSS riyaal (e) sittah bi-miitain baizah

3 (a) si:r (b) kart (c) buTaagah (d) Sarraaf (e) doolaar (f) risaalah (g) Taabi: (h) bank (i) chaik Column A: starliini

4 jinaihaat starliini
miitain w khamsiin jinaih
laish?
aruuH ayy waaHid min-hum?

Arabic script

A9 B5 C7 D6 E8 F2 G3 H1 I10 J4

Test yourself

1 kull **2** kull-haa **3** kull-hum **4** kull **5** kull-naa

6 wain mumkin aSraf miitain doolaar?

7 ariid aSraf chaik siyaaHii

8 ar-risaalah ila amriika bi-kam?

9 min faDHl-ak a:Tiini khamsa Tawaabi: bi thalaatha daraahim wa Taabi:ain bi khamsiin fils
10 fiih makiinat Sarf fii haadha l-bank?

Unit 13

Translations of dialogues

Dialogue 1

Janet	Be careful! Please pay attention to the road
taxi driver	(There's) no problem.
Janet	Slow down. Don't drive fast like this. This is the street . . . no, turn left at the second street.
taxi driver	This one here? Are you sure?
Janet	Yes. You've passed it! Go back a bit. This is it, in the big white building. Right. Stop here at the door.
taxi driver	Is this (here) right?
Janet	Yes fine. I'm going to deliver a letter here and I'll come back in five minutes. Stay in the car (and) don't go anywhere.
taxi driver	OK. I'll wait here.

Dialogue 2

Nasir	Is there a bus that goes to Doha please?
clerk	No, there isn't a bus that goes direct. You have to change in Hofuf.
Nasir	It doesn't matter. How much is the ticket?
clerk	Single or return?
Nasir	Return.
clerk	125 riyals.
Nasir	What time does the bus go?
clerk	Eight o' clock exactly.
Nasir	Right, and when does it arrive in Doha?
clerk	It gets to Hofuf at twelve noon, and the bus to Doha arrives at 7.05 in the evening.

Nasir	Give me a return ticket for tomorrow please.

Dialogue 3

Charlie	We have an idea to rent a car to go outside Dubai in order to see a bit of the country. Do you know a good firm that we can rent from?
Muhammad	Let me think. A lot of people from here have gone to the Capital Company, but some of them have said that their prices are a bit high. Why don't you go to the Gulf Car Company in Al-Wahdah Street? It's a well-known company, and their prices are reasonable.
Charlie	Good, thanks. I'll go and ask them.
car hire man	Good morning.
Charlie	Good morning, we want to rent a car. Which of your cars are suitable for the desert?
car hire man	How many people are you?
Charlie	Four (persons).
car hire man	The best would be a car with 4-wheel drive. I have a Toyota Land Cruiser, an excellent clean car that'll go anywhere.
Charlie	Does it have air-conditioning?
car hire man	Of course. All our cars have air-conditioning
Charlie	And how much is the rental per day?
car hire man	350 dirhams. How long do you want it for?
Charlie	We want it from Thursday morning until Saturday morning if possible.
car hire man	All right, I'll give you a special price. 600 dirhams for the whole period.
Charlie	Is that with insurance?
car hire man	Yes, and 300 km free.
Charlie	Fine. Can you deliver the car to us at the hotel or do we have to come and get it from here?
car hire man	We'll deliver it to the hotel. No problem.

Questions

1 (a) too fast (b) at the door (c) in the car

2 (a) no (b) SR125 (c) 19.05

3 (a) to make a trip outside the town in the desert (b) to take a 4-wheel drive/Toyota Land Cruiser (c) yes

Exercises

1 (a) How much it costs to rent per day (b) Whether this includes insurance (c) If he can deliver it to the airport
2 (a) :abbii-ha daizil min faDHl-ak (b) ariid khamasta:shar laitir mumtaaz (c) :aadi bi khamsah riyaalaat
3 (a) chayyik al-aayil wa l-maay (b) mumkin tiSalliH l-i banchar? (c) mumkin tiSalliH-ha l-yoom?
4 (a) false (b) true (c) false (d) false (e) true
5 mashghuul
maktab al-bariid
bi-sur:ah
khallii-k
siidah
liff
waggif
6 (a) For hire; (b) 1888; (c) Muscat.

Arabic script

(1) nafar (2) fundug (3) gab(i)l (4) faransa (5) filuus (6) ghurfah (7) masgaT (8) rag(a)m (9) dagiigah (10) gariib

Test yourself

1 khudh
2 ta:aali
3 ijlisu
4 titkallamii
5 ti:abbii
6 SabaaH al-khair. fiih baaS l-abu Dhabi bukrah ba:d aDH-DHuhr?
7 yooSal abu Dhabi s-saa:ah kam?
8 yoogaf fii makaan mumkin nashtari fii-h akl?
9 tadhkarat dhihaab bi-kam?
10 a:Tii-ni tadhkaratain dhihaab min faDHl-ak

Unit 14

Translations of dialogues

Dialogue 1

Abdel Aziz	Tell me what you think of the apartment
Amal	We liked it a lot. It's much bigger than the apartment we rent now.
Abdel Aziz	Where is it?
Salim	The building is next to our building. The apartment is on the fourth floor, and there are two more apartments on the same floor
Suad	How many rooms are there in it?
Salim	There's a sitting room, and dining room, and three bedrooms, and a kitchen and two bathrooms and a large hall.
Abdel Aziz	And how much is the rent per month?
Salim	The rent is 3,000 dirhams, that is 500 more than we pay now. And if we take it, we have to pay two months' rent in advance.
Abdel Aziz	So what are you going to do?
Salim	We'll think a little. We don't have to tell the landlord now.

Dialogue 2

Abdel Aziz	Is the apartment furnished?
Salim	No, we'll have to bring our (own) furniture. And we'll possibly have to buy new chairs for the sitting room. It's a big, spacious sitting room, and the chairs we have now are small.
Suad	What kind of electrical appliances are there?
Amal	There's a washing machine, a fridge and a new cooker. The landlord got a new one because the previous tenants broke it.
Salim	There's central air-conditioning, and a fan in the sitting room for the winter.
Abdel Aziz	And where will you put your car?

Salim	Downstairs. There's a big garage underneath the building and a lift that takes you upstairs to the apartment.

Dialogue 3

Amal	This green (stuff) here is excellent material. I like it. How much is it per metre?
shopkeeper	This is very good. It's 30 dirhams per metre, and 25 for making it up.
Amal	That's a lot. Can you give me a discount?
shopkeeper	OK. I'll give you a 20% discount. 24 dirhams and 20 for making it up.
Amal	Right. We want this pattern. Can you make them like these?
shopkeeper	Can you leave one with us so that we (can) know its pattern exactly?
Amal	This is the size I want for the sitting room, and I want this blue cloth for the bedroom. This is cotton, isn't it?
shopkeeper	Yes, cotton.
Amal	When will it be ready?
shopkeeper	Possibly . . . next Wednesday.
Amal	Can you make the green curtains first? Saturday maybe?
shopkeeper	Mmm . . . that's a bit difficult. All right, we'll finish the green ones for Saturday, and the other ones for Wednesday.
Amal	Thanks.

Questions

1 (a) 4th (b) 8 (c) 6000 Dh

2 (a) false (b) false (c) true (d) true

3 (a) 20% (b) blue (c) Saturday

Exercises

1 (a) beautiful apartment near the sea/living-room/small kitchen/two bed rooms/bathroom (b) villa/living room/dining room/three bedrooms/two bathrooms/big kitchen/garage/large garden/almond trees/mango trees/lot of flowers. (c) very small apartment/living room/kitchen/one bedroom/bathroom. (d) flat near the middle of town/two bedrooms/living-room/dining-room/bathroom/kitchen.

2 (a) askun fii shaggah Saghiirah fii-ha majlis, ghurfat noom waaHidah, maTbakh wa Hammaam (b) askun fii filla fii-ha majlis, ghurfat akil, arba: ghuraf noom, Hammaamain, maTbakh wa garaaj (c) askun fii bait fiih majlis kabiir, ghurfatain noom, Hammaam wa maTbakh

3 (a) tilifizyoon, maiz, sittah karaasi (b) thallaajah, SuHuun, Tabbaakhah, kabat (c) baraniiS, kabat, sariir (d) fuwaT (e) SuHuun, maiz, sittah karaasi

4 (a) fii-ha kam ghurfah? (b) hiyya mafruushah? (c) al-iijaar kam? (d) aish fii-ha min al-ajhizah l-kahrabaa'iyyah? (e) laazim adfa: kam mugaddam idha akhadht-ha?

5 Wordsearch:

aatháath	kabat
sariir	thallaajah
maiz	ghassaalah
kursi	gafshah
zooliyyah	sikkiin
tilifoon	raff
lambah	SaHn

6 haadha l-gumaash al-aHmar hina yi:jab-ni. al-mitir bi-kam?
haadha kathiir, mumkin ta:Tíi-ni takhfiiDH
zain, aakhudh-uh
mumkin tifaSSil l-i gamiiS mithl haadha?
ariid-uh aTwal min haadha shwayyah
mumkin tisawwíi-h bi-sur:ah?
zain, shukran.

Arabic script

1 halalah **2** kursi **3** mamlakah **4** mashhuur **5** shah(a)r **6** dukkaan **7** kahraba **8** hawa **9** fikrah **10** tadhkarah

Transcripts

Test yourself

1 jiib al-kitaab illi ishtarait-uh ams
2 haadhi hiya sh-shiggah illi ista'jart-haa
3 maa ya:jib-nii l-fustaan illi ishtaraitii-h
4 film shuft-uh yoom al-jum:ah
5 al-madiinah illi askun fii-haa jamiilah
6 shiggah kabiirah fii-haa arba: ghuraf noom
7 aSuHuun :ala l-maiz illi fi l-maTbakh
8 a:Tiini miftaaH yiftaH haadha l-baab
9 al-khayyaaT fi s-suug illi as:aar-uh ma:guulah
10 Taalib yigra haadha l-kitaab ya:raf yitkallam :arabi

Transcripts

Unit 1

Exercise 8

Jack	áhlan wa sáhlan
Salma	áhlan bii-k
Jack	kaif Háal-ich?
Salma	al-Hámdu li-l-láah.
Jack	ínti min wain? min ábu DHábi?
Salma	laa, ána min :umáan
Jack	áhlan wa sáhlan. aish ísm-ich?
Salma	ísm-i sálma
Jack	áhlan wa sáhlan bii-ch. titkallamíin inglíizi?
Salma	laa, :árabi

Unit 2

Exercise 3

(a) maktab al-bariid min wain? :ala l-yamiin (b) kaif aruuH fundug sii fyuu? ruuH siidah, ba:dain liff yisaar (c) al-miina min wain? aakhir ash-shaari: (d) al-jaami:ah min wain? ba:d ad-duwwaar ath-thaalith (e) maHaTTat al-baaS min wain? khudh thaani shaari: :a 1-yamiin, w maHaTTat al-baaS :ala l-yisaar

Unit 3

Exercise 1

(a) dubay thalaathah – al-baHrain Sifir (b) ash-shaarjah sab: ah – al-fujairah ithnain (c) al-kuwait arba:ah – abu DHabi arba:ah (d) jiddah sittah – Taayif ithnain (e) ad-dooHa waaHid – al-hufuuf Sifir

Exercise 2

(a) :ásharah (b) síttah wa thalaathíin (c) miitáin wa sáb:ah (d) tísa:ah míyyah wa iHdá:shar (e) ithnáin thaláathah wáaHid khámsah árba:ah Sífir (f) thaláathah árba:ah sáb:ah thamáaniyah Sífir síttah (g) sába:ah tís:ah thamáaniyah wáaHid ithnáin khámsah (h) thamáaniyah sáb:ah ithnáin síttah síttah Sífir

---

Unit 4

Exercise 1

(a) as-saa:ah waaHidah wa thilth (b) as-saa:ah sittah wa nuSS wa khams (c) as-saa:ah :asharah wa ruba: (d) as-saa:ah khamsah wa khams (e) as-saa:ah tisa:ah bi-l-lail

---

Unit 5

Exercise 1

(a) riyaaláin (b) thaláathah riyaaláat w miitáin baizah (c) tis:íin riyáal (d) khams miíyyat baizah (e) sáb:ah danaaníir

---

Unit 6

Exercise 1

1 (a) arba:ah shaay (b) ithnain :aSiir burtugaal w waaHid laimoon (c) waaHid Haliib bi-chaklait w waaHid laban (d) thalaathah kóola w waaHid :aSiir burtugaal (e) gahwah bi shikar w Haliib

Exercise 5

(a) aish tiriidúun?
wáaHid sandwíich baiDH w wáaHid gahwah min faDHlak
bi-shíkar w Halíib ?
Halíib bass
(b) múmkin asáa:id-kum?
thalaathah ayskriim, waaHid :aSiir burtugaal w waaHid laban
min faDHl-ak

(c) aish tiríid?
aríid dajáaj má:a baTáaTis w Halíib bi-chakláit min fáDHlak
(d) múmkin asáa:id-kum?
árba:ah sámak má:a baTáaTis min fáDHlak
má:a l-ásaf. maa :índ-na sámak. :índ-na báargar sámak bass n-zain. árba:ah bargaráat sámak má:a baTáTis.... w wáaHid :aSíir tuffáaH, ithnáin (:aSíir) burtugáal w wáaHid gahwah bi-dúun Halíib
(e) SabáaH al-khair. aish tiriidúun ?
SabáaH an-núur. naríid wáaHid bárgar, wa thaláathah bargar bi-l jibin má:a baTáaTis min fáDhlak
tiriidúun tishrabúun shay?
a:Tíi-na wáaHid :aSíir burtugáal wa thalaathah koola

Unit 7

Exercise 1

(a) ana Taalibah (b) ana SaaHib dukkaan fii dubay (c) ana ashtaghal fii sharikah (d) ana muwaDHDHaf fii wizaarat at-ta:liim (e) ana mudarrisah (f) ana Tabiib

Exercise 6

:aadatan aguum min an-noom as-saa:ah khamsah w aakul ar-riyuug. al-awlaad laazim yiruuHuun al-madrasah, w zoojat-i tiwaSSal-hum bi-sayyaarat-ha, w ana aruuH al-maktab. adaawim min as-saa:ah sab:ah li-ghaayat as-saa:ah waaHidah w nuSS. :aadatan aruuH al-bait, atghadda w ba:dain anaam saa:atain. as-saa:ah sittah tagriiban naruuH as-suug, aw nazuur al-:aa'ilah, aw nashuuf at-tilifizyoon. :aadatan nanaam as-saa:ah ithna:shar.

Unit 8

Exercise 1

(a) :ind-na Hajz li/ghurfah li shakhSain/lailatain/bi Hammaam (b) :ind-na Hajz/li ghurfah li shakhS waaHid/lailah waaHidah/ bi-duun Hammaam (c) maa :ind-na Hajz/li ghurfah li shakhSain

w ghurfatain li shakhS waaHid/lailah waaHidah/bi Hammaam
(d) maa :ind-na Hajz/li ghurfatain li shakhSain/thalaath layaali/ bi Hammaam

Exercise 7

fundug lu' lu' at al-khaliij fii-h takyiif kaamil. fii-h arba:ah w sittiin ghurfah w khamsat ajniHah, kull-ha fiih Hammaam wa miini baar wa tililfizyoon mulawwan w ittiSaal mubaashir li-l-khaarij bi t-tilifoon. fiih thalaathah maTaa:im min awwal darajah, bi T-Tabiikh al-:arabi, al-iTaali w al-hindi, w maqha maftuuHa arba:ah w :ishriin saa:ah. fiih baarain, w mumkin taakhudh mashruubaat aw sandwiich jamb al-masbaH. fiih qaa:ah kabiirah li l-iHtifaalaat aw al-mu'tamaraat. fundug lu'lu'at ash-sharg mathaali li-l-a:maal at-tijaariyyah aw wagt al-faraagh w yisudd kull Haajaat-kum.

Unit 9

Exercise 1

(a) al:ab skwaash (b) asbaH (c) al:ab booling (d) aruuH as-siinima (e) agra

Exercise 6

(a) shamaal manTigat al-khaliij yikuun fiih maTar. darajat al-Haraarah fi l-kuwait thamanta:shar darajah. (b) fi l-baHrain w gaTar yikuun fiih hawa w ghuyuum. darajat al- Haraarah thalaathah w :ishriin. (c) fi l-imaaraat shams, khamsah w :ishriin darajah, wa fii DHufaar shams, thamaaniyah w :ishriin darajah.

Unit 10

Exercise 4

Bill	aish ahamm khaSaa'iS ad-diin al-islaami?
Suleiman	asaas ad-diin al-islaami inn-uh Al-laah aHad, w muHammad rasuul-uh. niHna naguul: laa ilaaha

	illa l-llaah wa muHammadun rasuul Al-laah. haadha asaas ad-diin al-islaami - wa haadhi l-kalimaat maktuubah fii al-:alam as-sa:uudi.
Bill	w aish ghair?
Suleiman	al-muslim laazim yiSalli khams marraat fi l-yoom: al-fajr, aDH-DHuhur, al-:aSar, al-maghrib wa l-:isha ittijaah al-giblah
Bill	aish hiyya l-giblah?
Suleiman	al-giblah hiyya ittijaah makkah al-mukarramah.
Bill	w al-a:yaad al-islaamiyyah aish hiyya?
Suleiman	ahamm al-a:yaad ithnain. :iid al-fiTr, w :iid al-aDHHa.
Bill	aywah,sami:t :an :iid al-fiTr. haadha ba:d shahar ramaDHaan, laa?
Suleiman	bi DH-DHabT. al-muslimiin laazim yiSuumu Tuul shahar ramaDHaan, w kalimat 'fiTr' ma:naa-ha inn al-waaHid yifTur, ya:ni yaakul ba:d as-Soom.
Bill	w aish huwwa l-Hajj?
Suleiman	al-Hajj inn-uh yiruuH makkah l-mukarramah fii moosam al-Hajj w yizuur al-ka:bah. :iid al-aDHHa ba:d moosam al-Hajj mubaashiratan.

Unit 11

Exercise 1

(a) ruuH siidah, fawwit ad-duwwaar ath-thaani, wa tishuuf al-mustashfa :ala l-yamiin (b) :ind ad-duwwaar ath-thaani, liff yisaar. Tabiib al-asnaan :a l-yisaar. (c) khudh awwal shaari: :a l-yamiin, ba:dain awwal shaari: :a l-yisaar, w aT-Tabiib :a l-yisaar (d) ruuH siidah wa liff yisaar :ind ad-duwwaar ath-thaalith. khudh awwal shaari: :a l-yamiin, w al-:iyaadah :a l-yisaar

Exercise 2

(i) :indak Hubuub Hagg Sudaa:? (ii) :indak marham Hagg ladghat naHlah? (iii) ariid dawa Hagg waja: fi l-baTin (iv) fiih ma:juun al-asnaan?

Exercise 6

Omar	aish Saar l-ak?
Nabil	ta:awwart fii rijli ams. DHarabt-ha :ala Sakhrah
Omar	aish sawwait?
Nabil	akh-i Hasan waddaa-ni l-mustashfa, :ind aT-Tawaari'
Omar	sawwaa l-ak :aks eksrai?
Nabil	na:am, :ala shaan aT-Tabiib kaan yiftakir awwal inn-ha maksuurah. ba:dain gaal laa w HaTT fii-ha ribaaT. laakin hiyya maa zaal tooja:-ni. fi l-awwal maa kunt agdar amshi!
Omar	salamt-ak yaa akhi!

Unit 13

Exercise 1

(a) al-iijáar kam fi l-yoom? (b) haadha bi t-ta'miin? (c) mumkin tiwaddii-aa l-maTaar?

Unit 14

Exercise 1

(a) :ind-i shaggah jamiilah gariibah min al-baHar. fii-ha majlis, maTbakh Saghiir, ghurfatain maal noom w Hammaam.
(b) naskun fii filla. :ind-na majlis, ghurfat akil, thalaath ghuraf noom, Hammaamain wa maTbakh kabiir. fiih garaaj kamaan. wa fiih Hadiigah kabiirah fii-ha ashjaar maal looz w ambah, wa zuhuur kathiirah. (c) askun fii shaggah Saghiirah jiddan. fii-ha majlis, maTbakh, ghurfat noom waaHidah wa Hammaam.
(d) :ind-na shaggah gariibah min wasT al-madiinah. :ind-na ghurfatain maal noom, majlis, ghurfat akil wa Hammaam. ma:a maTbakh Tab:an.

Grammar summary

This grammar summary is intended to be used as a quick reference, and does not cover all the language given in the course.

1 Definite and indefinite

In Arabic all nouns and adjectives are either *definite* or *indefinite.*

Definite

(a) A definite noun is specific, and can be

- A proper noun, e.g. *Cairo*, *Mohammed.*
- A pronoun such as *I*, *you*, *they.*
- Preceded by the word **al-** *the*, called the *definite article.*

al- never changes for gender or number, and is always attached to the following noun or adjective, e.g. **al-bait** *the house.*

(b) **al-** is always the same in *written* Arabic. In pronunciation, if the preceding word ends in a vowel or **-ah**, the **a** of **al-** is omitted, e.g. **al-qáhwah l-ladhíidhah** *the delicious coffee.*

(c) If the word begins with one of the following Arabic letters:

n	l	DH	T	D	S	sh	s	z	r	dh	d	th	t

the **l** of the **al-** is omitted in pronunciation, and the following letter is *clearly doubled.*

Pronounced after a consonant	Pronounced after a vowel
ar-rájul	**r-rájul** *the man*
ash-shams	**sh-shams** *the sun*
an-nuur	**n-nuur** *the light*

Indefinite

There is no *indefinite article*, or word for *a*, in Arabic. **bait** in Arabic means *a house.*

2 Nouns

Masculine and feminine

In Arabic, nouns are either masculine or feminine in gender. Nouns ending in **-ah** are usually feminine, but

- A few feminine nouns do not have this ending, e.g. **umm** *mother.*
- A handful of masculine nouns end in **-ah**, e.g. **khalíifah** *Caliph.*

Singular and plural

The plural of Arabic words should be learned at the same time as the singular. The plural in Arabic refers to more than two (2+). For two of anything, see the section on the dual below.

(a) The *external masculine* plural, used in words for male human beings, is formed by adding **-iin** to the singular noun, e.g. **mudárris > mudarrisíin** (m.) *teachers.*

(b) The *external feminine/neuter* plural, used for the plural of most females and some other nouns, is formed by dropping the **-ah** (if there is one) and adding **-aat** to the singular word, e.g. **mudárrisah > mudarrisáat** (f.) *teachers.*

(c) The *internal plural*, used mainly for males and for things, is formed by altering the internal vowels of the word and/or by adding prefixes or suffixes. Although there is no general relationship between the singular word-shape and the plural word-shape, short words are more likely to take an internal plural, e.g. **gálam > agláam** *pens.*

(d) All plurals of things are regarded in Arabic as *feminine singular* for the purposes of agreement of adjectives and verbs.

Dual

The *dual* must be used when talking about two of anything, and is mostly regular for both nouns and adjectives. It is formed by adding an external suffix, similar to the masculine external plural, to the majority of nouns and adjectives.

Example			Suffix			
bait	*a house*	+	**-áin**	=	**baitáin**	*two houses*

(a) If a word has the feminine **-ah** ending, this changes to **-at** and the suffix **-áin** is added to it, e.g. **sayyáarah** a *car* becomes **sayyaaratáin** *two cars*.

(b) Adjectives must take the appropriate masculine or feminine dual ending and also agree with the noun, e.g. **sayyaaratáin kabiiratáin** *two big cars*. It is not usually necessary to insert the word for *two*.

3 Adjectives

Agreement of adjectives

(a) Adjectives must agree in number, gender and definiteness with the nouns they describe, e.g.:

al-fílm al-mumtáaz *the excellent film*
jáami:ah jáyyidah *a good university*

(b) In most cases, the feminine of an adjective is formed by adding **-ah** to the masculine, e.g. **Tawíil, Tawíilah** *tall, long*.

(c) If there is more than one adjective, it is added after the first one, agreeing with it and the noun, e.g.

al-fúndug al-kabíir al-jadíid *the big new hotel*
bint jamíilah Saghíirah *a beautiful young girl*

Adjectives of nationality

Adjectives indicating nationality are formed by adding **-ii/-íyyah** to the name of the country, e.g. **miSr** *Egypt*, **míSrii/miSríyyah** *Egyptian*.

Where the name of a country ends in **-aa** or **-ah**, this is omitted before the ending is added:

briiTáanya *Britain*
briiTáanii/briiTaaníyyah *British*

If the Arabic place name has the word **al-** *the* in front of it, this is omitted from the nationality adjective.

al-úrdun *Jordan* **úrdunii/urduníyyah** *Jordanian*

Singular and plural adjectives

The plurals of Arabic adjectives follow the same rules as nouns, adding the **-íin** (m.) or the **-áat** (f.) ending, or by means of internal plurals, which are given in the vocabulary with their singulars.

All plurals of things are regarded in Arabic as feminine singular, e.g.

aT-Túrug aT-Tawíilah *the long roads*

Noun	Adjective
Male human beings	*either* internal plural if it has one *or* + **-íin**.
Female human beings	+ **-áat**
Things/abstracts	+ **-ah** (f. sing.)

The primary colours are an exception (see Unit 5).

Word order

The adjective comes after the noun. In sentences with verbs, the verb usually (but not always) comes first.

4 Pronouns

Subject or personal pronouns

Subject pronouns are always definite.

Singular	Plural
ána *I*	**níHna** *we*
ínta *you* (m.)	**íntu** *you* (both genders)
ínti *you* (f.)	
húwwa *he*	**húmma** *they* (both genders)
híyya *she*	

The English *it* is translated into Arabic as *he* or *she*, depending on the gender of the word to which it refers.

Possessive pronoun suffixes

There is no equivalent in Arabic to English *mine*, *yours* etc. The words *my*, *your*, *his* etc. are expressed in Arabic as *suffixes* joined on to the object which is possessed, e.g. **bait-hum** *their house*, **akh-ii** *my brother*

Singular		Plural	
-i	*my*	**-na**	*our*
-ak	*your* (m.)	**-kum**	*your* (both genders)
-ich	*your* (f.)		
-uh	*his*	**-hum**	*their* (both genders)
-ha	*her*		

Object pronoun suffixes

Arabic uses the same pronoun suffixes as the possessive pronoun suffixes, with the exception of *me*, which is **-ni** after verbs.

The suffixes are added to the verb to express the *object* of the sentence, e.g.:

kallámt-uh ams *I spoke to him yesterday*
khabbár-ni náaSir *Nasser told me*

5 Saying *to have*

There is no verb *to have* in Arabic. Instead, this is expressed by using one of the prepositions **li-** *to/for*, or **:ind(a)** *with* (French *chez*) with a noun or pronoun, e.g. **li-l-wálad gálam** *the boy has a pen.*

The object of the English verb then becomes the subject of the Arabic sentence, e.g. *he has a car* **:ind-uh sayyáarah** (lit. *with him (is) a car*).

6 Verbs

Is/are sentences

There is no Arabic equivalent to the English *is/are*. Instead, a definite concept is simply followed by an indefinite one, e.g. **al-bait kabíir** *the house is big.*

Past tense

All Arabic verbs are derived from a root, usually a three-letter one, e.g. **k-t-b** which has the meaning of *writing*. Most verbs are formed from either a past or a present *stem*, with a standard set of *prefixes* and/or *suffixes*. The same prefixes and suffixes apply to every Arabic verb.

The Arabic past tense is used when the action of the verb is complete. To form the past tense, suffixes are added to the *he* form of the past stem, e.g. **katab** as follows:

Singular		Plural	
katáb-t	*I wrote*	**katáb-na**	*we wrote*
katáb-t	*you* (m.) *wrote*	**katáb-tu**	*you* (m. + f.) *wrote*
katáb-ti	*you* (f.) *wrote*		
kátab	*he wrote*	**kátab-u**	*they* (m. + f.) *wrote*
kátab-at	*she wrote*		

- If the subject is not stated as a noun, it is usually unnecessary to use a subject pronoun, since the suffix expresses the subject, e.g. **kátabat** *she wrote.*

- If the subject is a noun:
  (a) The normal (but not exclusive) word order in Arabic is V-S-O:

1 Verb	**2** Subject	**3** Object/the rest

(b) Verbs which come at the beginning of the sentence in Arabic can *only* have the *he* or *she* form, i.e. *always singular*, *never plural*, e.g. **zaar al-wúzara al-buyúut al-jadíidah** *the ministers visited the new houses*

Verb	Subject
he form for . . .	**1** One male being
	2 two or more male beings
	3 One object (grammatically m.)

she form for ...	**1** One female being
	2 Two or more female beings
	3 One object (grammatically f.)
	4 Two or more of any object

(c) If the sentence has two verbs, the word order is V1-S-O-V2:

1 1st Verb	**2** Subject	**3** Object (if any)	**4** 2nd Verb

The 1st verb is in the *he/she* form, and the 2nd verb follows the subject and agrees fully with it, e.g. **raaH l-awláad ilaa s-síinamaa wa-shaafuu l-film** *the boys went to the cinema and watched the film.*

A verb which for any reason comes *after* its subject must agree fully in number and gender.

Saying *was* and *were*

Although there is no verb in Arabic for *is/are*, the verb **kaan** is necessary for *was/were*.

The suffix endings are the same past tense ones used on all Arabic verbs.

Singular		Plural	
kun-t	*I was*	**kún-na**	*we were*
kun-t	*you* (m.) *were*	**kún-tu**	*you* (m. + f.) *were*
kún-ti	*you* (f.) *were*		
kaan	*he was*	**káan-u**	*they* (m. + f.) *were*
káan-at	*she was*		

kaan usually comes first in the sentence, e.g. **kaan wáalid-ii mudárris** *my father was a teacher.*

Present tense

The Arabic present tense is used if the action of the verb is incomplete. To form the present tense, prefixes – and suffixes for some parts – are added to the present tense stem, e.g. **ktib**, as follows:

Singular		Plural	
á-ktib	*I write*	**ná-ktib**	*we write*
tí-ktib	*you* (m.) *write*	**ti-ktib-úun**	*you* (m. + f.) *write*
ti-ktib-íin	*you* (f.) *write*		
yí-ktib	*he writes, is writing*	**yi-ktib-úun**	*they* (m. + f.) *write*
tí-ktib	*she writes*		

A full explanation of how to find the present stem of the verb is given in the section on **Arabic verbs**.

Future tense

Spoken Arabic expresses what you will do in the future by placing the prefix **b-** before the present tense verb. Before a consonant, a helping vowel, usually **-i**, is added, and the vowels of the present tense prefixes **t(i)-**, **y(i)-** and **n(a)-** are omitted to smooth out pronunciation.

Present		Future	
a-sáwwi	*I do*	**basáwwi**	*I shall/will do*
ti-sáwwi	*you* (m.) *do*	**bitsáwwi**	*you will do*
ti-saww-íin	*you* (f.) *do*	**bitsawwíi-n**	*you will do*
yi-sáwwi	*he does*	**biysáwwi** (or **byisáwwi**)	*he will do*
ti-sáwwi	*she does*	**bitsáwwi**	*she will do*
na-sáwwi	*we do*	**binsáwwi**	*we will do*
ti-sawwúun	*you* (pl.) *do*	**bitsawwúun**	*you will do*
yi-sawwúun	*they do*	**biysawwúun** (or **byisawwúun**)	*they will do*

Some dialects use the prefix **Ha-**. This works in the same way.

The past continuous/habitual

The past continuous is formed with **kaan** and the present tense verb. It is used to say what used to happen or what was habitual, e.g. **kunna narúuH s-suuq kull yoom.** *We used to go to the market every day.*

Arabic verbs

Arabic verbs have a basically simple underlying structure. There are no anomalies as in the English *go*, *went*, or *gone*. Arabic verbs all take the same prefixes and suffixes to form their tenses, of which there are only two, present and past (equivalent to English *I go*, *I am going* etc. and *I went*, *have gone*, etc.).

In the vocabulary boxes in this book, verbs are given in the 'he-form' of the present tense, followed by that of the past tense. There are two reasons for this. Firstly Arabic does not have what is called an infinitive form of the verb in (English *to go*, *to eat* etc). Secondly, the 'he-form' of the past is the simplest part of the Arabic verb, having neither prefixes or suffixes. So when you say *to write* = **kátab, yíktib** the Arabic words actually mean *he wrote/ has written*, *he writes/is writing* (The verb type is given after this in brackets: see below.)

Verb terms

To help describe verbs there are three main terms: prefixes, suffixes and stems. The first two should be self-explanatory, being bits added to the beginning and end of words respectively. The stem of a verb is its main 'core' which comes between the prefixes and suffixes. A rough analogy in English is to say that *like* is the verb stem, occurring also with the suffixes *-d* (*liked*), and *-s* (*likes*).

Verb agreement

English verbs change very little for the purposes of agreement – in fact in the vast majority of verbs you only add an *-s* or *-es* for the he/she/it form of the present tense (e.g. *I/you/we/they want, but he/she/it wants*). Arabic, like French and German, has different verb parts for each person, and these also sometimes differ for gender.

Because of this, as you will have seen in the units, it is not usually necessary to use the personal pronoun with a verb, i.e. instead of *we went*, the *we*-form of the verb is usually sufficient.

Past tense

Begin with this because it is structurally simpler than the present tense: it only has suffixes attached to a stem. (Some verbs have two stems as described below, but ignore this for now.)

Here is an example, using **kátab** (*wrote*), past stem **katab**. The past tense suffixes for all Arabic verbs are in bold and separated by a space for clarity. Note how the accent (marked) shifts.

Singular			*Plural*		
I wrote	katáb	**t**	*we wrote*	katáb	**na**
you (masc.) *wrote*	katáb	**t**	*you* (m. and f.) *wrote*	katáb	**tu**
you (fem.) *wrote*	katáb	**ti**			
he/(it) *wrote*	kátab		*they* (m. and f.) *wrote*	kátab	**u**
she/(it) *wrote*	kátab	**at**			

Notes

1 *I* and *you* masc. singular are identical.

2 The *he*-form has no suffix in most verb types and consists merely of the stem. The original suffix for this form was **-a**, and it is useful to remember this as it occurs in some types of verbs (see below).

3 It is very useful in dealing with certain types of verbs which have more than one stem to note now which suffixes begin with a consonant (*I*, *we* and *you*), and which with a vowel (*she*, *they* and also including the dropped **-a** of the *he* form).

4 The *they*-ending **-u** is pronounced in some dialects as **-oo** or **-aw**, but you will always be safe if you say **-u**.

5 Some conservative dialects preserve the fem. plural *you* and *they*, using the suffixes **-tan** and **-an** respectively. You may hear this, but

for practical purposes it can be ignored. The distinction masc./fem. in *you* singular (**-t/-ti**) is, however, compulsory in all dialects.

Present tense

This consists of a stem (usually different from that of the past tense) with a prefix (all parts) and a suffix (some parts). The present stem is the *he*-form stripped of its prefix (usually **yi-**).

Here again are the forms from **katab** *write*, present stem **ktib:**

Singular				*Plural*			
I write	**á**	ktib		*we write*	**ná**	ktib	
you (masc.) *write*	**tí**	ktib		*you* (masc./fem.) *write*	**ti**	ktib	**úun**
you (fem.) *write*	**ti**	ktib	**íin**				
he/(it) writes	**yí**	ktib		*they* (masc./fem.) *write*	**yi**	ktib	**úun**
she/(it) writes	**tí**	ktib					

Notes

1 *You* masc. and *she* are identical.

2 Speakers of Gulf Arabic often alter or even omit the vowel of the prefixes **yi-** and **ti-** to what they apparently think goes better with the stem, so you hear **yu-**, **tu-**, **ya-**, **ta-** or **y-**, **t-**. This makes no practical difference, so stick to **yi-** and **ti-** till your ear becomes attuned. (**a-** and **na-** do not change so readily.)

3 Some dialects habitually omit the final *n* of the endings **-iin** and **-uun**. Again stick to the forms given till you begin to absorb local speech characteristics.

4 As in the past tense above, it is very useful to notice the nature of the suffixes – in this case whether there is one or not. This helps when dealing with verbs which have more than one stem.

5 As with the past tense, some 'old fashioned' dialects preserve the feminine plural forms. These also end in **-an: ti-ktib-an** (*you* fem.) and **yi-ktib-an** (*they* fem.).

Verb types

Arabic verbs can be classified in four types (some with slight variants), except for a couple which can be called irregular. These type classifications depend on how many stems the verb has (varying between two and four*). Here is a brief explanation of how the various types work, so that you can fit newly acquired verbs into their correct category.

*Some verbs use only one stem for both past and present, but these have been regarded as having two 'identical' stems.

Type A

These have two stems, one past and one present. In most cases the prefixes and/or suffixes are merely added to the stem. The example **katab** (*write*) has been given above. Here are a few more. The stems are set in bold the first time they occur, and a few sample parts given:

Past		*Present*	
Tálab	Taláb-t, Tálab-u etc	yí-**Tlub**, yi-Tlub-úun	*request, ask for*
:áraf	:aráf-t, :áraf-u	yí-**:raf**, yi-:raf-úun	*know*
khábbar	khabbár-t, khábbar-u	yi-**khábbir**, yi-khabbir-úun	*tell, inform*
sáafar	saafár-t, sáafar-u	yi-**sáafir**, yi-saafir-úun	*travel*
takállam	takallám-t	yi-**takállam**	*speak*
intáDHar	intaDHár-t	yi-**ntáDHir**	*wait, wait for*
ishtághal	ishtaghál-t	yi-**shtághil**	*work*

These verbs present no difficulties as you only need to add the prefixes or suffixes to the relevant stem.

Type A has two minor variants which occur with a few common verbs. In the present tense of **akal** (*eat*) and **akhadh** (*take*) the vowel of the present prefixes is always elided before the stems **aakul** and **aakhudh**, hence **áakul** (*I eat*), **y-áakul** (*he eats*), **n-áakhudh** (*we take*), **y-aakhudh-úun** (*they take*).

The other variant is with verbs whose past stem begins with **w**, two common examples being **wáSal** (*arrive*), and **wágaf** (*stop, stand*). Here the **w** of the present stems (**wSal** and **wgaf**) combines with the prefix vowel to give an **oo** sound: **y-óoSal** (*he arrives*), and **y-óogaf** (*he stops*). Both of the above variants are simply to assist easy pronunciation.

Type B

These verbs have two distinct past stems and one present stem. The first past stem is used for *he*, *she* and *they* (see remarks about suffixes in the introduction above) and the second for all other parts. There are two subdivisions of this type: those which change the internal vowel (**B1**) and those whose second stem adds **-ai** (**B2**). Examples:

B1

Past	Present	Meaning
raaH/ruH	**ruuH**	*go*

raaH (*he went*), **ráaH-at** (*she went*), **ráaH-u** (*they went*), but **ruH-t** (*I/you* masc. *went*), **rúH-ti** (*you* fem. *went*), **rúH-na** (we went), etc.

Present tense is always **ruuH**: **yi-rúuH** (*he goes*), **na-rúuH** (*we go* etc.) Four other types of vowelling occur with this class, e.g.:

Past stems	*Present stem*	
jaab/jib	**jiib**	*bring*
naam/nim	**naam**	*sleep*
araad/arad	**riid**	*want, wish*
iSTaad/iSTad	**STaad**	*hunt*

Note: Although some of the vowel changes seem slight, you must preserve the distinctions between long and short.

B2

Habb/Habbai	**Hibb**	*like, love*

Hább (*he liked*), **Hább-at** (*she liked*), **Hább-u** (*they liked*), but **Habbái-t** (*I/you* masc. *liked*), **Habbái-ti** (*you* fem. *liked*), **Habbái-na** (we liked) etc.; present **yi-Híbb** (*he likes*), **ti-Híbb** (*you* masc./*she likes*), etc.

marr/marrai	**murr**	*pass by*

Note again the two vowelling possibilities in the present are, **i** or **u**.

Type C

These have two stems each for both past and present.

Past tense: stem 1 for *he*, *she* and *they* (as **B1** above) and stem 2 for all other parts.

In addition, the he-form takes a final **-a** (this is the restoration of the original suffix for this part, now dropped in all other types of verb).

Present tense: stem 1 for parts without a suffix, stem 2 for all other parts. (The second present stem is always the same as the first with the final vowel dropped.)

Past	*Present*	
saww/sawwai	**sawwi/saww**	*do, make*

sáwwa (*he did*), **sáww-at** (*she did*), but **sawwái-ti** (*you* fem. *did*), **sawwái-tu** (*you* plur. *did*).: in the present **yi-sáwwi** (*he does*), **ti-sáwwi** (*you* masc./*she does*), but **yi-sawwúun** (*they do*) etc.

Some examples:

mash/mashai	**mshi/msh**	*go, walk*
gar/garai	**gra/gr**	*read*
nas/nasii	**nsa/ns**	*forget*
ishtar/shtarai	**shtara/shtar**	*buy*
ibtad/ibtadai	**btadi/btad**	*begin*

Important note: For the sake of the sense, the *he*-form in the past tense has been given in the vocabularies with the added **-a**. This should be omitted in order to determine the stem.

Irregular verbs

There are only two verbs in Gulf Arabic which can be said to be irregular. These are **ja** or **aja** (*to come*) and **bagha** (*to want, wish for*).

Past Tense			
I came	**jiit**	*we came*	**jíina**
you (masc.) *came*	**jiit**	*you* (plural.) *came*	**jíitu**
you (fem.) *came*	**jíiti**		
he came	**ja**	*they came*	**ju**
she came	**jaat**		

Present Tense			
I come	**áaji**	*we come*	**náaji**
you (masc.) *come*	**tíiji**	*you* (plural.) *come*	**tiijúun**
you (fem.) *come*	**tiijíin**		
he comes	**yíiji**	*they come*	**yiijúun**
she comes	**tíiji**		

This verb has an irregular imperative from an entirely different root:
ta:áal, ta:áal-i, ta:áal-u

bagha behaves like a normal Type **C** in the past, but does all sorts of strange things in the present, depending on where you are in the region. It can be summarised as a Type **C** of two different possible kinds:

Past:
bagh/baghai

Present:
bgha/bgh (e.g. **yíbgha, yibghúun**)
b(b)i/b(b) (e.g. **yíb(b)i, yib(b)úun**)

To avoid difficulties you can always use the synonym **aráad, yiríid**, as has been done in this book.

Glossary of language terms

Although this book is written in as plain language as possible, some linguistic or grammatical terms have been used. It is worthwhile becoming used to these as they are often a quick way to express a complex idea. Here is a list of the main ones used, with particular reference to their use in relation to Arabic.

Accent See **stress**.

Adjectives Adjectives describe a person or thing, e.g. A *huge* building, I am *tired*. In Arabic these have the same properties as the noun (q.v.) and must agree with it in number, gender and definiteness. So: if a noun is feminine, its adjective must be feminine; if a noun is definite, its adjective must be definite, if a noun is plural its adjective must be plural.

Adverb Words which describe how (or sometimes when or where) the action of a verb occurs or has occurred. In English they usually end in *-ly* (He ran *quickly* up the stairs.). In Arabic they either end in **-an** or are phrases such as *with speed*, i.e. *quickly*.

Agreement This grammatical term for describing changes in one word caused by another mainly applies to nouns + adjectives (q. v.), and verbs which must agree with their subjects (feminine subject requires feminine verb etc.).

Article This refers to *a* or *an* (the *indefinite* article), and *the* (the definite article). Arabic does not have an indefinite article. To say *a book* you just say *book*, but it does have a definite article **al-** which is attached or prefixed to the following word.

Cardinal See **number**.

Comparative An adjective which compares two things. In English these end in *-er* or are preceded by the

	word *more* (she is *brighter/more intelligent* than him). *See also* **superlatives.**
Conjunctions	Words which join parts of sentences, such as *and*, *or*, *but* etc.
Consonant	The non-vowel letters: **b, d, g, dh, DH** etc. in this book.
Demonstrative	See **pronoun.**
Dual	A special form in Arabic to refer to *two* of anything, as opposed to one (singular) and more than two (plural).
Elision	Where part of a word, usually a vowel, is omitted to smooth speech.
Gender	Masculine or feminine. See **noun** and **adjective.**
Hidden 't'	The feminine ending of a noun **-ah**, which in certain contexts changes to **-at.**
Imperative	The form of a verb used when telling someone to do something.
Interrogative	Question words. See also **pronoun.**
Negatives	These are words used to negate or deny something: *no*, *not* etc. Arabic uses different words with nouns/adjectives and verbs.
Noun	A noun is the name of a person, thing, place or abstract concept, e.g. Hassan, boy, book, Dubai, economics. In Arabic a noun has three important properties: **1.** It is either masculine or feminine. (There is no 'neuter', or *it*, which you use in English to describe inanimate objects or abstracts etc.) This is called **gender** (q.v.). **2.** It is either singular (one only), dual (two only) or plural (more than two). English does not have a dual. This is called **number.** **3.** It is either definite or indefinite. This is simply logical: the word refers either to an unspecified person, thing etc. or to a specific one. In English, indefinites are often preceded by *a* or *an* (the indefinite article), but this is omitted in Arabic. Definites often have *the*, *this*, *that* etc., or *his*,

her. Names of people, places (words with capital letters in English) are automatically definite, e.g. Ahmed, Bahrain and so on. The concept of definiteness is very important in Arabic as it affects other words in the sentence. (Note: **pronouns** (q. v.) are always definite.)

Number See **noun** and **adjective**.

Numbers The numbers or numerals divide into two sets, *cardinal* (one, two, three, etc.) and *ordinal* (first, second, third).

Object The object of a verb is the thing or person which the action of the verb affects. It contrasts with the subject (q.v.), e.g. *the dog* (subject) *chased the cat* (object).

Ordinal See **number**.

Phrase A phrase is a part of a sentence, not necessarily making sense on its own, but a useful term in describing features of a language.

Pitch Pitch describes whether a word or part of a word is higher on the musical scale than another. It is mainly important in questions which, in Gulf Arabic, are often identical to statements except that the pitch rises towards the end of the phrase or sentence.

Plural In Arabic more than two. See **noun** and **adjective**.

Possessive When something owns or possesses something else. In English you either add *s* to the noun (Charlie's aunt), or use a possessive pronoun: *my* father, or the word *of*, e.g. the manager of the company.

Prefix A short part of a word added to the beginning of a noun or verb. In English for example you have *un-*, *dis-* or *pre-*. In Arabic prefixes alter the meaning of a verb.

Prepositions These are (usually) short words relating a noun to its place in space or time, e.g. English *in*, *on* etc. In Arabic a few common prepositions are prefixed to the word which follows them.

Pronouns Short words used as substitutes for nouns (q.v.). The most important is the personal pronoun. For example the English pronoun *he* has three distinct forms, *he*, *him* and *his* (in other pronouns such as *you* some of these forms have fused together). It will come naturally to you to say *he isn't at home* (not *him* or *his*), and also *I saw him* and *it is his house*. The first of these (*he*) is called a subject pronoun and these pronouns have equivalent words in Arabic. The other two (*him*, known as an object pronoun, and *his*, known as a possessive pronoun) share the same form in Arabic, and are not separate words, but endings or suffixes attached to their nouns. The personal pronouns are the most important, but there are other kinds such as demonstratives (*this*, *that* etc.), relatives (*who*, *which*, *that* in phrases like *the one that I like best*) and interrogatives *who*, *what* and *which* when used in questions like *who goes there*?

Relatives See **pronoun**.

Sentence A sentence is a complete utterance making sense on its own, e.g. *he is in his room*. In English these must contain a **verb** (q.v.), but sentences with *is* and *are* do not have a verb in Arabic. For instance, the sentence above would be in Arabic: *he in his room*.

Stem See **verb**.

Stress Also called accent. This is the part or syllable of a word which is most emphasised, e.g. the first *o* in English *photograph*. In the first few units of this book, stress has been marked with the acute accent: -á, ú, etc., and it is also given in the vocabularies and glossaries.

Subject The subject of a sentence is the person or thing which is carrying out the action. It can be a noun, pronoun or a phrase as in: *Bill* lives in Abu Dhabi, *he* works for the oil company, *the best picture* will win the prize.

Suffix An ending attached to a word which alters its meaning.

Superlative Applied to adjectives when they express the highest level of a quality. In English they end

	in *-est* or are preceded by *most* (*he is the brightest/ most intelligent boy in the class*). See also **comparatives.**
Tense	See **verb.**
Verb	A 'doing' word expressing an action (he *reads* the newspaper every day). Its most important features are: 1. *Tense.* This tells us when the action is/was performed. In Arabic there are only two tenses, present (*I go, am going*) and past (*I went, I have gone*). The future (*I shall go*) is the same as the present with a special prefix. 2. *Inflections.* This means that the prefix and/or suffix of the verb changes according to who is doing the action. In English, most verbs in, for instance, the present tense, undergo only one change: *I go, you go, they go* etc., but *he/she/it goes.* In Arabic there is a different verb part for each person, singular and plural. The part of the verb which remains constant in the middle of all the prefixes and suffixes is called the 'stem'. This is an important concept in learning Arabic, and may be compared to the *go-* part of *goes* in the example above. **Note:** a) that the verb *is/are* is omitted in Arabic, and b) the English verb *to have* is not a real verb in Arabic, but a combination of a *preposition* and a *pronoun* (q.v.).
Vowels	The sounds equivalent to *a, e, i, o, u* or combinations of them in English. Gulf Arabic has **a, i, u** and their long equivalents **aa, ii, uu,** and also **ai** occasionally **o** and **oo.** See also **consonant.**
Word order	In Arabic adjectives usually follow their nouns, e.g. *good man* becomes *man good.* Possessive pronouns are also suffixed to their nouns: *my book* becomes *book-my.*

Arabic–English glossary

Note: Nouns are given in the singular followed by plural in brackets, with **al-** included only in place names and other words where it is always present. The feminine and plural of adjectives is given only if they are irregular (i.e. not **-ah**, **-iin**). Verbs are given in the *he*-form of the past tense followed by the *he*-from of the present tense and the verb group shown in brackets. The order of entries does not take account of the symbols **:** and ’, or distinguish between capital and small letters.

a:máal (pl.) *business affairs*
á:Ta, yá:Ti (C) *to give*
:áa'ilah (-aat) *family*
:áadatan *usually, generally*
:áadi *regular (petrol)*
áakhir *last, end*
:áalam *world*
:aam (a:wáam) *year*
:áaSifah (:awáaSif) *storm*
:áaSimah (:awáaSim) *capital (city)*
áayil (*engine*) *oil*
ab *father*
ábadan *never*
:ábba. yi:ábbi (C) *to fill*
:abd (:ibáad) *worshipper*
abríil *April*
ábu DHábi *Abu Dhabi*
ábyaDH, f. báiDHa (biiDH) *white*
:áfwan *you're welcome, don't mention it; excuse me*
agáll *less, least*
aghúsTos *August*
:ágrab (:agáarib) *scorpion*
ágrab *nearer, nearest*
ágSar *shorter, shortest*

áh(a)l *family, kinsfolk*
ahámm *more/most important*
áhlan wa sáhlan *welcome, hello*
áHmar (f.) **Hámra** (**Húmur**) *red*
áHsan *better, best*
áhwan *better* (from an illness)
áHyáanan *sometimes*
:ain (**:uyúun**) *spring; eye*
aish *what*
aishgádd *how long, how much, what amount?*
:ájab, yí:jab (**A**) *to impress, please* (in the idiom *to like*)
ájnabi (**ajáanib**) *foreign, foreigner*
ákal, yáakul (**A**) *eat*
ák(i)l *food*
ákbar *bigger, biggest*
akh (**ikhwáan/ íkhwah**) *brother*
ákhadh, yáakhudh (**A**) *to take*
akhbáar (**pl.**) *news*
ákhDHar f. **kháDHra** (**khúDHur**) *green*
akíid *certain(ly)*
:aks eksrai *X-ray photograph*
al-'áan *now*
al-ándalus *Arab Spain*
al-baHráin *Bahrain*
al-gharb *the West*
al-gíblah *the direction of prayer, facing Mecca*
al-Hagíigah *really, actually*
al-Hámdu li-l-láah *praise (be) to God*
al-Híin *now*
al-híjrah *the Hegirah*
al-imaaráat al-:arabíyyah al-muttáHidah *the UAE*
al-isláam *Islam*
al-ká:bah *the Kaaba* (holy shrine in Mecca)
al-khalíij (**al-:árabi**) *the* (Arabian) *Gulf*
al-kuwáit *Kuwait*
Al-láah *God, Allah*
al-lail, bi l-lail *night, at night*
al-lúghah al-:arabíyyah *Arabic, the Arabic language*

al-madíinah *Medinah*
al-mámlakah l-muttáHidah *the United Kingdom*
al-mukárramah *Holy* (adjective used after Mecca)
al-munáwwarah *resplendent, illuminated* (used after Medinah)
al-qáahirah *Cairo*
al-qur'áan *the Koran*
al-yáman *Yemen*
al-yóom *today*
:ála *on*
:ála shaan *because, in order to*
:álam (a:láam) *flag*
:alf (aaláaf) *thousand*
:állam, yi:állim (A) *to teach*
almáani (almáan) *German*
ám(i)s *yesterday*
ámbah, hámbah *mango*
:amm (paternal) *uncle*
:ámmah (paternal) *aunt*
amríika *America*
:an *of, about*
ána *I*
ananáas *pineapple*
ánzal, yúnzil (A) *to reveal, send down* (literary usage)
ar-riyáaDH *Riyadh*
aráad, yiríid (B1) *to want, wish*
:árabi (:árab) *Arabic, Arab*
:áraf yí:raf (A) *to know*
árba:ah *four*
arba:atá:shar *14*
arba:íin *40*
árkhaS *cheaper, cheapest*
áS(a)l (uSúul) *origin*
:áS(i)r *late afternoon*
as-sa:udíyyah *Saudi Arabia*
aS-Siin *China*
aS-Súb(a)H *(in the) morning, forenoon*
asáas (úsus) *basis, fundamental belief*
asbríin *aspirin*

áSfar (f.) **Sáfra** (**Súfur**) *yellow*
áSghar *smaller, smallest*
ash-sháarjah *Sharjah*
ash-sharg al-áwsaT *the Middle East*
:ásha *dinner, supper*
:ásharah *ten*
:aSíir *juice*
ásra: *faster, fastest*
áswad (f.) **sóoda** (**suud**) *black*
aatháath (pl.) *furniture*
:aTsháan *thirsty*
áTwal *longer, longest*
aw *or*
awáa'il *the first, early part of*
áwHash *worse, worst*
áwwal *first*
áwwal ams *the day before yesterday*
áwwalan *firstly*
áyDHan *also*
ayskríim *ice cream*
áywa *yes*
ayy *which, any*
ázrag (f.) **zárga** (**zurg**) *blue*

ba:(a)dáin *afterwards, later, then*
ba:d aDH-Dhúh(u)r (in the) *afternoon*
ba:d *after*
ba:d búkrah *the day after tomorrow*
ba:DH *some*
ba:íid (:an) *far (from)*
baab (biibáan) *door, gate*
báagi *change, remainder of something*
báakir/búkrah *tomorrow*
baal *attention*
báarid *cold* (of things)
baaS (-aat) *bus*
baat, yibáat (B1) *to spend the night*
baddáalah *telephone exchange*

bádlah (-aat) *suit* (clothes)
bádri *early*
báH(a)r *sea, beach*
báiDHah (baiDH) *egg*
bait (buyúut) *house*
báitri (bayáatri) *battery*
baizáat *money* (Oman)
bálad (biláad) *town, village, country*
banáfsaji *violet* (colour)
bánchar *puncture*
bándar *town on the coast, port*
bánjari (banáajri) *bracelet*
bank (bunúuk) *bank*
bánnad, yibánnid (A) *to close*
banzíin *petrol*
bard *cold* (noun)
bardáan *cold* (of a person)
bárg *lightning*
bárgar bi l-jíbin *cheeseburger*
bárgar sámak *fishburger*
barnáamij (baráamij) *programme, plan of activity*
barnúuS (baraníiS) *blanket*
barr *land, desert*
bass *only, just, enough, that's all*
báT(i)n *stomach*
baTáaTis *chips, potatoes*
báTTah (baTT) *duck*
bi DH-DHábT *exactly*
bi- *with, by, in*
bi-dúun *without*
bi-kháir *well*
biláad (buldáan) (f.) *country*
bint (banáat) *girl, daughter*
biráik *brakes*
booling *bowling*
burtugáal *orange*
burtugáali *orange* (colour)
bustáan *garden, park*

buTáagah (-aat) *card, postcard*
buTáagah shakhSíyyah *identity card*

chaik (-aat) *cheque*
chaik siyáaHi *traveller's cheque*
chakláit *chocolate*
cháyyak, yicháyyik (A) *to check*
chingáal (chanagíil) *fork*

dáa'irah (dawáayir) (government) *department*
dáawam, yidáawim (A) *to keep office hours*
dáayman *always,*
dábal *4-wheel drive*
dáfa:, yídfa: (A) *to pay*
dagíigah (dagáayig) *minute*
dáirah *Deira* (the commercial quarter of Dubai)
dáizil *diesel*
dajáajah (dajáaj) *chicken*
dállah (dlaal) *coffee pot*
dárajah (-aat) *degree, class, step*
dáras, yídrus (A) *to study*
dárras, yidárris (A) *to teach*
dáwa (adwiyah) *medicine*
dáwlah (dúwal) *state, country, nation*
dáwli *international*
DHáabiT (DHubbáaT) *officer*
DHáh(a)r *back*
dháhab *gold*
DHaif (DHuyúuf) *guest*
DHárab, yíDHrab (A) *to hit, strike, knock*
DHarb *multiplication*
dhiháab *going, single* (ticket)
dhiháab w iyáab *return* (ticket)
DHúh(u)r *noon*
DHuhúur *emergence, appearance*
diin (adyáan) *religion*
disámbar *December*

doktóor (dakáatrah) *doctor*
dooláar (-aat) *dollar*
door (adwáar) *floor, storey*
dráiwil (draiwilíyya) *driver*
dubáy *Dubai*
dukkáan (dakaakíin) (small) *shop*
duwwáar (-áat) *roundabout*

fa *so*
fáaDHi *free, empty*
fáakihah (fawáakih) *fruit*
fáDHDHah *silver*
fáDHDHal, yifáDHDHil (A) *to prefer*
fáj(i)r *dawn*
fákkar, yifákkir (A) *to think*
faláafil *fried bean patties*
faríig (furúug) *team*
fáSSal, yifáSSil (A) *to make, fashion, tailor*
fátaH, yíftaH (A) *to open, conquer*
fáTar, yífTur (A) *to break a fast; have breakfast*
fáwran *immediately, right now*
fáwwat, yifáwwit (A) *to pass, go past* (a place)
fibráayir *February*
fii amáan Al-láah: *goodbye*
fii amáan al-karíim *goodbye* (reply to above)
fii *in*
fiih *there is*
fíkrah (afkáar) *thought, idea*
fíl(i)m (afláam) *film*
fílfil *pepper*
filúus *money*
finjáan (fanajíin) (small coffee) *cup*
foog *above, upstairs*
fúndug (fanáadig) *hotel*
fustáan *(lady's) dress*
fuTúur *breakfast*
fúuTah (fúwaT) *towel*

gá:ad, yíg:ad (A) *to sit, stay, remain*
gáa:ah *hall, large room*
gáadim *next, coming*
gaal yigúul (B1) *to say*
gaam, yigúum (B1) *to rise, get up* (from sleep)
gaas, yigíis (B1) *to measure*
gáb(i)l *before*
gabíilah (gabáayil) *tribe*
gádar, yígdar (A) *to be able*
gadíim *old*
gáfshah (gfáash) *spoon*
gáhwah *coffee*
gála:, yígla: (A) *pull out*
gálam (agláam) *pen*
galóon (-aat) *gallon*
gamíiS (gumSáan) *shirt*
gára, yígra (C) *to read*
garáaj *garage*
garíib min *near* (to)
garn (gurúun) *century*
gaSíir *short*
gáTar *Qatar*
gháali *expensive*
gháda *lunch*
gháilam *turtles* (in Oman; elsewhere **Hámas**)
ghaim or **ghuyúum** *clouds*
ghair *other than, else*
ghassáalah (-aat) *washing machine*
ghooS *diving*
ghraam (-aat) *gram*
ghúrfah (ghúraf) *room*
ghúrfat (ghúraf) ákil *dining room*
ghúrfat (ghúraf) noom *bedroom*
giláas (glaasáat) (drinking) *glass*
giTáar *train*
goolf/lá:bat al-goolf *golf*
gumáash (ágmisha) *cloth, material*
gúTun *cotton*

háadha, (f.) **háadhi (haadhóol)** *this, these*
haadháak, (f.) **haadhíik (haadhooláak)** *that, those*
háadi *quiet, peaceful*
Háajah (-aat) *need* (noun).
háajar, yiháajir (A) *to emigrate*
Háal (aHwáal) *condition*
Haarr *hot*
Háasis bi- *feeling (e.g. illness)*
Habb, yiHíbb (B2) *to like, love*
Hábbah (Hubúub) *pill*
Had *someone*
Hadíigah (Hadáayig) *garden, park*
Hagg *for, belonging to*
Hájaz, yíHjiz (A) *to book, reserve*
Hajj *pilgrimage; pilgrim*
Hálag *earrings*
Halíib *milk*
hámbargar (-aat) *hamburger*
Hammáam (-aat) *bathroom*
Haráami (-iyya) *thief*
Haráarah *heat, temperature*
Harr *heat*
Hásab, yíHsab (A) *to reckon, count, calculate*
HáSSal, yiHáSSil (A) *to get, find, obtain*
HaTT, yiHúTT (B2) *to put, place*
Hátta *until, so that, in order to*
háwa *wind, air*
Hawáali *about, approximately*
hawáayah (-aat) *interest, hobby*
Háwwal, yiHáwwil (A) *to change, exchange*
Hayyáa-k Al-láah *goodbye*
Hiin *when, at the time when*
Hilw *sweet, pleasant, pretty*
hína/híni *here*
hináak *there*
Hisn *fort*
híyya *she, it*
Húmma *fever*

húmma *they*
Húrmah (**Haríim**) *woman*
húwwa *he, it*

ibtáda, yibtádi (C) *to begin, start*
ídha, ídha kaan *if*
ídhan *so, therefore*
iftákar, yiftákir (A) *to think, consider, be of the opinion that*
iHdá:shar *eleven*
iHtáaj, yiHtáaj (B1) **íla** *to need*
iHtifáal (**-aat**) *celebration, party, function*
iHtimáal (lit. *possibility*) *possible, perhaps*
:iid (**a:yáad**) *Eid, religious festival*
iid (dual **iidáin**) *hand, arm*
ijáazah (**-aat**) *holiday*
iksbráis *express*
ílla *except for, less*
ílli *who/which, the one who/which*
:imáarah (**-aat**) *apartment building, block*
imáarah (**-áat**) *emirate*
in shaa' Al-láah *if God wills*
inbásaT, yinbásiT min (A) *to enjoy*
:ind *at, with* (used for to have)
:índ-ma *when, while*
ingiltérra *England*
inglíizi (pl. **ingliiz**) *English*
inn *that* (conjunction)
ínta/ínti/íntu *you* (m., f. and pl.)
intáDHar, yintáDHir (A) *to wait*
intáshar, yintáshir (A) *to spread, spread out*
ís(i)m (**asáami**) *name*
isbáanya *Spain*
:ísha *evening prayer*
isháal (pronounced **is-háal**) *diarrhœa*
:ishríin *20*
ishtághal, yishtághal (A) *to work*
ishtára, yishtári (C) *to buy*
iskutlánda *Scotland*

isláami *Islamic*
istá'jar, yistá'jir (A) *to hire, rent*
iSTáad, yiSTáad (B1)(**sámak**) *to hunt* (fish), *to fish*
istáma:, yistámi: íla (A) *to listen to*
istaráaH, yistaríiH (B1) *to rest, relax, take one's ease*
ithná:shar *12*
ithnáin, (f.) **thintáin** *two*
ittáSal, yittáSil (A) **fii** *to phone, contact*
ittijáah *direction, facing, in the direction of*
:iyáadah (-aat) *clinic*

jaa yíiji (C irreg.) *to come*
jaab, yijíib (B1) *to bring, get, collect, obtain*
jáahil (jihháal) *child*
jáahiz *ready*
jáami: (jawáami:) (big) *mosque*
jáami:ah (-aat) *university*
jábal (jibáal) *mountain, desert*
jadd (ajdáad) *grandfather* (ancestors)
jáddah *grandmother*
jadíid (júdad, jidáad) *new*
jaish (juyúush) *army*
jámal (jimáal) *camel*
jamb *next to*
jamíil *beautiful*
jánTah *suitcase* (alternative to **shánTah**)
janúub *south*
jawáaz as-sáfar *passport*
jáwlah (-aat) *tour*
jaww *air, atmosphere, weather*
jáyyid *good* (quality)
jázar *carrots*
jazíilan *copious, very much* (used only after **shúkran** *thanks*)
jazíirah (jazáayir/júzur) *island*
jazíirat al-: árab *the Arabian peninsula*
jíb(i)n *cheese*
jíddan *very*
jiháaz (ájhizah) *appliance, piece of equipment*

jináaH (**ájniHah**) *suite, wing*
jináih (**-aat**) **starlíini** *pound sterling*
jís(i)r (**jusúur**) *bridge*
joo:áan *hungry*
júndi (**junúud**) *soldier*

káamil *complete*
káamira (**-aat**) *camera*
kaan, yikúun (B1) *was* (present tense *will/would be*)
káatib (**kuttáab**) *clerk*
kábat (**-aat**) *cupboard, wardrobe*
kabíir (**kibáar**) *big*
kaHH, yikúHH (B2) *to cough*
káhrab(a) *electricity*
kahrabáa'i *electrical*
kaif *how*
kaik *pastry, cake*
kalb (**kiláab**) *dog*
kálimah (**-aat**) *word*
kam *how much, how many*
kamáan *also, as well*
kandáishan *air-conditioning*
karíim (**kiráam**) *generous, noble* (after Koran *holy*)
kart (**kurúut**) *card*
kásar, yíksir (A) *to break*
kasláan *lazy*
kássar, yikássir (A) *to break up, smash*
kátab, yíktib (A) *to write*
kathíir *much, many, a lot, often, frequently*
khaal *maternal uncle*
kháalah *maternal aunt*
kháaliS *pure*; (after negative) *at all*
kháarij *outside*
khábbar, yikhábbir (A) *to tell, inform*
kháffaf, yikháffif (A) *to lighten, reduce*
khafíif *light* (in weight)
kháimah (**khiyáam**) *tent*
khálla, yikhálli (C) *to let, leave*
khállaS, yikhálliS (A) *to finish, complete something*

khamastá:shar *15*
khámsah *five*
khamsíin *50*
khánjar (khanáajir) *dagger*
kharbáan *broken down, not working*
khaSáarah *a pity*
khaSíiSah (khaSáa'iS) *characteristic, feature*
kháTar (akhTáar) *danger*
khayyáaT (-iin/khayaayíiT) *tailor*
khídmah (khidmáat) *service*
kídha, chídha, chídhi *like this, so*
kíilo, kiiloghráam *kilogram*
kíilo, kiilomít(i)r *kilometre*
kitáab (kútub) *book*
kull *all, each, every*
kúrah, (more formally) **kúrat al-gádam** *football*
kúrsi (karáasi) *chair*
kúuli (kuulíyya) *coolie, labourer*

lá:ab yíl:ab (A) *to play*
laa . . . wála *neither . . . nor*
laa *no*
laa shay *nothing*
láakin *but*
láazim *necessary*
lában *yoghourt drink*
ládagh, yíldagh (A) *to sting*
ládghat náHlah *bee-sting*
ladhíidh *delicious*
laff, yilíff (B2) *to turn* (direction)
láH(a)m *meat*
láHDHah (laHaDHáat) *moment*
lail *night* in general; **láilah (layáali)** *a night, nights*
laimóon *lemon, lime*
láisan (layáasin) *licence*
láisan maal siwáagah *driving licence*
laish *why*
lait (-aat) *light* (of a car, street lamp)
láitir, lítir (-aat) *litre*

lámbah (-aat) *lamp*
lándan *London*
law samáHt *if you please*
law, loo *if*
li'ánn *because*
li-, la- *to, for*
li-gháayat *up to, until*
li-múddat aish *for how long*
líHyah *beard*
lóobi *lobby* (hotel)
lóoHah (-aat) *board,* (framed) *picture*
loon (alwáan) *colour*
looz *almonds*
lúbsah (-aat) (lady's) *dress*
lúghah (-aat) *language*
lúghat al-úmm *mother tongue* (lit. *language of the mother*)

má:a *with, along with, together with*
má:a l-ásaf *sorry*
má:a s-saláamah *goodbye*
ma:gúul *reasonable*
ma:júun al-asnáan *toothpaste*
má:na *meaning*
maa :aláish *it doesn't matter*
maa *not* (before verbs)
maa sháa' alláah! *good heavens!*
maa yikháalif *that's OK, it doesn't matter*
maa zaal *still* (continuing something)
máaDHi *past, last* (year, week etc.)
maal *belonging to, associated with*
maay *water*
máayo *May*
máblagh (mabáaligh) *sum, amount* (money)
maDHbúuT *exact, correct*
mádrasah (madáaris) *school*
mafrúuDH *obligatory, required, should be done*
mafrúush *furnished*
maftúuH *open*

magáas *size*
magfúul *closed, shut*
mágha (pronounced **mág-ha**) (**magáahi**) *café*
mágli *fried*
magsúumah :ala *divided by*
maHáll (-aat) (large) *shop*
maHáTTah (-aat) *station*
maHáTTat al-baaS *bus station*
maHjúuz *booked, reserved*
maiz (amyáaz) *table*
majjáanan *free, gratis*
majlis (majáalis) *sitting-, reception room;* also *council*
makáan (-aat) *place*
makháddah (-aat) *pillow*
mákHalah (pronounced **mák-Halah**) *kohl pot*
makhSúuS *special*
makíinat Sarf *cash machine*
mákkah *Mecca*
maksúur *broken*
máktab (makáatib) *office, desk*
máktab al-baríid *post office*
maktúub *written*
málak, yímlik (A) *to own*
málik (mulúuk) *king*
man, min *who*
mánTigah (manáaTig) *area, region*
mára (niswáan) *woman*
márHab *welcome, hello*
márham *cream* (pharmaceutical)
maríiDH (márDHa) *ill; sick person, patient*
márkaz (maráakiz) *centre*
márkaz ash-shúrTah *police station*
márkaz tijáari *shopping centre*
márkazi *central*
márrah (-aat) *time, occasion*
mars *March*
márwaHah (maráawiH) *fan*
máS(i)r *Egypt*

másbaH (masáabiH) *swimming pool*
másha, yímshi (C) *to walk*
mashghúul *busy*
mashhúur *famous, well known*
mashruubáat *drinks*
másjid (masáajid) (small) *mosque*
máT:am (maTáa:im) *restaurant*
máta *when?* (in questions)
maTáar (-aat) *airport*
máTar *rain*
máTbakh (maTáabikh) *kitchen*
mátHaf (matáaHif) *museum*
máthalan *for example*
matrúus *full*
máw:id (mawa:íid) *appointment;* (pl. *schedule, operating hours*)
mawjúud *present, here*
mawlúud *born*
mázra:ah (mazáari:) *farm, country estate*
miftáaH (mafatíiH) *key*
míghsalah *washbasin, sink*
miiláadi *pertaining to the birth of Christ, AD.*
míina (mawáani) *port, harbour*
míjmar (majáamir) *incense burner*
milyóon (malaayíin) *million*
min fáDHl-ak/-ich/-kum *please*
min *from; who* (also **man**)
min gábil *before, beforehand*
min Hiin íla Hiin *now and then, occasionally*
miráayah (-aat) *mirror*
míS:ad (maSáa:id) *lift, elevator*
mísa *afternoon, evening*
mit'ákkid *sure*
mit:áwwid :ála *used to, accustomed to*
míth(i)l *like, similar to*
mitzáwwaj *married*
míyyah, (also **ímya**) *hundred*
móosam (mawáasim) *season*
mooz *bananas*

mu'támar (-aat) *conference, convention*
mu:áaSir *contemporary*
mubáasharatan *directly*
mubáashir *direct*
mudárris (-íin) *teacher* (m.)
mudárrisah (-aat) *teacher* (f.)
múddah *period of time*
mudíir (**múdara**) *manager*
mufíid *effective, beneficial*
mugáddam *in advance*
muhándis (-íin) *engineer*
mujtáhid *hard-working, diligent*
muláwwan *coloured*
múmkin *possible*
mumtáaz *excellent; super, premium* (petrol)
munáasib *suitable, convenient*
murúur *traffic*
múshkilah (**masháakil**) *problem*
musíiga *music*
mustáshfa (**mustashfayáat**) *hospital*
mut'ákkid *sure*
mut(a)'ássif *sorry*
muu, mub *not* (before nouns and adjectives)
muwaaSaláat *communications, transport*
muwáDHDHaf (-iin) *official*

náfar (**anfáar**) *individual, person* (used in counting)
ná:am *yes*
náagiS *minus*
naam, yináam (B1) *to sleep, go to sleep*
naas *people*
nábi (**anbiyáa'**) *prophet*
naDHDHáarah (-áat) (pair of) *glasses*
naDHDHáarah maal shams (pair of) *sun-glasses*
naDHíif *clean, in good condition*
náfa:, yínfa: (A) *to be suitable, useful*
nafs *self, same*
nafs ash-shay *the same thing*

náHla (náHal) *bee*
nákhlah (nakhíil) *palm tree*
narjíil *coconuts*
níHna *we*
noom *sleep* (noun)
nufámbar *November*
nuSS *half*

októobar *October*

pánkah or **bánkah (-aat)** *ceiling fan*

ra'y (aaráa) *opinion*
rá:(a)d *thunder*
ráabi: *fourth*
ráagid (adj.) *in bed* (lit. *lying down*)
raaH, yirúuH (B1) *to go*
raas (ruus) *head, headland*
raas al-kháimah *Ras al-Khaimah*
raff (rufúuf) *shelf*
rág(a)m (argáam) *number*
rágad, yírgad (A) *to lie down, stay in bed*
rája:, yírja: (A) *to return, come back, go back*
rájja:, yirájji: (A) *to return something, give back*
rajjáal (rajajíil) *man*
rakhíiS *cheap*
raSáaS *lead* (metal)
rasúul Al-láah *the Apostle of God* (i.e. the Prophet Muhammad)
ribáaT (rúbaT) *bandage*
ríHlah (-aat) *outing, trip, journey*
rijl (rujúul) *foot, leg*
rimáal *sands* (sing. **rám(a)l**)
risáalah (rasáayil) *letter*
riyáaDHah (-aat) *sport*
riyúug *breakfast*
rúba: *quarter*
rúkhSat siwáagah *driving permit*

sá'al, yis'al (A) *to ask*
Sá:(a)b *difficult*
sa:úudi *Saudi*
sáa:ad, yisáa:id (A) *to help*
sáa:ah (-aat) *hour, clock, watch*
Saabúun *soap*
sáafar, yisáafir (A) *to travel*
saag, yisúug (B1) *to drive*
SáaHib (aSHáab) *master, owner; friend*
SáaHib al-milk *landlord*
sáakhin *warm, hot*
sáakin (-iin) (adj.) *staying;* (noun) (pl. **sukkáan**) *inhabitant. resident*
Sáalah *hall* (of a house)
Saam, yiSúum(B1) *to fast*
Saar, yiSíir (B1) *to become, happen*
sáar, yisíir (B1) *to go, travel*
sáawa, yisáawi (C) *to equal, add up to*
sáb:ah *seven*
sab:atá:shar *17*
sab:íin *70*
SabáaH *morning*
SabáaH al-kháir *good morning*
SabáaH an-núur (reply to **SabáaH al-kháir**)
sábaH, yísbaH (A) *to swim, bathe*
sabtámbar *September*
Sadíig (áSdiga) *friend* (m.)
Sadíigah (-aat) *friend* (f.)
sáfar *travel*
safíinah (súfun) *ship*
safíir (súfara) *ambassador*
Saghíir (Sugháar) *small, young*
SáH(a)n (SuHúun) *plate*
SaHíiH *correct, right*
Said as-sámak *fishing*
Saif *summer*
sákan, yískun (A) *to live, reside*
Sákhrah (Sukhúur) *rock*

SálaTah *salad*
Sálla Al-láahu :alái-hi wa sállam *peace be upon Him (used after the mentioning the name of the Prophet Muhammad)*
Sálla, yiSálli (C) *to pray, say one's prayers*
SállaH, yiSálliH (A) *to repair*
Sálsah *sauce*
sámak *fish*
sámi:, yísma: (A) *to hear*
sámma, yisámmi (C) *to call, name*
sánah (sanawáat/siníin) *year*
sand(A)wíich (-áat) *sandwich*
Sáraf, yíSraf (A) *to cash, change money*
saríir (saráayir) *bed*
Sarráaf (-iin) *cashier; money changer*
sáwwa, yisáwwi (C) *to do, make*
sawwáag (also **dráiwil**) *driver*
Sáwwar, yiSáwwir (A) *to photograph, take photographs*
Saydalíyyah (-aat) *pharmacy*
sayyáarah (-aat) *car*
shaaf, yishúuf (B1) *to see, watch, look at*
sháari: (shawáari:) *street*
shaay, chaay *tea*
shadíid *violent, acute*
shággah/shíggah (shígag) *flat, apartment*
sháh(a)r (shuhúur) *month*
shájarah (ashjáar) *tree*
shák(i)l (ashkáal) *appearance; shape, type, kind*
shakhS (ashkháaS) *person, individual*
shamáal *North*
shams (f.) *sun*
shánTah (shúnuT) *bag, suitcase*
shárab, yíshrab (A) *to drink*
sharg *East*
shárikah (-aat) *company, firm*
shárshaf (sharáashif) (bed) *sheet*
shawármah *sliced roast lamb, doner kebab*
shay (ashyáa) *thing*
shay ghair *something else, other*

shibs *crisps, chips*
shíishah/maHaTTat banzíin *filling station*
shíkar *sugar*
shíta *winter*
shúgh(u)l (ashgháal) *work, working* (pl. *public works, road works*)
shúkran *thanks, thank you*
shúrTah *police*
shwáyyah *a little, some*
si:r (as:áar) *price, exchange rate*
sibáag al-jimáal *camel racing*
sibáaHah *swimming*
sifáarah (-aat) *embassy*
Síf(i)r *zero*
síidah *straight on, straight ahead*
síinima (-aat) *cinema*
sikkíin (sakaakíin) *knife*
sikritáirah (-aat) *secretary* (f.)
sílsilah (saláasil) *chain*
sinn (asnáan) *tooth*
sitáarah (satáayir) *curtains*
sittá:shar *16*
síttah *six*
sittíin *60*
siwáagah, siyáagah *driving* (car)
Soom *fast, fasting*
Sudáa: *headache*
Sufríyyah (Safáari) *pan* (cooking)
suhúulah *ease*
súr:ah *speed*
Suuf *wool*
suug (aswáag) *market*
Súurah (Súwar) *picture, photograph*

ta'míin *insurance*
ta:áal/i/u *come! (imperative)*
tá:ab, yít:ab (A) *to tire*
ta:állam, yit:állam (A) *to learn*
ta:áwwar, yit:áwwar (A) *to be, get wounded*

ta:báan *tired, ill*
ta:líim *education*
Táabag (Tawáabig) *floor, storey*
Táabi: (Tawáabi:) *(postage) stamp*
Táalib (Tulláab or **Tálabah)** *student* (m.)
Táalibah (-aat) *student* (f.)
taaríikh *date, history*
taayr (-aat) *tyre*
Táb:an *of course, naturally*
Tábakh, yíTbukh (A) *to cook*
Tabbáakhah (-aat) *cooker*
Tabíib (aTíbba) *doctor*
Tabíib al-asnáan *dentist*
Tabíikh *cooking, cuisine*
tádfi'ah *heating*
tádhkarah (tadháakir) *ticket*
t(a)fáDHDHal *here you are, help yourself*
tafSíil *making, fashioning*
taghádda, yitghádda (C) *to lunch, eat lunch*
tagríiban *approximately*
táH(i)t *underneath, below, downstairs*
Tair (Thyúur) *bird*
takállam, yitkállam (A) *to speak*
takhfíiDH (-aat) *discount, reduction*
takyíif *air conditioning*
Tála:, yíTla: (A) *to leave, depart, go out*
Tálab, yíTlub (A) *to order* (something), *ask for*
tánis *tennis*
tánki *tank* (car)
táras, yítrus (A) *to fill*
Tard (Turúud) *parcel, package*
Taríig (Túrug) *road, way*
Tárrash, yiTárrish (A) *to send*
tashkíil (-aat) *selection, variety*
Tawáari' (pl.) *casualty, emergency*
Tayyáarah (-aat) *plane*
Táyyib *good, well, fine, OK*
tháalith *third*

tháani *second*
thaláathah *three*
thalaathíin *30*
thalaathtá:shar *13*
thalj *ice*
thalláajah (-aat) *refrigerator*
thamáan(i)yah *8*
thamaaníin *80*
thamantá:shar *eighteen*
thilth *third* (fraction)
Tibb (the science of) *medicine*
tijáarah *commerce*
tijáari *commercial*
tilifóon *telephone*
tilifizyóon *television*
tís:ah *nine*
tis:atá:shar *19*
tis:íin *90*
tuffáaH *apples*
Tuul *throughout*

ukht (akhawáat) *sister*
:úm(u)r *life, age*
:umáan *Oman*
:úmlah (-aat) *currency*
umm (ummaháat) *mother*
urúbba *Europe*
usbúu: (asabíi:) *week*
ustráalya *Australia*
úula fem. of **áwwal** *first*

víidiyoo or **fíidiyoo (viidiyooháat)** *video*
vílla or **fíllah (vílal, fílal)** *villa*

wa, w *and*
wa-l-láahi *by God!*
wáadi (widyáan) *wadi, dried-up river bed, valley*
wáaHa (-aat) *oasis*

wáaHid *one*
wáajid *much, many*
wáalid *father*
wáalidah *mother*
waalidáin *parents*
wáarim *swollen*
wáasi: *spacious*
wádda, yiwáddi (C) *to take to, deliver*
wag(i)t *time*
wágaf, yóogaf (A) *to stop, come to a stop*
wágga:, yiwággi: (A) *to sign*
wággaf, yiwággif (A) *to stop* (a car, etc.)
wagt al-faráagh *leisure* (time)
wain *where*
wája: *ache, pain*
wája: al-asnáan *toothache*
wája:, yóoja: (A) *to give pain*
wájabah (-aat) *meal*
wála *nor* (lit. *and not*)
wálad (awláad) *boy, son;* (pl. *children*)
wáragah (awráag) (sheet of) *paper*
wárshah (-aat) *workshop*
wás(a)T *middle, centre*
wás(i)kh *dirty*
wáSal, yóoSal (A) *to arrive*
wáSSal, yiwáSSil (A) *to transport, take to*
wáTan (awTáan) *nation, homeland*
wáTani *national*
wazíir (wúzara) *minister*
wazn (awzáan) *weight*
wíyya *with, together with*
wizáarah (-aat) *ministry*
wizáarat ad-daakhilíyyah *Ministry of the Interior*
wizáarat al-i:láam *Ministry of Information*
wizáarat al-khaarijíyyah *Ministry of Foreign Affairs*
wizáarat aS-SíHHah *Ministry of Health*
wizáarat at-ta:líim *Ministry of Education*
wizáarat ath-thaqáafah *Ministry of Culture*

yaa (used before names when addressing people)
yamíin *right* (direction)
yanáayir *January*
yímkin *maybe*
yisáar *left* (direction)
yoom (ayyáam) *day*
yoom al-áHad *Sunday*
yoom al-árba:ah *Wednesday*
yoom al-ithnáin *Monday*
yoom al-júma:ah *Friday*
yoom al-khamíis *Thursday*
yoom ath-thaláathah *Tuesday*
yoom as-sabt *Saturday*
yúulyo *July*
yúunyo *June*

záa'ir or **záayir (zuwwáar)** *visitor*
zaa:, yizúu: (B1) *to vomit*
záar, yizúur (B1) *to visit*
záayid *plus*
zain *OK, good*
ziyáadah *more, increase*
zooj *husband*
zóojah *wife*
zoolíyyah (zawáali) *carpet*
zuhúur *flowers*
zukáam *a cold*

English–Arabic glossary

a little, some **shwáyyah**
a pity **khaSáarah**
A.D. **miiláadi**
about, approximately **Hawáali**
above, upstairs **foog**
ache, pain **wája:**
after **ba:d**
afternoon **ba:d aDH-DHúhur**
afterwards, later, then **ba:(a)dáin**
age **:úm(u)r**
air conditioning **kandáishan, takyíif**
air, atmosphere, weather **jaww**
airport **maTáar (-aat)**
all, each, every **kull**
almonds **looz**
also **áyDHan, kamáan**
always **dáayman**
ambassador **safíir (súfara)**
America **amríika**
and **wa, w**
any **ayy**
apartment building **:imáarah (-aat)**
appearance; type, shape, kind **shák(i)l (ashkáal)**
apples **tuffáaH**
appliance **jiháaz (ájhizah)**
appointment **máw:id (mawa:íid)**
approximately **tagríiban, Hawáali**
April **abríil**
Arabic, Arab **:árabi (:árab)**
Arabic, the Arabic language **al-lúghah al-:arabíyyah**
area, region **mánTigah (manáaTig)**
army **jaish (juyúush)**
arrive **wáSal, yóoSal (A)**

ask sá'al, yís'al (A)
aspirin asbríin
attention baal
August aghúsTos
aunt, paternal :ámmah, *maternal* kháalah
Australia ustráalya

back DHáh(a)r
bag, suitcase shánTah (shúnuT)
Bahrain al-baHráin
bananas mooz
bandage ribáaT (rúbaT)
bank bank (bunúuk)
basis asáas (úsus)
bathroom Hammáam (-aat)
battery báitri (bayáatri)
be kaan (past), yikúun (future) (B1); not used in the present)
be able gádar, yígdar (A)
be suitable, useful náfa:, yínfa: (A)
be, get wounded ta:áwwar, yit:áwwar (A)
beard líHyah
beautiful jamíil
because li'ánn, :ála shaan
become, happen Saar, yiSíir (B1)
bed saríir (saráayir)
bedroom ghúrfat (ghúraf) noom
bee náHla (náHal)
bee-sting ládghat náHlah
before gáb(i)l
beforehand min gábil
begin ibtáda, yibtádi (C)
belonging to, associated with maal
better, best áHsan; (from an illness) áhwan
big kabíir (kibáar)
bigger, biggest ákbar
bird Tair (Tuyúur)
black áswad f. sóoda (suud)
blanket barnúuS (baraníiS)

blue ázrag f. zárga (zurg)
board, (framed) *picture* lóoHah (-aat)
book kitáab (kútub)
book, reserve Hájaz, yíHjiz (A)
booked, reserved maHjúuz
born mawlúud
*boy, son; (*pl. *children)* wálad (awláad)
bracelet bánjari (banáajri)
brakes biráik
break kásar, yíksir (A)
break up, smash kássar, yikássir (A)
breakfast fuTúur, riyúug
breakfast (to eat) fáTar, yífTur (A)
bridge jís(i)r (jusúur)
bring, get jaab, yijíib (B1)
broken maksúur
broken down, not working kharbáan
brother akh (ikhwáan)
bus baaS (-aat)
bus station maHáTTat al-baaS
busy mashghúul
but láakin
buy ishtára yishtári (C)

café mágha (magáahi), gáhwah
Cairo al-qáahirah
cake kaik
call, name sámma, yisámmi (C)
camel jámal (jimáal)
camel racing sibáag al-jimáal
camera káamira (-aat), áalat taSwíir
capital (city) :áaSimah (:awáaSim)
car sayyáarah (-aat)
card kart (kurúut)
card, postcard buTáagah (-aat)
carpet zoolíyyah (zawáali)
carrots jázar
cash, change money Sáraf, yíSraf (A)

cash machine makíinat Sarf
cashier; money changer Sarráaf (-iin)
casualty, emergency Tawáari' (pl.)
ceiling fan pánkah or bánkah (-aat), márwaHah (maráawiH)
celebration, party, function iHtifáal (-aat)
central márkazi
centre márkaz (maráakiz)
century garn (gurúun)
certain(ly) Táb(a):an, akíid
chain sílsilah (saláasil)
chair kúrsi (karáasi)
change, exchange Háwwal, yiHáwwil (A)
change, remainder of something báagi
characteristics khaSáa'iS
cheap rakhíiS
cheaper, cheapest árkhaS
check cháyyak, yicháyyik (A)
cheese jíb(i)n
cheque chaik (-aat)
chicken dajáajah (dajáaj)
child jáahil (jihháal)
China aS-Siin
chips, potatoes baTáaTis
chocolate chakláit
cinema síinima (-aat)
clean naDHíif
clerk káatib (kuttáab)
clinic :iyáadah (-aat)
clock, watch sáa:ah (-aat)
close bánnad, yibánnid (A)
closed, shut magfúul, mubánnad
cloth, material gumáash (ágmisha)
clouds ghaim/ghuyúum
coconuts narjíil
coffee gáhwah
coffee pot dállah (dlaal)
cold (illness) zukáam
cold (noun) bard

cold (adj. of a person) **bardáan**
cold (of things) **báarid**
colour **loon (alwáan)**
coloured **muláwwan**
come **jaa, yíiji** (C irreg.)
come! (imperative) **ta:áal/i/u**
commerce **tijáarah**
commercial **tijáari**
communications **muwaaSaláat**
company, firm **shárikah (-aat)**
complete **káamil**
condition **Háal (aHwáal)**
conference **mu'támar (-aat)**
contemporary **mu:áaSir**
cook **Tábakh, yíTbukh** (A)
cooker **Tabbáakhah (-aat)**
cooking, cuisine **Tabíikh**
coolie, labourer **kúuli (kuulíyya)**
correct, right **SaHíiH**
cotton **gúTun**
cough **kaHH, yikúHH** (B2)
country **biláad (buldáan)** (f.)
cream (pharmaceutical) **márham**
crisps, chips **shibs**
cup (small coffee) **finjáan (fanajíin)**
cupboard, wardrobe **kábat (-aat)**
currency **:úmlah (-aat)**
curtain **sitáarah (satáayir)**

dagger **khánjar (khanáajir)**
danger **kháTar (akhTáar)**
date **taaríikh**
dawn **fáj(i)r**
day **yoom (ayyáam)**
day after tomorrow **ba:d búkrah**
day before yesterday **áwwal ams**
December **disámbar**
degree, class, step **dárajah (-aat)**

delicious **ladhíidh**
dentist **Tabíib al-asnáan**
department (government) **dáa'irah (dawáayir)**
desk **máktab (makáatib)**
diarrhœa **isháal** (pronounced **is-háal)**
diesel **dáizil**
difficult **Sá:(a)b**
dining room **ghúrfat (ghúraf) ákil**
dinner **:ásha**
direction of prayer **al-gíblah**
direction; facing, in the direction of **ittijáah**
direct **mubáashir**
directly **mubáasharatan**
dirty **wás(i)kh**
discount **takhfíiDH (-aat)**
divided by **magsúumah :ala**
diving **ghooS**
do, make **sáwwa, yisáwwi (C)**
doctor **doktóor (dakáatrah), Tabíib (aTíbba)**
dog **kalb (kiláab)**
dollar **dooláar (-aat)**
door, gate **baab (biibáan)**
dress (lady's) **lúbsah (-aat)/fustáan (fasatíin)**
drink **shárab, yíshrab (A)**
drinks **mashruubáat**
drive **saag, yisúug (B1)**
driver **sawwáag (-iin), dráiwil (draiwilíyya)**
driving **siwáagah, siyáagah**
driving licence **láisan maal siwáagah**
duck **báTTah (baTT)**

each **kull**
early **bádri**
earrings **Hálag**
ease **suhúulah**
east **sharg**
education **ta:líim**
effective, beneficial **mufíid**

egg **báiDHah (baiDH)**
Egypt **máS(i)r**
Eid, religious festival **:iid (a:yáad)**
eight **thamáan(i)yah**
18 **thamantá:shar**
80 **thamaaníin**
electrical **kahrabáa'i**
electricity **káhrab(a)**
11 **iHdá:shar**
else **ghair**
embassy **sifáarah (-aat)**
emigrate **háajar, yiháajir** (A)
emirate **imáarah (-áat)**
engineer **muhándis (-íin)**
England **ingiltérra**
English **inglíizi (inglíiz)**
enjoy **inbásaT, yinbásiT min** (A)
equal, add up to **sáawa, yisáawi** (C)
Europe **urúbba**
every **kull**
evening **mísa**
evening prayer **:ísha**
exact, correct **maDHbúuT**
exactly **bi DH-DHabT**
excellent; super, premium (petrol) **mumtáaz**
except **ílla**
exchange (telephone) **baddáalah**
expensive **gháali**
eye **:ain (:uyúun)** (f.)

family **:áa'ilah, :áayilah (-aat)**
family, kinsfolk. **áh(a)l**
famous **mashhúur**
fan **márwaHah (maráawiH)**
far(from) **ba:íid (:an)**
farm, country estate **mázra:ah (mazáari:)**
fast, quickly **bi-súr(a):ah**
fast, fasting **Soom**

fast **Saam, yiSúum** (B1)
faster, fastest **ásra:**
father **ab, wáalid**
February **fibráayir**
feeling (illness) **Háasis bi-**
fever **Húmma**
15 **khamastá:shar**
50 **khamsíin**
fill **táras, yítrus** (A), **:ábba, yi:ábbi** (C)
filling station **shíishah** or **maHáTTat banzíin**
film **fíl(i)m (afláam)**
finish, complete **khállaS, yikhálliS** (A)
first **áwwal,** fem. **úula**
firstly **áwwalan**
fish **sámak**
fish **iSTáad, yiSTáad** (B1) **sámak**
fishing **Said as-sámak**
five **khámsah**
flag **:álam (a:láam)**
flat, apartment **shággah** or **shíggah (shígag)**
floor, storey **door (adwáar), Táabag (Tawáabig)**
flowers **zuhúur**
food **ák(i)l**
foot, leg **rijl (rujúul)**
football **kúrah,** or more formally **kúrat al-gádam**
for example **máthalan**
for, belonging to **Hagg, maal**
foreign, foreigner **ájnabi (ajáanib)**
fork **chingáal (chanagíil)**
fort **Hisn**
40 **arba:íin**
four **árba:ah**
14 **arba:atá:shar**
fourth **ráabi:**
4-wheel drive **dábal**
free, empty **fáaDHi**
free, gratis **majjáanan**
Friday **yoom al-júma:ah**

fried **mágli**
friend (f.) **Sadíigah (-aat)**
friend (m.) **Sadíig (áSdiga)**
from **min**
fruit **fáakihah (fawáakih)**
full **matrúus**
furnished **mafrúush**
furniture **aatháath** (pl.)

gallon **galóon (-aat)**
garage **garáaj**
garden, park **Hadíigah (Hadáayig), bustáan**
German **almáani (almáan)**
get, find, obtain **HáSSal, yiHáSSil** (A)
girl, daughter **bint (banáat)**
give **á:Ta, yá:Ti** (C)
give back, return **rájja:, yirájji:** (A)
give pain **wája:, yóoja:** (A)
glass (drinking) **giláas (glaasáat),** *pane of* **jáamah**
glasses **naDHDHáarah (-áat)**
go **raaH yirúuH (B1), sáar, yisíir** (B1)
God, Allah **Al-láah**
gold **dháhab**
golf **goolf** or **lá:bat al-goolf**
good (quality) **jáyyid**
goodbye **má:a s-saláamah**
good morning **SabáaH al-kháir,** (reply **SabáaH an-núur**)
good, well, fine, OK **zain, Táyyib**
gram **ghraam (-aat)**
grandfather (ancestors) **jadd (ajdáad)**
grandmother **jáddah**
green **ákhDHar** f. **kháDHra (khúDHur)**
guest **DHaif (DHuyúuf)**
Gulf, the (Arabian) **al-khalíij (al-:árabi)**

half **nuSS**
hall (of a house) **Sáalah**
hand, arm **iid (iidáin)**

harbour, port míina (mawáani)
hard-working, diligent mujtáhid
have :ind (plus noun or pronoun suffix)
he, it húwwa
head, headland, raas (ruus)
headache Sudáa:
hear sámi:, yísma: (A)
heat Harr, Haráarah
heating tádfi'ah
Hegirah, the al-híjrah
help sáa:ad, yisáa:id (A)
here hína or híni; *present* mawjúud
hire, rent istá'jar yistá'jir (A)
hit, strike DHárab, yíDHrab (A)
holiday ijáazah (-aat)
hospital mustáshfa (mustashfayáat)
hot Haarr
hotel fúndug (fanáadig)
hour sáa:ah (-aat)
house bait (buyúut)
how kaif
how much, how many kam, aishgádd
hundred míyyah, (also ímya)
hungry joo:áan
husband zooj

I ána
ice thalj
ice cream ayskríim
identity card buTáagah shakhSíyyah
if ídha, ídha kaan, law, loo, in
ill; sick (person), *patient* maríiDH (márDHa)
immediately fáwran
impress, please :ájab, yí:jab (A)
in fii
in advance mugáddam
in order to :ála shaan
incense burner míjmar (majáamir)

individual, person (used in counting) **náfar (anfáar)**
inside **dáakhil**
insurance **ta'míin**
interest, hobby **hawáayah (-aat)**
international **dáwli**
Islam **al-isláam**
Islamic **isláami**
island **jazíirah (jazáayir or júzur)**
it **húwwa, híyya**
it doesn't matter **maa :aláish, maa yikháalif**

January **yanáayir**
juice **:aSíir**
July **yúulyo**
June **Yúunyo**

key **miftáaH (mafatíiH)**
kilogramme **kíilo, kiiloghráam**
kilometre **kíilo, kiilomít(i)r**
king **málik (mulúuk)**
kitchen **máTbakh (maTáabikh)**
knife **sikkíin (sakaakíin)**
know **:áraf yí:raf** (A)
kohl box **mákHalah**
Koran, the Holy **al-qur'áan al-karíim**

lamp **lámbah (-aat)**
land, desert **barr**
landlord **SáaHib al-milk**
language **lúghah (-aat)**
*last (*year, week etc.) **máaDHi**
lazy **kasláan**
lead (metal) **raSáaS**
learn **ta:állam, yit:állam** (A)
leave, depart, go out **Tála:, yíTla:** (A)
left (direction) **yisáar**
leisure (time) **wagt al-faráagh**
lemon, lime **laimóon**

less, least agáll
let, leave khálla, yikhálli (C)
letter risáalah (rasáayil)
licence láisan (layáasin)
lie down rágad, yírgad (A)
life, age :um(u)r
lift, elevator míS:ad (maSáa:id)
light (in weight) khafíif
light (of a car, street lamp) lait (-aat)
lighten, reduce kháffaf, yikháffif (A)
lightning bárg
like this, so kídha, chídha, chídhi
like, love Habb, yiHíbb (B2)
like, similar to míth(i)l
listen to istáma: yistámi: íla (A)
litre láitir, lítir (-aat)
live, reside sákan, yískun (A)
London lándan
longer, longest áTwal
lunch gháda
lunch, eat lunch taghádda, yitghádda (C)

make, do sáwwa, yisáwwi (C)
man rajjáal (rajajíil)
manager mudíir (múdara)
mango ámbah, hámbah
March mars
market suug (aswáag)
married mitzáwwaj
master, owner SáaHib (aSHáab)
May máayo
maybe múmkin, yímkin
meal wájabah (-aat)
meaning má:na
measure gaas, yigíis (B1)
meat láH(a)m
Mecca mákkah
medicine dáwa (adwíyah), (the science of) Tibb

Medinah al-madíinah
Middle East, the ash-sharg al-áwsaT
middle wás(a)T
milk Halíib
million milyóon (malaayíin)
minister wazíir (wúzara)
ministry wizáarah (-aat)
Ministry of Culture wizáarat ath-thaqáafah
Ministry of Education wizáarat at-ta:líim
Ministry of Foreign Affairs wizáarat al-khaarijíyyah
Ministry of Health wizáarat aS-SíHHah
Ministry of Information wizáarat al-i:láam
Ministry of the Interior wizáarat ad-daakhilíyyah
minus náagiS
minute dagíigah (dagáayig)
mirror miráayah (-aat)
moment láHDHah (laHaDHáat)
Monday yoom al-ithnáin
money filúus, baizáat
month sháh(a)r (shuhúur)
more ziyáadah
more/most important ahámm
morning SabáaH, Súb(a)H
mosque (big) jáami: (jawáami:), (small) másjid (masáajid)
mother umm (ummaháat), wáalidah
mother tongue lúghat al-úmm
mountain, desert jábal (jibáal)
much, many kathíir, wáajid
museum mátHaf (matáaHif)
music musíiga

name ís(i)m (asáami)
nation wáTan (awTáan)
national wáTani
near (to) garíib min
nearer, nearest ágrab
necessary láazim
need iHtáaj, yiHtáaj (B1) íla

need (noun) **Háajah (-aat)**
neither ... nor **laa... wála**
never **ábadan**
new **jadíid júdad, jidáad)**
news **akhbáar** (pl.)
next, coming **gáadim**
next to **jamb**
night (in general) **lail;** (single night) **láilah (layáali)**
nine **tís:ah**
19 **tis:atá:shar**
90 **tis:íin**
no **laa**
noon **DHúh(u)r**
North **shamáal**
not (before nouns and adjectives) **muu, mub,** (before verbs) **maa**
nothing **laa shay**
November **nufámbar**
now **al-Híin, al-'áan**
now and then, occasionally **min Hiin íla Hiin**
number **rág(a)m (argáam)**

oasis **wáaHa (-aat)**
obligatory **mafrúuDH**
October **októobar**
of **min;** *of, about* **:an**
of course, naturally **Táb:an**
office **máktab (makáatib)**
officer **DHáabiT (DHubbáaT)**
official **muwáDHDHaf (-iin),** (adj.) **rásmi**
oil (engine) **áayil;** (petroleum) **nafT, bitróol;** (cooking) **zait**
OK, good **zain**
old **gadíim**
on **:ála**
one **wáaHid**
only, just, enough, that's all **bass**
open **fátaH, yíftaH** (A)
open (adj.) **maftúuH**
opinion **ra'y (aaráa)**

or **aw**
orange **burtugáal**
orange (colour) **burtugáali**
order (something), *ask for* **Tálab, yíTlub** (A)
origin **áS(a)l (uSúul)**
other than, else **ghair**
outing, trip **ríHlah (-aat)**
outside **kháarij**
own, to **málak, yímlik** (A)

palm (tree) **nákhlah (nakhíil)**
pan (cooking) **Sufríyyah (Safáari)**
paper (sheet of) **wáragah (awráag)**
parcel **Tard (Thrúud)**
parents **waalidáin**
pass, go past **fáwwat, yifáwwit** (A)
passport **jawáaz as-sáfar**
pay **dáfa:, yídfa:** (A)
pen **gálam (agláam)**
people **naas**
pepper **fílfil**
person **shakhS (ashkháaS)**
petrol **banzíin**
pharmacy **Saydalíyyah (-aat)**
phone **tilifóon**
phone **ittáSal, yittáSil** (A) **fii**
photograph **Sáwwar, yiSáwwir** (A)
picture, photograph **Súurah (Súwar)**
pilgrimage; pilgrim **Hajj**
pill **Hábbah (Hubúub)**
pillow **makháddah (-aat)**
pineapple **ananáas**
place **makáan (-aat)**
plane **Tayyáarah (-aat)**
plate **SáH(a)n (SuHúun)**
play **lá:ab yíl:ab** (A)
please **min fáDHl-ak/-ich/-kum**
plus **záayid**

police shúrTah
possible múmkin
potatoes áalu, baTáaTis
post baríid
post office máktab al-baríid
pound sterling jináih (-aat) starlíini
pray Sálla, yiSálli (C)
prefer fáDHDHal, yifáDHDHil (A)
price si:r (as:áar)
problem múshkilah (masháakil)
programme barnáamij (baráamij)
puncture bánchar
put HaTT, yiHúTT (B2)

quarter rúba:
quick saríi:
quickest ásra:
quickly bi-súr(a):ah
quiet, peaceful háadi

rain máTar
read gára, yígra (C)
ready jáahiz
really, actually al-Hagíigah
reasonable ma:gúul
reckon, count, calculate Hásab, yíHsab (A)
red áHmar (f.) Hámra (Húmur)
refrigerator thalláajah (-aat)
regular :áadi
religion diin (adyáan)
repair SállaH, yiSálliH (A)
resident, inhabitant sáakin (sukkáan)
rest, relax, take one's ease istaráaH, yistaríiH (B1)
restaurant máT:am (maTáa:im)
return, come back, go back rája:, yírja: (A)
return ticket tádhkarat dhiháab w iyáab
right (direction) yamíin
rise, get up gaam, yigúum (B1)

road, way Taríig (Túrug)
rock Sákhrah (Sukhúur)
room ghúrfah (ghúraf)
roundabout duwwáar (-áat)

salad SálaTah
same thing, the nafs ash-sháy
sands rimáal, (sing. rám(a)l)
sandwich sand(a)wíich (-áat)
Saturday yoom as-sabt
sauce Sálsah
Saudi Arabia as-sa:udíyyah
say gaal, yigúul (B1)
school mádrasah (madáaris)
scorpion :ágrab (:agáarib)
sea báH(a)r
season móosam (mawáasim)
second, other tháani
secretary (f.) sikritáirah (-aat)
see, watch, look at shaaf, yishúuf (B1)
self, same nafs
send Tárrash, yiTárrish (A)
September sabtámbar
service khídmah (khídmáat)
seven sáb:ah
17 sab:atá:shar
70 sab:íin
she, it híyya
sheet (bed) shárshaf (sharáashif)
shelf raff (rufúuf)
ship safíinah (súfun)
shirt gamíiS (gumSáan)
shop (large) maHáll (-aat), (small) dukkáan (dakaakíin)
shopping centre márkaz tijáari
short gaSíir
shorter, shortest ágSar
sign wágga:, yiwággi: (A)
silver fáDHDHah

single ticket tádhkarat dhiháab
sister ukht (akhawáat)
sit, stay, remain gá:ad, yíg:ad (A)
sitting room májlis (majáalis)
six síttah
16 sittá:shar
60 sittíin
size magáas
sleep (noun) noom
sleep, go to sleep naam, yináam (B1)
small, young Saghíir (Sugháar)
smaller, smallest áSghar
so fa, idhan
so that, in order to :ála shaan, Hátta
soap Saabúun
soldier júndi (junúud)
some ba:DH, shwáyyat
someone Had
something else, other shay ghair
sometimes aHyáanan
sorry mut(a)'ássif, ma:a l-ásaf
South janúub
spacious wáasi:
speak takállam, yitkállam (A)
special makhSúuS
speed súr:ah
spend the night baat, yibáat (B1)
spoon gáfshah (gfáash)
sport riyáaDHah (-aat)
spread out intáshar, yintáshir (A)
spring (water) :ain (:uyúun) (f.)
stamp (postage) Táabi: (Tawáabi:)
state, country, nation dáwlah (dúwal)
station maHáTTah (-aat)
still (continuing) maa zaal
sting ládghah (-aat)
sting ládagh, yíldagh (A)
stomach báT(i)n

stop (a car etc.) **wággaf, yimággif** (A)
stop, come to a stop **wágaf, yóogaf** (A)
storm **:áaSifah (:awáaSif)**
straight ahead **síidah**
street **sháari: (shawáari:)**
student (f.) **Táalibah (-aat)**
student (m.) **Táalib (Tulláab or Tálabah)**
study **dáras, yídrus** (A)
sugar **shíkar**
suit (of clothes) **bádlah (-aat)**
suitable, convenient **munáasib**
suitcase **shánTah, jánTah (shúnuT)**
sum, amount (money) **máblagh (mabáaligh)**
summer **Saif**
sun **shams** (f.)
Sunday **yoom al-áHad**
super (petrol) **mumtáaz**
sure **mit'ákkid**
sweet, pleasant, pretty **Hilw**
swim, bathe **sábaH, yísbaH** (A)
swimming **sibáaHah**
swimming-pool **másbaH (masáabiH)**
swollen **wáarim**

table **maiz (amyáaz)**
tailor **khayyáaT (-iin/khayaayíiT)**
take **ákhadh, yáakhudh** (A irreg.)
take someone, give them a lift **wáSSal, yiwáSSil** (A)
take, deliver **wádda, yiwáddi** (C)
tank **tánki**
tea **shaay, chaay**
teach **:állam, yi:állim** (A)
teach **dárras, yidárris** (A)
teacher (f.) **mudárrisah (-aat)**
teacher (m.) **mudárris (-íin)**
team **faríig (furúng)**
telephone **tilifóon**
television **tilifizyóon**

tell, inform khábbar, yikhábbir (A)
ten :ásharah
tennis tánis
tent khaimah (khiyáam)
thanks, thank you shúkran
that (conjunction) inn
that, those haadháak, (f). haadhíik (haadhooláak)
there hináak
there is/are fiih
they húmma
thief Haráami (-iyya)
thing shay (ashyáa)
think, ponder fákkar, yifákkir (A)
think, be of the opinion iftákar, yiftákir (A)
third tháalith
third (fraction) thilth
thirsty :aTsháan
13 thalaathtá:shar
30 thalaathíin
this, these háadha, (f.) haadhi (haadhóol)
thought, idea fíkrah (afkáar)
thousand alf (aaláaf)
three thaláathah
throughout Tuul
thunder rá:ad
Thursday yoom al-khamíis
ticket tádhkarah (tadháakir)
time wag(i)t; *occasion* márrah (-aat), *period of* múddah
tire tá:ab, yít:ab (A)
tired, ill ta:báan
to, for li-, la-
today al-yóom
tomorrow báakir/búkrah
tooth sinn (asnáan)
toothache wája: al-asnáan
toothpaste ma:júun al-asnáan
tour jáwlah (-aat)
towel fúuTah (fúwaT)

town, village, country bálad (biláad)
traffic murúur
train giTáar
transport, take wáSSal, yiwáSSil (A)
travel sáfar
travel, to sáafar, yisáafir (A)
travellers' cheque chaik siyáaHi
tree shájarah (ashjáar)
tribe gabíilah (gabáayil)
Tuesday yoom ath-thaláathah
turn, to (direction) laff, yilíff (B2)
turtles (in Oman) gháilam; elsewhere Hámas
twelve ithná:shar
twenty :ishríin
two ithnáin, f. thintáin
tyre taayr (-aat)

UAE al-imaaráat al-:arabíyyah al-muttáHidah
UK al-mámlakah al-muttáHidah
uncle, paternal :amm, *maternal* khaal
underneath, below, downstairs táH(i)t
university jáami:ah (-aat)
until Hátta, li-gháayat
used to, accustomed to mit:áwwid :ála
usually, generally :áadatan

very jíddan, wáajid
video víidiyoo/fíidiyoo (viidiyoohaát)
villa vílla/fíllah (vílal, fílal)
violent, acute shadíid
violet (colour) banáfsaji
visit záar, yizúur (B1)
visitor záa'ir or záayir (zuwwáar)
vomit zaa:, yizúu: (B1)

wadi wáadi (widyáan)
wait intáDHar, yintáDHir (A)
walk másha, yímshi (C)

want, wish aráad, yiríid (B1)
warm, hot sáakhin
washbasin, sink míghsalah
washing machine ghassáalah (-aat)
water maay
we níHna
Wednesday yoom al-árba:ah
week usbúu: (asabíi:)
weight wazn (awzáan)
welcome, hello áhlan wa sáhlan, márHab
well bi-kháir
west gharb
what aish
when Hiin; (in questions) máta
where wain
which ayy
while :índ-ma
white ábyaDH, (f.) báiDHa (biiDH)
who man, min
why laish
wife zóojah
wind, air háwa
winter shíta
with, together with má:a, wíyya; *by means of* bi-
with, by, in bi-
without bi-dúun
woman Húrmah (Haríim), már'a (niswáan)
wool Suuf
word kálimah (-aat)
work ishtághal, yishtághal (A)
work shúgh(u)l (ashgháal)
workshop wárshah (-aat)
world :áalam
worse, worst áwHash
worshipper :abd (:ibáad)
write kátab, yíktib (A)
written maktúub

X-ray photograph **:aks éksrai**

year **sánah (sanawáat/siníin); :aam (a:wáam)**
yellow **áSfar** (f.) **Sáfra (Súfur)**
yes **áywa, ná:am**
yesterday **ám(i)s**
you (m., f. and pl.) **ínta/ínti/íntu**

zero **Síf(i)r**

Index

References take the form 5.Gp4, where the first number refers to the unit, the letter(s) refer to the section within the unit (e.g. Gp for 'Grammar points'), and the second number refers to the point within that section. For example, 10.D2.2 indicates Unit 10, Dialogue 2, Note 2 (in the Notes section following Dialogue 2); 10.D1.Ct refers to the 'Cultural tips' section at the end of Dialogue 1. Other references are in the form 1. As, where the number is the unit and the letter(s) refer to the section within the unit (in this case 'Arabic script'), and there are no numbered points within the section. The abbreviations for sections within the units are as follows:

As	Arabic script
D1 etc.	Dialogue 1 etc.
Ct	Cultural tips
E	Exercises
Gp	Grammar points
Kp	Key phrases